REIMAGINING
A MORE
Perfect Union

REIMAGINING A MORE
Perfect Union

A *Better* Constitution
for Modern America

Richard S. Order

ISBN: 979-8-9917195-0-6 - Paperback
eISBN: 979-8-9917195-1-3 - eBook

♾This paper meets the requirements of ANSI/NISO Z39.48-1992 (Permanence of Paper)

032825

To Denise, my wife and the love of my life,
and our wonderful sons, Jonathan and Daniel.

Some men see things as they are and ask, "Why?"
I dream things that never were and ask, "Why not?"

Robert F. Kennedy, Sr., 1968

CONTENTS

PART THREE

★OVERVIEW

After years of servicing, repairing, and replacing parts for a car, there comes a point when you finally give up and get a new car.

The United States Constitution (the "Constitution") is a 235-year old jalopy that has been tinkered with right from the start. While some scholars and judges view it as a living, organic document that can and should be adapted and updated to the present, others refuse to deviate from the original intent, whatever that may mean when applying it in an era with space travel, robotic surgery, and artificial intelligence.

Instead of continuing to patch and reinterpret the Constitution to address situations never envisioned by its Framers, it is time to trade it in for a new model with all the modern bells and whistles.

Let's consider a new, reorganized Constitution that reflects modern concerns and priorities, assembles into unified Articles a number of related provisions presently scattered throughout multiple amendments, cures deficiencies, fills in gaps, and modifies the structure of the federal government, while retaining provisions that are still sensible and work reasonably well.

Part One presents the entire text of the new Constitution, which is entitled, the "Restated United States Constitution" or "Restated Constitution," for short, borrowing a term from corporate legal documents.

The Restated Constitution starts off in Article I with a new Bill of Rights that codifies personal rights, liberties, and freedoms and appears first to emphasize its importance.

Article II establishes a new independent agency called, the "Commission on National Elections and Compensation," which creates geographic Districts and Regions for election of Members of Congress and the Commission itself, administers national elections, determines compensation for national officers, and selects federal judges.

Article III reconfigures Congress into a single chamber of 100 Members who are elected to four-year terms staggered with the President's four-year terms and whose service is capped at 16 years.

Article IV gathers together the provisions concerning the President and the Vice President from Article II and the 12th, 20th, 22nd, and 25th Amendments[1] of the Constitution. It also abolishes the Electoral College in favor of election of the President and the Vice President by popular vote, makes a person ineligible to serve as President or Vice President while incarcerated, prohibits Presidents from pardoning themselves or their co-conspirators, requires the President to abide by the new Constitution, amplifies on impeachment and its effects, and strips Presidents of criminal immunity.

Article V sets a service limit for federal judges of 25 years or reaching the age of 75, whichever occurs first, establishes a new system for appointing judges through a Judicial Appointment Council, and subjects Supreme Court justices to a Code of Conduct.

Article VI collects the various provisions of the Constitution regarding the States.

Article VII provides for amendment and ratification of the Restated Constitution by popular vote.

Article VIII joins provisions of Article VI and the 14th Amendment of the Constitution relating to the supreme law of the land and ineligibility of certain persons for holding national office.

Finally, Article IX defines ratification of the Restated Constitution, the effect of ratification, and the effective date of the Restated Constitution.

Part Two explains every new aspect, concept, and wrinkle of Articles I through IX of the Restated Constitution. This discussion is expressed in plain, straightforward language that can be readily followed without any formal legal training. **In fact, if it seems too daunting to read the entire text of the Restated Constitution straight through, just skip Part One and go directly to the section-by-section analysis in Part Two.**

Part Three proposes an action plan for replacing the Constitution with the Restated Constitution.

Because the discussion of the changes in the Restated Constitution often explains the historical context, the current Constitution appears in **Appendix A** as a convenient reference.

So, with that overview, let's take the Restated Constitution for a test drive.

PART ONE

THE RESTATED UNITED STATES CONSTITUTION

*In the following text of the Restated Constitution, new provisions, concepts, and language appear in **bold type.** Language carried over from the Constitution appears in regular type, with a citation in brackets to its source location in the Constitution. Citations to concepts in the Constitution on which new language in bold is based appear at the end of a section. Bold type is not used where punctuation, spelling, or grammar of the Constitution has been modernized or where slight modifications have been made that do not alter the meaning, such as replacing male pronouns with gender-neutral language.*

WHEREAS, the United States Constitution (the "Constitution") was ratified in 1788; and

WHEREAS, the Constitution has been amended 27 times and interpreted and reinterpreted countless times by countless courts since then; and

WHEREAS, the United States and the world have changed dramatically since ratification, and, as a result, the Constitution, as amended, needs to be updated to address current and future needs and technology;

NOW, THEREFORE, WE THE PEOPLE of the United States of America, in accordance with Article V of the Constitution, hereby amend, repeal, and restate the

3

Constitution by superseding and replacing it in its entirety with this Restated United States Constitution (the "Restated Constitution") as follows:

ARTICLE I

PERSONAL RIGHTS, LIBERTIES, AND FREEDOMS

1.   All persons shall have a right to privacy, and no United States, State, or local government (collectively, "Government") shall interfere with a person's right to privacy, which shall include, by way of example, freedom of worship and religion; freedom of sexual relationships between consenting adults; freedom of marriage between consenting adults regardless of sex, sexual orientation, gender identity, race, or religion; freedom of gender identity; and freedom to prescribe, sell, purchase, possess, and use contraceptives. [1st Amend.]

2.   Every female, regardless of age or parental consent, shall have an absolute right to abort a fetus she is carrying up to the beginning of the third trimester of pregnancy. After the beginning of the third trimester of pregnancy, every female shall have the right to abort a fetus she is carrying if the pregnancy or birth poses a reasonably high danger to her physical or mental health or the fetus has a severe medical defect or condition, as determined in consultation with her medical providers, or if she is the victim of a rape or incest. All qualified medical providers shall have the right to perform any such

4

abortions. No Government shall interfere with such rights to an abortion or to perform abortions.

3.   All persons born or naturalized in the United States and subject to the jurisdiction thereof, **including its possessions and territories,** are citizens of the United States. **All persons born outside the United States or its possessions or territories to at least one parent who was a United States citizen at the time of their birth and who previously resided in the United States are citizens of the United States. All persons domiciled or residing in the United States or its possessions or territories on the Effective Date of this Restated Constitution who entered or have remained in the United States illegally shall be deemed citizens of the United States.** No State shall make or enforce any law that abridges the privileges, **rights, liberties, freedoms,** or immunities of citizens of the United States. [14th Amend., Sect. 1]

4.   The right of United States citizens who are 18 years of age or older to vote **in any election or primary** shall not be denied or abridged by the Government on account of age, race, color, sex, **sexual orientation, gender identity, literacy, payment of a fee or tax of any kind, conviction of or imprisonment for any crime, homelessness, or lack of any Government issued identification. Notwithstanding the foregoing, election officials may require that voters provide proof of identity and domicile.** [15th, 19th, 24th and 26th Amend.]

5.   All persons shall have the right to exercise freedom of speech, freedom to assemble peacefully, and freedom to petition the Government for a redress of grievances. The media shall likewise enjoy freedom of expression. **Notwithstanding the foregoing, the Government may restrict or punish hate speech, hate crimes, and speech advocating the overthrow of the Government by force. Similarly, targets and victims of hate speech or hate crimes shall have the right to sue civilly the perpetrators of such hate speech or hate crimes. This Section shall not affect common law claims such as infliction of emotional distress, defamation, and invasion of privacy.** [1ˢᵗ Amend.]

6.   **All persons shall enjoy freedom of safety and freedom from violence. In furtherance of such rights, after the Effective Date of this Restated Constitution, no civilian shall have the right to carry any firearm in any area reasonably declared by the Government to be gun-free and off-limits to firearms. Moreover, commencing one year after the Effective Date of this Restated Constitution, no civilian shall have the right to use, carry, or possess any weapon of war, including assault weapons and high-capacity magazines or ammunition. The two preceding sentences shall not apply to the military, the National Guard, or Government law enforcement personnel acting in their official capacities.**

7.   The right of the people to be secure in their persons, houses, **places of business, automobiles,** papers, **electronically stored information,** and effects against unreasonable searches and seizures shall not be

violated, and no warrants shall issue but upon probable cause supported by oath or affirmation and particularly describing the place to be searched and the persons or things to be seized. [4th Amend.]

8.   **All persons charged with a crime shall be deemed innocent until proven guilty beyond a reasonable doubt. Accordingly,** excessive bail shall not be required. **Bail shall be set within defendants' reasonable ability to pay, unless they are flight risks or pose a danger to the public. No bail shall be required for misdemeanor charges.** [8th Amend.]

9.   No person shall be held to answer for a **felony**, unless on a presentment or indictment of a grand jury, except in cases arising in the land or naval forces or in the **National Guard** when in actual service in time of War or public danger. No persons shall be subject for the same offense to be twice put in jeopardy of life or limb, nor shall be compelled in any criminal case to be a witness against themselves, nor be deprived of life or liberty without due process of law. [5th Amend.; 14th Amend., Sect. 1]

10.   In all criminal prosecutions, the accused shall enjoy the right to a speedy and public trial by an impartial jury of the State and district wherein the crime shall have been committed, which district shall have been previously ascertained by law, and to be informed of the nature and cause of the accusation. Accused persons shall have the right to be confronted with the witnesses against them, to have compulsory process for

obtaining witnesses in their favor, and to have the assistance of counsel for their defense. [6ᵗʰ Amend.]

11. **In criminal cases,** excessive fines **shall not be** imposed, nor cruel and unusual punishments inflicted. **No Government shall impose on any incarcerated person a fee related to the cost of housing, feeding, or providing medical care to such person during or arising out of the incarceration. No Government shall execute any person as punishment for any crime.** [8ᵗʰ Amend.]

12. In suits at common law, where the value in controversy shall exceed **$5,000,** the right of trial by jury shall be preserved, and no fact tried by a jury shall be otherwise re-examined in any court of the United States, other than according to the rules of the common law. [7ᵗʰ Amend.]

13. No person shall be deprived of property without due process of law. No private property shall be taken for public use without just compensation. **All persons are entitled to** equal protection of the laws **regardless of sex, sexual orientation, gender identity, race, or religion, and all persons are entitled to freedom from discrimination based on sex, sexual orientation, gender identity, race, or religion. For purposes of this Section, corporate entities, such as companies and partnerships, shall be considered "persons" solely with respect to laws regarding property and criminal liability and not with respect to individual civil rights, liberties, and freedoms.** [5ᵗʰ Amend.; 14ᵗʰ Amend., Sect. 1]

14. **Slavery is banned, including involuntary servitude as punishment for a crime. Consequently, the Government must pay prisoners at least minimum wage for work they perform.** [13th Amend.]

15. **All persons are entitled to basic human necessities, including healthcare, housing, food, clothing, and education.**

16. The enumeration in **this Restated Constitution** of certain rights, **liberties, and freedoms** shall not be construed to deny or disparage others retained by the People, **and the Government shall respect, shall be bound by, and shall not violate, infringe, or abridge the personal rights, liberties, and freedoms in this Article.** [9th Amend.]

ARTICLE II

COMMISSION ON NATIONAL ELECTIONS AND COMPENSATION

1. **Upon ratification of this Restated Constitution,** there shall be established a new independent and auto- nomous agency called, the "Commission on National Elections and Compensation" (the "Commission"), comprised of 20 members who shall be called, "Commissioners." Half of the Commissioners must not be affiliated with or a member of any political party. The initial 20 Commissioners shall be appointed by the House of Representatives within 30 days after ratification of this Restated Constitution in accordance

with the requirements of eligibility provided in the following Section of this Article. Because no Regions will have been established at the time of the appointment of the initial Commissioners, the House of Representatives shall appoint two Commissioners to represent each geographical area consisting of approximately one-tenth of the population of the nation based on the most recent national census. Upon appointment, the Commissioners shall divide the United States and its possessions and territories into ten Regions, each consisting of approximately one-tenth of the population of the nation, and ten Districts of approximately equal population within each Region based on locale and not on political affiliation.

2.   Only a citizen who is 35 years or older, who has been a United States citizen for more than eight years prior to election, and who is at the time of election domiciled in the Region may be elected to represent that Region on the Commission. When a vacancy occurs in the Commission before a national election, the Commission shall hold a special election by the people in the affected Region to fill the vacancy until the next national election.

3.   The Commission shall hold elections for the President and Vice President on the first Saturday and Sunday following the first Monday of November in the four-year cycle in effect on the Effective Date of this Restated Constitution. The Commission shall hold the initial national election for Members of Congress and Commissioners on the first Saturday and Sunday following the first Monday of November

in the year that is two years after the next election for President and Vice President following the Effective Date of this Restated Constitution. Subsequent national elections for Members of Congress and Commissioners shall be held on the first Saturday and Sunday following the first Monday of November every four years and shall include a vote on any amendments to this Restated Constitution proposed in accordance with Article VII. The Commission shall hold and monitor national elections and Presidential elections and shall work with the Department of Justice in enforcing all election laws.

4.   The initial Commissioners shall serve until noon on the third day of January following the initial national election by popular vote for Commissioners. At the initial national election, two Commissioners shall be elected by popular vote in each Region as representatives of that Region and shall serve for a term of four years each. One of the two Commissioners from each Region must not be affiliated with or a member of any political party. Each initial Commissioner may run for election in the initial election. Thereafter, the Commissioners shall be elected at each national election. No Commissioner may serve on the Commission for more than a total of 12 years after the initial election. The terms of each Commissioner shall end at noon on the third day of January following an election, and the terms of their successors shall then begin.

5.   The Commission shall determine the initial boundaries of the Regions based on the most recent

national census. A national census shall be conducted in every year ending in a zero, and the Commission shall redraw the boundaries of the Regions and Districts within two years after and based on each new census.

6.   The Commission shall administer and conduct all elections for the President and Vice President, for Members of Congress, and for Commissioners, shall count all ballots cast in such elections, and shall determine and declare, on or before the 15th day of December following each election, the winners of the elections for the President, Vice President, and Members of Congress based on the popular vote. The Commission shall declare as the victor the person receiving the most votes in each of these elections, regardless of whether the candidate received a majority of the votes.

7.   To avoid any appearance of a conflict of interest, within ten days after the Commission declares the winners of the elections for Congress, the then sitting Congress shall determine and declare, as the victors of the election for the Commissioners, the two persons, subject to the conditions of Section 4 of this Article, receiving the most votes in each Region resulting from the popular vote within each Region regardless of whether they received a majority of the votes.

8.   The Commission shall select and appoint judges from the list of eligible and highly qualified candidates prepared by the Judicial Appointment Council in accordance with Article V.

9.   The Commission shall determine and fix the compensation of the President, the Vice President, Members of Congress, and the members of the Judicial Appointment Council, whose compensation shall neither be increased nor decreased during their terms, and any change in their compensation shall take effect only after their next election or appointment. The Commission shall also determine and fix the compensation of the judges of the United States, which **may be increased but** shall not be diminished during their continuance in office. [Art. II, Sect.1; Art. III, Sect. 1; 27th Amend.]

10.   The Commissioners shall receive compensation for their services, to be ascertained by Congress. Their compensation shall neither be increased nor decreased during their terms, and any change in their compensation shall take effect only after their next election or appointment.

11.   The Commissioners shall in all cases, except treason, felony, and breach of the peace, be privileged from arrest during their attendance at any session of the Commission and in going to and returning from the same, and for any speech or debate in the Commission, they shall not be questioned in any other place.

12.   No Commissioners shall, during the time for which they were elected, be appointed to any civil office under the authority of the United States, which shall have been created, or the emoluments whereof shall have been increased, during such person's time

on the Commission. Similarly, no persons holding any office under the United States shall be Commissioners during their continuance in office.

ARTICLE III

LEGISLATIVE BRANCH

1.   **The legislative branch of the United States government shall be called, "Congress."** [Art. I, Sect. 1]

2.   **Congress shall be comprised of a single chamber with 100 "Members." Each District shall elect one Member of Congress by popular vote to represent that District for a term of four years, which** shall end at noon on the third day of January **following each national election,** and the terms of their successors shall then begin. **The terms of all Senators and Representatives elected before the initial national election held pursuant to Section 3 of Article II shall end at noon on the third day of January following the initial national election, regardless of whether certain Senators may have any years remaining in their terms as of the date of the initial national election. No Member may serve in Congress for more than a total of 16 years, whether or not consecutive, after the initial national election held following the Effective Date. When a vacancy occurs in Congress, the Commission shall hold a special election to fill the vacancy.** [20th Amend.]

3.   Only a citizen who is 25 years or older, who has been a United States citizen for more than **eight**

years prior to election, and who is at the time of election **domiciled in** the **District** may be elected to represent that **District in and serve as a Member of Congress**. [Art. I, Sect. 2]

4.   Congress shall choose its Speaker and other officers. The Vice President of the United States shall be President of **Congress** but shall have no vote except to break a tie. [Art. I, Sects. 2 and 3]

5.   **Congress** shall have the sole power of impeachment, **by a majority vote, of any United States officer or official, including judges, Commissioners, members of the Judicial Appointment Council, and Members of Congress**, and to try all impeachments. When trying an impeachment, Members shall be on oath or affirmation. When the President of the United States is tried, the Chief Justice of the Supreme Court shall preside. No person shall be convicted except upon a vote of at least two-thirds of the Members present. **A conviction of impeachment shall serve to remove such convicted persons from any current office and ban them from any future office or position in the United States government. Congress may impeach and convict any United States officers or officials subject to this Section even after they have resigned from such positions or after their terms have expired. A conviction or acquittal under this Section is not a defense to any criminal charges or civil claims based on the same facts and shall not serve as a reason for dismissal of criminal charges on the grounds of double jeopardy.** [Art. I, Sects. 2 and 3]

6.   Congress shall assemble at least once in every year, and such meeting shall begin at noon on the third day of January, unless it shall by law appoint a different day. A majority of the Members of Congress shall constitute a quorum to conduct business, but a smaller number may adjourn from day to day and may be authorized to compel the attendance of absent Members in such manner and under such penalties as Congress may provide. **Except as otherwise provided in this Restated Constitution, all votes shall be determined by a simple majority of those Members present. No filibusters shall be permitted.** [Art. I, Sects. 4 and 5; 20th Amend., Sect. 2]

7.   Congress may determine the rules of its proceedings, punish its Members for disorderly behavior, and, upon a two-thirds vote of the entire Congress, expel a Member. [Art. I, Sect. 5]

8.   Congress shall keep a journal of its proceedings and from time to time publish the same, excepting such parts as may in their judgment require secrecy. The yeas and nays of the Members on any question shall, at the desire of one-fifth of those present, be entered on the journal. **Meetings of Congress shall be open to the public, with reasonable restrictions, unless national security requires closed sessions.** [Art. I, Sect. 5]

9.   During session, Congress shall not adjourn for more than three days, nor to any other place than **the Capitol Building in Washington, D.C.** or any other place in which it shall be sitting. [Art. I, Sect. 5]

10.   The Members shall receive compensation for their services, to be ascertained by Law, and paid out of the Treasury of the United States. Their compensation shall neither be increased nor decreased during their terms **and shall be determined and fixed by the Commission**. They shall in all cases, except treason, felony, and breach of the peace, be privileged from arrest during their attendance at any session of Congress and in going to and returning from the same, and, for any speech or debate in Congress, they shall not be questioned in any other place. No Members shall, during the time for which they were elected, be appointed to any civil office under the authority of the United States, which shall have been created, or the emoluments whereof shall have been increased, during such time **in Congress**. Similarly, no persons holding any office under the United States shall be a Member during their continuance in office. [Art. I, Sect. 6; 27th Amend.]

11.   Every bill which shall have passed Congress shall, before it becomes law, be presented to the President of the United States. If the President approves the bill, the President shall sign it, but, if not, the President shall return it with any objections to Congress, which shall enter the objections at large on its journal and proceed to reconsider it. If after such reconsideration, two-thirds of Congress shall agree to pass the bill, it shall become law. The votes shall be determined by yeas and nays, and the names of the persons voting for and against the bill shall be entered on the journal. If any bill shall not be returned by the

President within ten business days after it shall have been presented to the President, it shall become law as if the President had signed it, unless Congress by its adjournment prevents its return, in which case it shall not become law. The same procedure shall be followed for every order, resolution, or vote that may require the approval of the President. [Art. I, Sect. 7]

12.   Congress shall have the power and authority:

a.   to lay and collect taxes, including taxes on incomes (from whatever source derived, without apportionment among the States and without regard to any census or enumeration), duties, imposts, and excises to pay the debts and operations of the United States and provide for the common defense and general welfare of the United States; but all duties, imposts, and excises shall be uniform throughout the United States;

b.   to borrow money on the credit of the United States;

c.   to regulate commerce with foreign nations, among the States, and with Indian tribes;

d.   to establish a uniform rule of naturalization;

e.   to establish uniform laws on the subject of bankruptcies throughout the United States;

f.   to coin money, regulate the value thereof, and of foreign coin, and fix the standard of weights and measures;

g.   to provide for the punishment of counterfeiting the securities and current coin of the United States;

h.   to establish Post Offices and post roads;

i.   to promote the progress of science and useful arts by securing for limited times to authors and inventors the exclusive right to their respective writings and discoveries;

j. to constitute tribunals inferior to the Supreme Court;

k. to define and punish piracies and felonies committed on the high seas and offenses against the law of nations;

l. to declare war, grant letters of marque and reprisal, and make rules concerning captures on land and water;

m. to raise and support armies, but no appropriation of money to that use shall be for a longer term than two years;

n. to provide and maintain a navy;

o. to make rules for the government and regulation of the land, **air,** and naval forces;

p. to provide for calling forth the **National Guard** to execute the laws of the union, suppress insurrections, and repel invasions;

q. to provide for organizing, arming, and disciplining the **National Guard** and for governing such part of them as may be employed in the service of the United States, reserving to the States, respectively, the appointment of the officers and the authority of training the **National Guard** according to the discipline prescribed by Congress;

r. to exercise exclusive legislation in all cases whatsoever over **Washington, the District of Columbia,** as the seat of the government of the United States, and to exercise like authority over all places within **Washington, the District of Columbia,** for the erection of forts, magazines, arsenals, dock yards, and other needful buildings; and

s. to make all laws that shall be necessary and proper for carrying into execution the foregoing powers and all other powers vested by this Restated Constitution in the government of the United States or in any department or officer thereof. [Art. I, Sect. 8; 16th Amend.]

13. Congress' powers and authority shall be restricted as follows:

a. the privilege of the writ of habeas corpus shall not be suspended, unless, when in cases of rebellion or invasion, the public safety may require it;

b. no bill of attainder or ex post facto law shall be passed;

c. **aside from taxes on income**, no capitation or other direct tax shall be laid, unless in proportion to the census;

d. no tax or duty shall be laid on articles exported from any State;

e. no preference shall be given by any regulation of commerce or revenue to the ports of one State over those of another, nor shall vessels bound to or from one State be obliged to enter, clear, or pay duties in another;

f. no money shall be drawn from the Treasury, but in consequence of appropriations made by law, and a regular statement and account of the receipts and expenditures of all public money shall be published from time to time;

g. no title of nobility shall be granted by the United States, and no person holding any office of profit or trust under them shall, without the consent of the Congress, accept any present, emolument, office, or title of any kind whatever from any king, prince, or foreign state;

h. the validity of the public debt of the United States, authorized by law, shall not be questioned.

i. [Art. I, Sect. 9; 14th Amend., Sect. 4; 16th Amend.]

14. No State shall:

a. enter into any treaty, alliance, or confederation; grant letters of marque and reprisal; coin money; emit bills of credit; make anything but gold and silver coin a tender in payment of debts; pass any bill of attainder, ex post facto law, or law impairing the obligation of contracts, or grant any title of nobility;

b. without the consent of the Congress, lay any imposts or duties on imports or exports, except what may be absolutely necessary for executing its inspection laws, and the net produce of all duties and imposts laid by any State on imports or exports shall be for the use of the Treasury of the United States, and all such laws shall be subject to the revision and control of the Congress; and

c. without the consent of Congress, lay any duty of tonnage, keep troops or ships of war in time of peace, enter into any agreement or compact with another State or with a foreign power, or engage in war, unless actually invaded or in such imminent danger as will not admit of delay. [Art. I, Sect. 10]

15. Congress shall have power to enforce **and implement Articles I and II** by appropriate legislation. [13th, 14th, 15th, 19th, 24th, and 26th Amend.]

ARTICLE IV

EXECUTIVE BRANCH

1.   The executive power shall be vested in a President of the United States of America. **The President and the Vice President shall hold office** during a term of four years **and shall be elected as a team, provided they are not domiciled in the same State, based on the national popular vote of citizens 18 years of age or older without regard to the boundaries of the States, Districts, Regions, possessions, and territories. The Commission shall declare as the victor the team receiving the most votes in the Presidential election, regardless of whether that team receives a majority of the votes. The Electoral College is hereby abolished.** [Art. II, Sect. 1; 12th Amend.]

2.   Only a natural born citizen who is 35 years or older and has resided within the United States for at least 14 years before the national election shall be eligible to serve as President or Vice President. **No person may hold the office of President or Vice President while incarcerated.** [Art. II, Sect. 1; 12th Amend.]

3.   The President **and the Vice President** shall, at stated times, receive compensation for their services, which **shall be determined by the Commission and** shall neither be increased nor diminished during the period for which they shall have been elected. They shall not receive within that period any other compensation or emolument from the United States or any State. **They shall not accept, without the consent of**

the Congress, any present, emolument, office, or title of any kind whatever from any king, prince, or foreign state. [Art. I, Sect. 9; Art. II, Sect. 1]

4.   Before entering on the execution of office, the President shall take the following Oath or Affirmation: "I do solemnly swear (or affirm) that I will faithfully execute the Office of President of the United States and will, to the best of my ability, preserve, protect, defend, **and abide by** the **Restated** Constitution of the United States." [Art. II, Sect. 1]

5.   The terms of the President and the Vice President shall end at noon on the 20th day of January, and the terms of their successors shall begin at that time. [20th Amend., Sect. 1]

6.   If, at the time fixed for the beginning of the term of the President, the President elect shall have died, the Vice President elect shall become President. If a President elect shall have failed to qualify, **as determined by the Commission,** then the Vice President elect shall act as President until a President shall have qualified. Congress may by law provide for the case wherein **both a President elect and a Vice President elect shall have died or** neither a President elect nor a Vice President elect shall have qualified, **as determined by the Commission,** declaring who shall then act as President and the manner in which one who is to act shall be selected, and such person shall act accordingly until a President or Vice President shall have qualified. [20th Amend., Sect. 3]

7.   Congress may by law provide for the case of the death of any of the persons from whom it may choose a President or Vice President whenever the right of choice shall have devolved upon it. [20th Amend., Sect. 4]

8.   No person shall be elected to the office of the President more than twice, and no person who has held the office of President, or acted as President, for more than two years of a term to which some other person was elected President shall be elected to the office of the President more than once. [22nd Amend.]

9.   In case of the removal of the President from office or of the President's death or resignation, the Vice President shall become President. [25th Amend., Sect. 1]

10.   Whenever there is a vacancy in the office of the Vice President, the President shall nominate a Vice President who shall take office upon confirmation by a majority vote of Congress. **Congress may by law provide for the case wherein a President dies while the office of Vice President is vacant, declaring who shall then act as President and Vice President.** [25th Amend., Sect. 2]

11.   Whenever the President transmits to the Speaker of Congress a written declaration that the President is unable to discharge the powers and duties of the office, and until the President transmits to the Speaker a written declaration to the contrary, such powers and duties shall be discharged by the Vice President as Acting President. [25th Amend., Sect. 3]

12.   Whenever the Vice President and a majority of either the principal officers of the executive department or of such other body as Congress may by law provide transmit to the Speaker their written declaration that the President is unable to discharge the powers and duties of the office, the Vice President shall immediately assume the powers and duties of the office as Acting President. [25th Amend., Sect. 4]

13.   Thereafter, if the President transmits to the Speaker a written declaration that no inability exists, the President shall resume the powers and duties of office unless the Vice President and a majority of either the principal officers of the executive department or of such other body as Congress may by law provide transmit within four days to the Speaker their written declaration that the President is unable to discharge the powers and duties of the office. Thereupon, Congress shall decide the issue, assembling within forty-eight hours for that purpose if not in session. If the Congress, within 21 days after receipt of the latter written declaration, or, if Congress is not in session, within 21 days after Congress is required to assemble, determines by two-thirds vote that the President is unable to discharge the powers and duties of the office, the Vice President shall continue to discharge the same as Acting President. Otherwise, the President shall resume the powers and duties of the office. [25th Amend., Sect. 4]

14.   The President shall be Commander in Chief of the **armed forces** of the United States and of the State **National Guards**, when called into the actual service of the United States. The President may require the

opinion, in writing, of the principal officer in each of the executive departments upon any subject relating to the duties of their respective offices. [Art. II, Sect. 2]

15.   The President shall have power to grant reprieves and pardons for offenses against the United States, except in cases of impeachment. **The President may not, however, grant himself, herself, or a co-conspirator a reprieve or pardon.** [Art. II, Sect. 2]

16.   The President shall have power, by and with the advice and consent of Congress, to make treaties, provided two-thirds of the Members present concur. The President shall nominate, and by and with the advice and consent of Congress, shall appoint ambassadors, other public ministers and consuls, and all other officers of the United States, whose appointments are not herein otherwise provided for and which shall be established by law. Congress may by law vest the appointment of such inferior officers, as they think proper, in the President alone. The President shall have power to fill up all vacancies that may happen during the recess of Congress by granting commissions which shall expire **when Congress reconvenes**. [Art. II, Sect. 2]

17.   The President shall from time to time give to Congress information of the State of the Union and recommend to their consideration any necessary and expedient measures. The President may, on extraordinary occasions, convene Congress and may adjourn Congress to a proper time. The President shall receive ambassadors and other public ministers. The President shall take care that the

laws be faithfully executed and shall commission all the officers of the United States. [Art. II, Sect. 3]

18.   **In accordance with Section 5 of Article III,** the President, Vice President, and all civil officers of the United States shall be removed from office on impeachment for and conviction of treason, bribery, **sedition, fomenting rebellion or insurrection, advocating the overthrow of the United States government by force,** or other **felonies. A conviction of impeachment shall serve to remove such convicted persons from any current office and ban them from any future office or position in the United States government. Congress may impeach and convict any United States officers or officials subject to this Section even after they have resigned from such positions or after their terms have expired. A conviction or acquittal under this Section is not a defense to any criminal charges or civil claims based on the same facts and shall not serve as a reason for dismissal of criminal charges on the grounds of double jeopardy.** [Art. II, Sect. 4]

19.   **Presidents are absolutely immune from civil suit for any act they committed while in office. They are not, however, immune whatsoever from criminal prosecution for any act they committed while in office. Nevertheless, no such criminal prosecution may be initiated until a President has left office as President, at which time any applicable statute of limitations shall begin to run.**

ARTICLE V

JUDICIAL BRANCH

1.   The judicial power of the United States shall be vested in one Supreme Court **comprised of a Chief Justice and eight Associate Justices** and in such inferior courts as the Congress may from time to time ordain and establish, **including trial courts, special subject matter courts, and intermediate courts of appeal**. [Art. III, Sect. 1]

2.   **Only a citizen who is 45 years or older, has resided within the United States for at least 14 years before appointment, and is an attorney in good standing admitted to any State bar or the bar of a possession or territory shall be eligible to serve as a judge in the courts of the United States.**

3.   **No judge shall serve in any courts of the United States for more than 25 years in the aggregate or beyond the age of 75 years, whichever occurs sooner. The positions of Senior Judge and Senior Justice are hereby abolished. Notwithstanding the foregoing, for the purpose of calculating the remaining terms of judges serving as of and prior to the Effective Date, only half of the previous service time shall count toward the 25-year limit and no age limit shall be imposed.** The judges of the courts of the United States shall hold their offices during good behavior **within their terms as defined in this Section,** and shall, at stated times, receive for their services, a compensation, which **may be increased but**

shall not be diminished during their continuance in office **and which the Commission shall determine and fix.** [Art. III, Sect. 1]

4. **Upon ratification of this Restated Constitution, a Judicial Appointment Council (the "Council") of 20 persons shall be established for the purpose of compiling and updating lists of recommended candidates deemed eligible and highly qualified to serve as judges in the courts of the United States. The Council shall be comprised of five judges of the courts of the United States appointed by the Judicial Conference of the United States (notwithstanding any provision in this Restated Constitution to the contrary), five non-governmental attorneys appointed by Congress, five persons who are not attorneys appointed by Congress, and five persons appointed by the President, and they shall serve for a term of five years and may be reappointed by the same or a different appointing authority for a second term of five years but shall serve no more than ten years. If a vacancy occurs on the Council, the entity that appointed the vacated seat shall appoint another person to fill that vacancy and such person shall be eligible for reappointment but in no event may serve more than 12 years. The Commission shall select and appoint judges to fill vacancies and new positions in the courts of the United States only from the lists compiled by the Council. The Commission shall determine and fix the compensation of the Council members, which shall neither be increased nor diminished during their continuance in office.**

5.   **A Code of Conduct for United States Judges shall be issued by the Judicial Conference of the United States and shall apply to all United States judges and magistrate judges, including the Justices of the Supreme Court.**

6.   The judicial power shall extend (a) to all cases, in law and equity, arising under this **Restated** Constitution, the laws of the United States, and treaties made, or which shall be made, under their authority; (b) to all cases affecting ambassadors, other public ministers, and consuls; (c) to all cases of admiralty and maritime jurisdiction; (d) to controversies to which the United States shall be a party; (e) to controversies between two or more States, (f) to controversies between citizens of different States, and (g) to controversies between citizens of the same State claiming lands under grants of different States. [Art. III, Sect. 2]

7.   The judicial power of the United States shall not be construed to extend to any suit, in law or equity, commenced or prosecuted against one of the States by citizens of another State or by citizens or subjects of any foreign state. [11th Amend.]

8.   In all cases affecting ambassadors, other public ministers, and consuls, and those in which a State shall be a party, the Supreme Court shall have original jurisdiction. In all the other cases before mentioned, the Supreme Court shall have appellate jurisdiction, both as to law and fact, with such exceptions and under such regulations as Congress shall make. [Art. III, Sect. 2]

9.   The trial of all crimes, except in cases of impeachment, shall be by jury, and such trial shall be held in the State where the said crimes shall have been committed, but when not committed within any State, the trial shall be at such place or places as Congress may by law have directed. [Art. III, Sect. 2]

10.   Treason against the United States shall consist only in levying war against it or in adhering to its enemies, giving them aid and comfort. No person shall be convicted of treason unless on the testimony of two witnesses to the same overt act or on confession in open court. Congress shall have power to declare the punishment of treason, but no attainder of treason shall work corruption of blood or forfeiture during the life of the person attainted. [Art. III, Sect. 3]

ARTICLE VI

THE STATES

1.   Full faith and credit shall be given in each State to the public acts, records, and judicial proceedings of every other State. Congress may by general laws prescribe the manner in which such acts, records, and proceedings shall be proved and the effect thereof. [Art. IV, Sect. 1]

2.   The citizens of each State shall be entitled to all privileges, **rights, liberties, freedoms,** and immunities of citizens in the several States. [Art. IV, Sect. 2]

3.   Persons charged in any State with treason, felony, or other crime, who shall flee from justice and be found in another State, shall on demand of the executive authority of the State from which they fled, be delivered up to be removed to the State having jurisdiction of the crime. [Art. IV, Sect. 2]

4.   New States may be admitted by Congress into this Union, but no new State shall be formed or erected within the jurisdiction of any other State; nor any State be formed by the junction of two or more States or parts of States, without the consent of the legislatures of the States concerned as well as of Congress. [Art. IV, Sect. 3]

5.   Congress shall have power to dispose of and make all needful rules and regulations respecting the territory or other property belonging to the United States, and nothing in this Restated Constitution shall be so construed as to prejudice any claims of the United States or of any particular State. [Art. IV, Sect. 3]

6.   The United States shall guarantee to every State in this Union a republican form of government and shall protect each of them against invasion and, on application of the State legislature or of the State executive (when the legislature cannot be convened), against domestic violence. [Art. IV, Sect. 4]

7.   **Each State shall maintain a National Guard unit.** [2nd Amend.]

8.   The powers not delegated to the United States by **this Restated** Constitution, nor prohibited by it to the States, are reserved to the States, respectively, or to the People. [10th Amend.]

ARTICLE VII

AMENDMENT

1.   **This Restated Constitution is intended to be a living document to be adapted to future times.**

2.   **A proposal for amendment to this Restated Constitution may be made by:**
   a. a two-thirds vote of Congress;
   b. a convention for proposing amendments called for by the legislatures of two-thirds of the several States; **or**
   c. **a resolution or referendum by popular vote of two-thirds of the several States.** [Art. V]

3.   **After a proposal for an amendment has satisfied any of these requirements, the proposed amendment shall be submitted for a popular vote in the next national election conducted by the Commission. If three-fourths or more of the States vote in favor of the amendment, it shall become part of this Restated Constitution. A vote in favor of the amendment by more than half of the votes cast in a State shall be deemed by the Commission to be a vote by that State in favor of the amendment.**

ARTICLE VIII

SUPREME LAW OF THE LAND

1.   This **Restated** Constitution, the laws of the United States made pursuant thereto, and all treaties made under the authority of the United States shall be the supreme law of the land, and the judges in every State shall be bound thereby, anything in the constitution or laws of any State to the contrary notwithstanding. [Art. VI]

2.   The Members of Congress, **the Commissioners, the members of the Council**, the members of the several State legislatures, and all executive and judicial officers, both of the United States and of the several States, shall be bound by oath or affirmation to support **and abide by** this Restated Constitution, but no religious test shall ever be required as a qualification to any office or public trust under the United States. [Art. VI]

3.   No person shall be a Member of Congress, **President, Vice President, Commissioner, judge, or member of the Council** or hold any office, civil or military, under the United States or under any State, who, **as determined by the Commission in the case of offices of the United States, has** engaged in **treason, sedition,** insurrection, rebellion, **advocating the overthrow of the United States government by force, or similar conduct** against the **United States** or given aid or comfort to the enemies thereof. **Nevertheless,** Congress may by a vote of two-thirds remove such disability. [14th Amend., Sect. 3]

ARTICLE IX

RATIFICATION AND EFFECTIVE DATE

1.   **This Restated Constitution shall be deemed ratified** when approved by the legislatures or conventions of **three-fourths of the** States **and shall take effect two years after its ratification (the "Effective Date"). Upon the Effective Date, this Restated Constitution shall be binding on all States, possessions, and territories, including those States that have not approved it, and shall supersede and replace the original Constitution and its amendments in their entirety.** [Art. V; Art. VII]

PART TWO

EXPLICATION
AND COMMENTARY

T he Restated Constitution adds personal rights, liberties, and freedoms, transforms the way we elect the President and the Vice President, revamps the structure of Congress and the tenure of its Members, alters the method of selecting judges and takes away their lifetime tenure, and adds provisions to make this organic document protect and serve the needs and rights of the people. While the Restated Constitution presents fundamental changes in the structure of the government, many of the nuts-and-bolts elements of the national government continue in place. After all, even a new model car with cutting-edge technology like autonomous driving, electric power, and Bluetooth still retains the basic concept of a chassis with wheels, seats, and windows.

Part Two explains the import of the proposed changes and why they are necessary. To borrow Thomas Jefferson's introduction to the Declaration of Independence, "a decent Respect to the Opinions of Mankind requires that [we] should declare the causes which impel [us]" to overhaul the Constitution.

Due to familiarity, most Americans assume we have the perfect Constitution and that the Founders and Framers were geniuses to devise a political system that anticipated every circumstance and would endure forever.

During Donald Trump's presidency, however, he repeatedly said or did something that sent political analysts running to the Constitution to consult obscure clauses relating to the powers of the President. Day after day, he would unleash his "stable genius" mind on Twitter or in front of any camera he could find and spew out comments that showed he either did not know about or understand provisions to the contrary in the Constitution or was simply flouting them. This disregard for the Constitution from someone who had sworn to "preserve, protect and defend" it was infuriating.

For example, Trump defied the emoluments clause (Art. I, Sect. 9) by receiving huge payments from foreign governments under the guise of lavish expenditures at the Trump Hotel several blocks up Pennsylvania Avenue and abused Presidential pardons and reprieves (Art. II, Sect. 2) when he rescued his co-conspirators and cronies, Paul Manafort, Roger Stone, and Steve Bannon.

Similarly, polls show that people are dissatisfied with the Supreme Court as an institution and its recent decisions, either because they feel the decisions were wrong or because they find the Constitution, itself, lacking. An example of both is *Dobbs v. Jackson Women's Health Organization*, which overturned *Roe v. Wade* and which will be discussed in the section regarding Article I, below.

Searching for provisions in the Constitution pertinent to Trump's rants and unhinged musings will uncover other provisions that seem antiquated, ambiguous, or plainly wrong. Yet, still thinking inside the box, people tend to think the best and only approach would be to focus on the most urgent issue and push Congress to propose a single amendment or two, such as expressly stating that instigating an insurrection is an impeachable offense. In struggling to narrow general discontent to a single most crucial amendment or two, however, it becomes apparent that a major reconstruction and not arthroscopic surgery is required.

Two years after his defeat, Trump made yet another bombastic statement on social media in support of his claim that the election results should be overturned: "A Massive Fraud of this type and magnitude allows for the termination of all rules, regulations, and articles, even those found in the Constitution. Our great 'Founders' did not want, and would not condone, False & Fraudulent Elections!"[2]

Trump was actually correct that the Constitution has problems that need to be fixed. Of course, he failed to explain what is wrong with the Constitution and how to fix it. Presumably, he meant that the process for electing the President should be amended so that the sitting President and his minions can manipulate or overrule the Electors of the Electoral College to remain in power. Needless to say, this proposed Restated Constitution differs as to what is wrong and how to fix it.

During Trump's initial campaign in 2016, he kept preparing his excuses for a probable loss by predicting that the process was "rigged" in Hillary Clinton's favor. After he won by garnering more Electoral votes but losing the popular vote by 3 million, political cartoonists had a golden opportunity to revisit the comments he made during the campaign. Picture a caricature of Trump with his swept dyed-blond hair, snarling lips, oversized torso, and little hands standing in front of a monitor showing the final tally of Electoral votes for Trump and Clinton (304-227) with a speech bubble stating, "See, I told you it was rigged!"

Neither Trump nor his supporters complained in 2016 that the Constitution should be "terminated" to prevent someone from becoming President after being outvoted by

3 million citizens. Years after he lost both the popular and Electoral votes in 2020, however, he continues his obsessive ravings about fraudulent elections and the need to "terminate" the Constitution.

Eventually, some Republican leaders criticized such comments. It is sickening, though, to listen to these self-righteous Republican Senators and Congressmen distance themselves from Trump and pay lip service to the sanctity of the Constitution. Where were they when they shirked their duty "to support this Constitution" (Article VI) by voting to acquit Trump of impeachment for his role in inciting the January 6th insurrection? Their after-the-fact comments are too little, too late.

So, the makeover of the Constitution begins by first pulling together all the rights, liberties, and freedoms from various provisions, primarily in the Amendments, and adding more. Then, a different methodology is established for electing and running our national government and appointing our judges. Provisions are retained if they seem to work satisfactorily, either verbatim or with some adjustments that supplement, clarify, or modernize.

The temptation to thoroughly research more than 200 years of jurisprudence on each article and section of the Constitution was rejected because that would have taken years to do and the resulting mammoth treatise would have been incomprehensible and inaccessible to the public. Likewise, the Enlightenment philosophers like Jean-Jacques Rousseau, John Locke, and Baron de Montesquieu who influenced the Framers of the Constitution were not consulted, nor was time spent reading later political philosophers.

Rather, the Restated Constitution was drafted with a little legal knowledge of the problems and issues inherent in the original text and its interpretations over the years and with some intellect, common sense, and, mostly, heart and soul.

It is crucial to get the conversation rolling now to stimulate a popular grassroots movement that can actually effect much needed change as soon as possible. Article V of the Constitution sets up a methodology for amendment that has proven over the years to be dominated by politicians who will not like these proposals for changing Congress and, as a result, will have no desire or incentive to disrupt their cushy fiefdoms even for the betterment of the country. Consequently, this book is an appeal to the People to push for dramatic change.

The following sections explain the changes being proposed in the Restated Constitution or the reasons for not making changes.

★ A NEW
BILL OF RIGHTS

ARTICLE I

PERSONAL RIGHTS, LIBERTIES, AND FREEDOMS

A sk people what they think is the most important thing the Constitution provides, and many will say it protects them from an overreaching Government. Perhaps, they are thinking of the Bill of the Rights contained in the first ten Amendments, or they simply view the Constitution as the embodiment of our freedoms in general even though they have never read or grasped its meaning, nuances, or judicial interpretations over the years.

They would be surprised to learn that the original seven articles of the Constitution just set up the national government and courts with a smattering of provisions relating to the States and slavery. In fact, some of the objections to ratification of the Constitution were based on its lack of individual protections. After all, what did the colonialists fight the tyranny of King George III for if their Constitution did not protect them from the new government?

Consequently, three years after the ratification of the Constitution in 1788, it was amended by adding the Bill of Rights.

In restating the Constitution, let's not make that mistake again. Let's make it clear that our personal rights, liberties, and freedoms are paramount by enumerating and enshrining them at the very beginning in Article I of the Restated Constitution. This new Bill of Rights uses the terms "rights," "liberties," and "freedoms" interchangeably and applies the one that sounds the best with the particular right/liberty/freedom.

RIGHT TO PRIVACY

1.   **All persons shall have a right to privacy, and no United States, State, or local government (collectively, "Government") shall interfere with a person's right to privacy, which shall include, by way of example, freedom of worship and religion; freedom of sexual relationships between consenting adults; freedom of marriage between consenting adults regardless of sex, sexual orientation, gender identity, race, or religion; freedom of gender identity; and freedom to prescribe, sell, purchase, possess, and use contraceptives. [1ˢᵗ Amend.]**

Ask Americans whether they believe the Constitution protects them from the Government intruding into their bedrooms and telling them what they cannot do there, and they will undoubtedly say "yes." Ask them to find specific language in the Constitution regarding a right to privacy, and they will not be able to because it is not there. Perhaps, they will say that the Constitution provides us with the right to life, liberty, and the pursuit of happiness, thinking of the most famous line of the Declaration of Independence, not the Constitution: "We hold these truths to be self-evident, that all Men are created equal, that they are endowed by their Creator with certain unalienable Rights, that among these are Life, Liberty, and the Pursuit of Happiness . . . ."

After all, doesn't the phrase, "life, liberty, and the pursuit of happiness," represent and convey the core of our sense of freedom under natural, rather than man-made, law? Wasn't that what the colonialists fought the Revolutionary War for? Consequently, if the concept of "life, liberty, and the pursuit of happiness" isn't in the Constitution, shouldn't it be?

A similar phrase appears in the 14th Amendment's prohibition against the States depriving "any person of life, liberty or property, without due process of law," but that formulation is different. First, protection of property is not as extensive as protection of the right to pursue happiness. Second, the 14th Amendment simply ensures life, liberty, and property will not be taken away *except through legal proceedings*, such as eminent domain, and, therefore, falls far short of an "unalienable" right.

The Supreme Court addressed the right to privacy in *Griswold v. Connecticut*, 381 U.S. 479 (1965). In that case, the Executive Director and the Medical Director of the Planned Parenthood League of Connecticut were convicted of violating a Connecticut statute prohibiting aiding and abetting the use of contraceptives when they prescribed a contraceptive device to a married couple. In writing for the Court, Justice William Douglas stated that "specific guarantees in the Bill of Rights have penumbras, formed by emanations from those guarantees that help give them life and substance. . . . Various guarantees create zones of privacy." 381 U.S. at 484.

What the heck is a "penumbra"? The word comes from the Latin words *"paene,"* meaning "almost" (a "peninsula" is almost an island), and *"umbra,"* meaning "shadow" (like what an umbrella produces under sunlight). A penumbra,

47

therefore, is a murky, vague, indefinite substance that is not even quite a shadow cast by something else.

In *Griswold*, Douglas relied on penumbras stemming from the 1st, 3rd, 4th, 5th, and 9th Amendments in the Bill of Rights that protect a marriage "lying within the zone of privacy created by several fundamental constitutional guarantees." 381 U.S. at 485. He asked, "Would we allow the police to search the sacred precincts of marital bedrooms for telltale signs of the use of contraceptives? The very idea is repulsive to the notions of privacy surrounding the marriage relationship." 381 U.S. at 485-86.

In a concurring opinion, Justice Arthur Goldberg focused more on the 9th Amendment as providing a basis for the right to privacy than relying on penumbras. The 9th Amendment, which is preserved in Section 16 of Article I of the Restated Constitution, provides, "The enumeration in the Constitution of certain rights shall not be construed to deny or disparage others retained by the people." Goldberg explained that James Madison proposed this amendment to make sure that no one viewed the mention of certain rights in the Constitution as an exhaustive list. There is a legal principle for interpreting statutes based on the Latin maxim, *expressio unius est exclusio alterius*, meaning the expression of one thing is the exclusion of another. For example, a sign on a door saying, "Ladies' Room," means not only a facility for women but also that no men allowed. So, the 9th Amendment was designed to prevent reading the Constitution as banning or not supporting other personal rights not expressly mentioned.

In any event, to avoid any possible argument that there is no penumbra and, accordingly, no right to privacy or zone of privacy in the Constitution, such as stated in *Dobbs v. Jackson Women's Health Organization* and discussed in the next Section, the right to privacy is written in stone in the very first Section of the first Article of the Restated Constitution. In other words, the right to privacy is coming out of the shadows and into bright daylight.

In the hope of avoiding future litigation over the meaning of the term "privacy," several examples of the right to privacy are expressly stated, namely, "freedom of worship and religion; freedom of sexual relationships between consenting adults; freedom of marriage between consenting adults regardless of sex, sexual orientation, gender identity, race, or religion; freedom of gender identity; and freedom to prescribe, sell, purchase, possess, and use contraceptives." This list is not exhaustive.

Freedom of Worship and Religion

Freedom of worship and religion is borrowed from the 1st Amendment but recast as an affirmative personal freedom rather than a ban on Congress making any "law respecting an establishment of religion, or prohibiting the free exercise thereof." The 1st Amendment's ban on Congressional laws interfering with religious practices, on the other hand, seems a more passive or backdoor approach to expressing a freedom.

Plus, the 1st Amendment initially banned only Congress from restricting religious practices and did not stop the States from doing so. In fact, in Connecticut, state law prohibited the worship of any religion other than the Congregational Church. Other Christian churches, such as Catholic churches, were not allowed until adoption of the new state constitution in 1818, and Jewish synagogues were not officially permitted until well into the 19th Century.[3] After the ratification of the 14th Amendment in 1868, providing equal protection of the laws, most of the amendments in the Bill of Rights were eventually considered binding on the States.

Nevertheless, to ensure that the rights, liberties, and freedoms enumerated in Article I of the Restated Constitution are not misinterpreted to lessen those in the Constitution or court interpretations of the Constitution, this Section also provides that "**no United States, State, or local government (collectively, 'Government') shall interfere with a person's right to privacy.**" The term "Government" is defined in the first sentence of the Restated Constitution and then used throughout to encompass government at every level to avoid the issue of whether a provision applies to only the national government but not the States. Also, Section 16 of Article I states that "the Government shall respect, shall be bound by, and shall not violate or infringe the personal rights, liberties, and freedoms in this Article." In this manner, we retain the 1st Amendment concept that the Government shall not make laws "respecting an establishment of religion, or prohibiting the free exercise thereof."

The term "freedom of worship and religion" conjures up President Franklin D. Roosevelt's Four Freedoms Speech in his 1941 State of the Union Address and Norman Rockwell's depictions of each freedom capturing their essence.

The use of the term "freedom of worship and religion" is intended to incorporate and continue all previous case law interpreting the 1st Amendment's establishment clause, as well as the freedom to not worship and to not be required by the Government to participate in any religious act or observance, such as school prayer.

Freedom of worship and religion is listed as an example of the right to privacy because worship and religion, as well as atheism, are spiritual beliefs that are deeply personal by nature and define our identities. Throughout history, people have been persecuted for their religious beliefs, and many have been martyred. Their courageous adherence to their religion of choice and refusal to convert in the face of discrimination, torture, and death confirm the centrality of religion to their sense of who they are.

Freedom of Sexual Relationships, *Marriage, Gender Identity, and Contraceptives*

In the *Dobbs* decision, Justice Clarence Thomas implied in a concurring opinion that the erosion of the right to privacy established in *Griswold* should lead to re-examination by the Court of rights that it had found based on the right to privacy, such as the rights to gay sex, to gay marriage, and to contraceptives. This view is so out of touch with the overwhelming public opinion in favor of these personal rights that it almost seems not necessary to spell them out here, but to avoid future technical and legalistic arguments, they are included as examples of the right to privacy to ensure they are not undermined in the future, particularly by crazy State legislatures.

It seems hypocritical of Justice Thomas to threaten an attack on these particular rights but not on the right of interracial marriage established in *Loving v. Virginia*, 388 U.S. 1 (1967), which has allowed him, a black man, to be married to a white woman and live in Virginia. Of course, he would probably distinguish that case by pointing out it was decided on equal protection and due process grounds rather than the right to privacy. A distinction without a difference.

With all the progress that has been made in gay rights, the latest cause is transgender issues and protections. We should expressly include them in the right to privacy, as well.

Protection for sexual activity is expressed as the "freedom of sexual relationships between consenting adults" with no qualifiers as to gender, sexual orientation, gender identity, race, or religion because an adult is any person qualified solely by age and regardless of any of these other characteristics. Each State may determine the age of an "adult." The only modifier attached to "adult" is that all involved must consent to the acts. Thus, excluded from protection are rape, including date rape, and statutory rape, where the willing but underage participant is deemed too young to make a well-informed and intelligent decision to consent.

The same approach is applied to marriage between consenting adults to protect kids from marrying too young and to prevent any forced marriages, such as in cults. Again, each State may determine the legal age of an adult. Because of the past legal problems with interracial and gay marriage, it makes sense to protect them expressly here. This Section uses the terms "sex," meaning one's anatomy, "sexual orientation," meaning the sex of the person to whom one is sexually attracted, and "gender identity," meaning the gender one identifies as regardless of anatomy or physical characteristics. That should cover it all and prevent any out-of-touch State politicians from legislating around the right to privacy.

Religion is included in the list because although there doesn't appear to be a problem currently, the Government should not regulate marriage on religious grounds. Plus, the litany of "regardless of sex, sexual orientation, gender identity, race, or religion" is employed in the equal protection clause in Section 13 of Article I, and consistent phraseology should avoid any debate about the significance of omitting religion here.

ABORTION

2. **Every female, regardless of age or parental consent, shall have an absolute right to abort a fetus she**

is carrying up to the beginning of the third trimester of pregnancy. After the beginning of the third trimester of pregnancy, every female shall have the right to abort a fetus she is carrying if the pregnancy or birth poses a reasonably high danger to her physical or mental health or the fetus has a severe medical defect or condition, as determined in consultation with her medical providers, or if she is the victim of a rape or incest. All qualified medical providers shall have the right to perform any such abortions. No Government shall interfere with such rights to an abortion or to perform abortions.

The placement of abortion rights in Section 2 does not mean to suggest that they are more important than other rights, such as freedom of speech or the right against self-incrimination. Abortion rights appear in Section 2 because they flow from the right to privacy and could have been included in Section 1 but deserve independent treatment in light of the long battle over *Roe v. Wade*.

Finally, we get to *Dobbs v. Jackson Women's Health Organization*, 597 U.S. 215 (2022). Polls show that two-thirds or more of Americans strongly disagree with that decision overturning the right of abortion established in 1973 in *Roe v. Wade*, 410 U.S. 113 (1973). Most likely, an overwhelming percentage of those disagreeing with *Dobbs* have never read *Dobbs* or *Roe* and are basing their opinions simply on their understandings of what they have been told are the holdings of each case.

From a strictly legal point of view, however, it is hard to argue with much of Justice Samuel Alito's technical reasoning. He basically observed that abortion is not mentioned specifically anywhere in the Constitution, that some colonies made abortion illegal before ratification of the Constitution, and that most States continued to make it illegal after ratification up until *Roe*. Of course, he fails to observe that all those laws criminalizing abortion were enacted by white, landowning men with little interest in the physical and mental well-being of women, particularly, in many instances, Black slaves whom they had raped. Thus, he should not have held those laws up as a basis for demonstrating a longstanding tradition of legitimate and commendable American values. Justice Alito criticized *Roe* for relying on the right to privacy from *Griswold* and, more harshly, for its rules governing abortions based on trimesters and viability of the fetus outside the womb.

Since *Roe* was handed down, the Supreme Court has been criticized for acting like a legislature in determining rules on abortions that go well beyond a court's usual powers and purposes. Even worse, the Court did so without fact-finding and without holding public hearings. Try reading *Roe*, and good luck understanding the legal bases for its holdings and trimester differentiations.

The problem of facing unwanted pregnancies is nothing new, and abortions go back thousands of years. The sexual revolution of the Sixties exacerbated the problem. Preaching sexual abstinence has never resulted in total sexual abstinence because it is just plainly contrary to human nature, desires, and compulsions. Knowledge about, access to, and actual use of birth control were and remain challenges dependent on all sorts of socio-economic factors, not to mention sex under the influence of recreational drugs and alcohol undermining the ability to make good decisions.

Roe was issued at a time when women and teenage girls were dying from or being maimed by illegal abortions performed by people, including themselves, lacking medical training in non-clinical environments without proper medical equipment. Clearly, unwanted pregnancies were a huge social issue at the time. Under the circumstances, *Roe* was hailed as a huge step forward in recognizing women's rights, in general, and in their right to control their own bodies, specifically.

Not only did *Roe* rely on the vague right to privacy in holding that women were entitled to abortions, but it went further and set up rules for the circumstances under which women could have abortions. The right to abortion was deemed absolute within the first trimester of pregnancy. During the second trimester, a State could regulate but not ban abortions. In the final trimester, a State could prohibit abortion except when necessary to protect the woman's health.

Many articles and books have been written on the controversy over abortion. Rather than attempt to address all aspects of the controversy, the following discussion focuses on several of the main points that call for the rights proposed in this Section of the Restated Constitution.

Two questions of major significance in any discussion of abortion are when life begins and when a fetus is viable outside the womb. Those two questions then raise the question of when a State should exercise its duty as *parens patriae*, a Latin phrase meaning "parent of the country," to protect children whose biological parents are failing to protect their interests. For example, States act as *parens patriae* when they remove children from the custody of abusive or neglectful parents or appoint a guardian *ad litem* to represent children in a nasty divorce.

Philosophers and religious scholars have debated when life begins for thousands of years. For many years, the

Roman Catholic Church taught that life began at "quickening," when a mother felt movement in the womb, usually not earlier than 13-16 weeks after conception. In the 19th Century, the Church decided that life began much earlier at the moment of conception.

In *Roe,* Justice Blackmun discussed viability of the fetus to live outside the womb. In 1973, viability was considered to occur at 28 weeks. He used that threshold as a basis for his demarcation of rules regarding abortion. Today, thanks to scientific and technological developments, viability is deemed to occur at 23 or 24 weeks. So, should we move up the right of a State to ban abortion after 24 weeks?

Roe represents a compromise of competing interests. On the one hand, a woman should have the right to control her own body. On the other hand, a State should have the right to protect a child who lacks an advocate. At what point during a pregnancy do the State's rights and duties override the woman's rights, if at all? Until *Dobbs,* the fight has been over this question, as conservative States have continually pushed the limits of the second trimester middle ground of *Roe* by imposing restrictions on access to abortions in multiple ways, including by age, parental consent, and providers. In fact, even in *Dobbs,* the primary issue was whether Mississippi could ban most abortions after 15 weeks, not whether the Court should overrule *Roe* in its entirety.

While many people believe that *Roe* correctly found a right to abortion, albeit on the somewhat shaky premise of a penumbral right to privacy, the Court arguably exceeded normal judicial functions in setting up rules for abortions based on trimester stages. It should have left those rules up to State legislatures.

Similarly, while Justice Alito was correct in the way he

technically dismantled *Roe*, Chief Justice Roberts' concurrence makes a strong argument that Alito went too far in deciding the case in front of the Court. The Court could have and should have decided the case simply by upholding the Mississippi statute banning most abortions after 15 weeks. There was no need to go further and overturn *Roe* completely. In fact, just as Justice Alito criticized *Roe* for exceeding judicial functions, he violated the standard Supreme Court practices of following its own precedents and of deciding cases narrowly, particularly when Constitutional rights are concerned.

Justice Alito tried to rationalize his overruling of a 50-year precedent by arguing that the Court is obligated to correct wrongly decided precedents. As an example, he pointed to the overturning of the "separate but equal" principle announced in the 1896 decision in *Plessy v. Ferguson*, 163 U.S. 537 (1896), when 58 years later the Court decided that separate was inherently not equal in *Brown v. Board of Education*, 347 U.S. 483 (1954), which required integration of public schools with "all deliberate speed." What he failed to acknowledge was that *Brown* corrected a 58-year old <u>wrong</u> that deprived Blacks equal rights. *Dobbs* did just the opposite—it deprived women of a 49-year old <u>right</u>.

The judicial principle of *stare decisis*, meaning to stand by previous decisions and adhere to precedents, is the very basis of old English common law on which our judicial system has always been based. Essentially, English law developed through judges relying on decisions in earlier, similar cases. This approach served a few purposes. First, it provided notice to and assured the public that certain conduct would be treated the same way in the future, thereby providing certainty and guidance in how to conduct oneself. Second, it avoided reinventing the wheel and coming up with a different result each time.

In fact, the Supreme Court has rarely completely overruled its own precedent, particularly a longstanding precedent. One example of adherence to *stare decisis* shows how firm the principle can be. In *Federal Baseball Club of Baltimore, Inc. v. National League of Professional Baseball Clubs*, 259 U.S. 200 (1922), Justice Oliver Wendall Holmes, Jr. held in 1922 that the federal antitrust laws did not apply to professional baseball teams because each game was played solely within one state, despite the fact that the visiting team had usually traveled from another state, and, therefore, the games did not affect interstate commerce, which was the Constitutional basis (found in Section 8 of Article I) empowering Congress to enact the antitrust statutes. This became known as baseball's antitrust exemption.

Eventually, however, the Supreme Court modified its view of what constitutes and affects interstate commerce when faced repeatedly with the issue of the constitutionality of President Roosevelt's New Deal statutes and programs during the Great Depression in the 1930s. Thus, the concept of interstate commerce expanded, and the Court found the antitrust laws applicable to other forms of entertainment presented in only one State at a time such as theater productions, boxing, football, and basketball. Each of these decisions questioned the logic of Justice Holmes' reasoning in *Federal Baseball*, construed it narrowly to apply only to baseball, and refused to overrule it.

This line of cases culminated in the 1972 decision in *Flood v. Kuhn*, 407 U.S. 258 (1972), in which Curt Flood sued Major League Baseball when he was traded against his will, claiming its reserve clause violated the antitrust laws. Justice Blackmun acknowledged that *Federal Baseball* was wrongly decided under modern views of the commerce clause. He decided, however, that *Federal Baseball's* holding that

Congress did not intend the antitrust laws to apply to baseball had endured for 50 years, that Congress had not amended the antitrust laws to cover baseball despite the ruling in *Federal Baseball,* and that the principle of *stare decisis* militated against overturning such a long-tenured precedent.

So, 50 years ago, the Supreme Court decided it would not correct a longstanding but poorly reasoned decision involving the game of baseball, but now it has decided to overrule a longstanding but somewhat flawed decision involving a woman's right to control her own body. While baseball is still a popular sport despite falling way behind football and even basketball as our national pastime, our society should clearly consider it more important to protect a woman's right to determine what is going on with and in her body than to preserve baseball's antitrust exemption.

The Federal Rules of Civil Procedure direct trial courts to strive for a just result and to construe pleadings "so as to do justice." While those rules do not apply to Supreme Court cases, the Supreme Court should adhere to the mission and goal of doing justice. *Dobbs* failed to do justice, and the Restated Constitution needs to rectify the injustice it committed.

One can understand the logic and sincerity of some pro-life proponents who truly believe that life begins at conception, that abortion is the murder of a poor, defenseless human being, and that the mother's wishes and right to control her own body cannot justify the termination of the fetus' life. After all, who would claim that it is okay to kill a baby once it has been born? Clearly, the State has a strong and legitimate interest in protecting the baby's life after birth.

Many pro-lifers, however, do not truly value human life. They want to nuke Iran and North Korea. They tend to also believe in other conservative views, such as capital punishment and unqualified rights to own guns that destroy human lives. True, there is a big difference between a defenseless, innocent fetus and convicted murderers and terrorists, but, as discussed below in the context of capital punishment, a human life is a human life and no one, not even the Government, should take a human's life. The questions, as stated before, are whether a fetus is a viable human life and at what point it becomes one.

Additionally, many pro-lifers are also hard on crime and believe that criminals should be locked up for a long time. In the 50 years since *Roe*, however, crime has steadily decreased and the decrease has been linked in part to fewer unwanted births and the resulting unwanted and neglected children who turn to crime.

Another characteristic of many pro-lifers is an aversion to the welfare state. Banning abortion, however, would increase dependence on welfare for many single mothers and their unwanted children.

The hardest thing to reconcile, though, is pro-lifers' view that they and the Government may decide whether a woman can get an abortion while at the same time believing that the Government and public should keep the heck out of other people's lives. Some of these pro-lifers believe that owning a gun is a God-given right that the Government must not regulate or that no Government can force them to be vaccinated. If they believe so strongly in an individual's rights and choices, who are they to prohibit a woman from having a procedure on her own body, at least during the first two trimesters?

Accordingly, an anti-abortion stance actually undermines other positions that many pro-lifers hold and reveals them for the hypocrites they are.

It is absurd that so many pro-lifers are men. Who are they to force a female to carry an unwanted baby to full term? They come off as self-righteous and, if they ever impregnated a girlfriend, would most likely insist she get an abortion, just like Hershel Walker did the several times that we know of.

In the end, it is difficult to draw absolute bright-line rules on abortion. As a society, we must reach a compromise that recognizes a woman's right to control her own body and a State's right and duty to protect a fetus. The beauty of *Roe* was that it found a compromise, although the Court probably went beyond its power in doing so.

Consequently, in this Section, abortion is protected as an express right with certain limitations, following somewhat the *Roe* formula. As in *Roe*, all abortions are absolutely legal in the first trimester. Unlike *Roe*, that absolute right continues through the second trimester. *Roe*'s balancing of individual and State's interests in the second trimester has provided conservative States incentives to impose excessive restrictions on abortions that serve to nullify the right to abortions.

To make sure that "absolute right" means "absolute," the absolute right extends to "[e]very female, regardless of age or parental consent." This language addresses two areas that some States have used to deny abortions. The term "female" is used instead of "woman" to avoid a debate over when a girl becomes a woman and to cover many females who are in the direst need of abortions precisely because they are adolescents who lacked judgment and knowledge of or access to contraceptives.

This Section also gives them the right to an abortion regardless of parental consent because many are too embarrassed to tell their parents of their pregnancies and many of their parents would override their decision to obtain an abortion. While our society gives parents pretty much total control over their kids, a pregnancy is so personal that even young girls should be entitled to decide on their own whether to go through with a pregnancy.

Some people may argue that underage girls are too young to make a decision of this magnitude. If, however, they are deemed too young to decide whether to have an abortion, they should likewise be deemed to have been too young to make an informed decision to have unprotected sex with the high risk of pregnancy and should not be forced by their parents to continue the pregnancy. In fact, this concept is the basis for deeming underage girls incapable of giving consent to sex under statutory rape laws.

In the third trimester, the State begins to have a legitimate interest in protecting a fetus because it would most likely be viable outside the womb, as medical science has demonstrated in the case of premature births and emergency cesarean sections. Thus, the right to abortion is not absolute in the third trimester, but a right to abortion continues **"if the pregnancy or birth poses a reasonably high danger to her physical or mental health or the fetus has a severe medical defect or condition, as determined in consultation with her medical providers, or if she is the victim of a rape or incest."** Most Americans believe that abortion should be legal in these situations, and the needs and legitimacy for such abortions are obvious. Of course, this Section would not prevent a State from providing greater rights and continuing the absolute right to all abortions into the third trimester.

To make sure that States do not try to get around the right to abortion by placing onerous restrictions on abortion medical providers and facilities, this Section protects all qualified medical providers.

Finally, to make sure that these rights to an abortion are not simply ethereal or philosophical rights, this Section provides that "no Government shall interfere with such rights to an abortion or to perform abortions." This may seem redundant of Article I, Section 16, but the battle over abortion has been going on too long and this provision can be viewed as emphatic rather than simply repetitive.

Long ago, abortion opponents cleverly dubbed themselves "pro-life" rather than "anti-abortion" to convey the message that they were charitable and selfless individuals and to imply that abortion rights advocates were, conversely, against life and were baby killers. Abortion rights advocates similarly dubbed themselves "pro-choice" to send the message that they were not encouraging abortions but rather supporting the right to choose whether to undergo an abortion.

This Section simply provides the option for an abortion. The Government and the public in general should interfere as little as possible when it comes to our rights to privacy and self-determination for our own bodies, and the choice of whether to abort a fetus should be made in accordance with a female's own personal beliefs, circumstances, plans, and desires.

This Section also addresses the right to abort a fetus that doctors detect is deformed or disabled. While those conditions can often be determined well before the third trimester, developments and detection may not occur until the third trimester. Consequently, such a fetus may be aborted in the third trimester in consultation with medical providers.

In the wake of *Dobbs*, voters in California, Michigan, and Vermont approved amendments preserving the right to abortion in their constitutions. Even more telling were the convincing defeat of a measure in conservative Kansas to remove the right to abortion from its constitution and the defeat of a measure to ban abortion in the constitution of another red State, Kentucky.

All told, there are about a dozen States where the right to abortion is expressly provided in their constitutions or where their Supreme Courts have held that such a right is covered by the right to privacy in their constitutions.[4] In light of all the emotional warfare, manipulative State legislation, and inconsistent court rulings in the 50 years since *Roe* despite the views of a supermajority of Americans favoring the right to abortion, it is now time to enshrine the right to abortion in the Restated Constitution.

Perhaps, Section 2 should just declare a right to abortion without all the detailed circumstances, but in the 50 years since *Roe*, State legislatures have proven too clever at whittling away the right to abortion. We can't let that happen again.

CITIZENSHIP

3.   All persons born or naturalized in the United States and subject to the jurisdiction thereof, **including its possessions and territories,** are citizens of the United States. **All persons born outside the United States or its possessions or territories to at least one parent who was a United States citizen at the time of their birth and who previously resided in the United States are citizens of the United States. All persons domiciled or residing in the United States or its possessions or territories on the Effective Date of this Restated Constitution who entered or have remained in the United States illegally shall be deemed citizens of the United States.** No State shall make or enforce any law

that abridges the privileges, **rights, liberties, freedoms,** or immunities of citizens of the United States. [14th Amend., Sect. 1]

Citizenship

Citizenship is the very foundation of the political structure of our country. Yet, citizenship is barely mentioned and not even defined in the original Constitution.

Under Sections 2 and 3 of Article I of the Constitution, only a citizen of at least seven years is eligible to serve in the House of Representatives and only a citizen of at least nine years is eligible to serve in the Senate. There is no explanation of how such citizens attain citizenship.

The requirement for President and Vice President is even more stringent. Under Section 1 of Article II, the President must be a natural born citizen or a citizen at the time of the adoption of the Constitution in 1788 and must have been a resident within the United States for 14 years prior to election. Thus, George Washington through the ninth President, William Henry Harrison, plus the twelfth President, Zachary Taylor, who were all born before 1788, were eligible because they were citizens of former colonies in 1788. Alexander Hamilton, who was born on the Caribbean island of Nevis was also eligible because he had been living in New York since 1772. All other Presidents have been eligible because they were born in the United States. Foreigners who become citizens through naturalization are not eligible to become President.

Interestingly, Article III of the Constitution contains no requirement that federal judges be citizens. Section 2 of Article III establishes federal court jurisdiction over various situations involving citizens of the States.

Section 2 of Article IV of the Constitution states that the

"Citizens of each State shall be entitled to all Privileges and Immunities of Citizens in the several States." This provision is a cornerstone of federalism and requires each State to treat citizens of other States as if they were their own citizens. So, a State cannot enact laws that favor its citizens or discriminate against citizens of another State. This provision appears in Section 2 of Article VI of the Restated Constitution.

That's about it for treatment of citizens in the original Constitution. In fact, one of the greatest rights of citizenship, the right to vote, is not described in terms of citizenship. Rather, "the People of the several States" elect the Representatives in Section 2 of Article I. Senators were originally chosen by State legislatures until the 17th Amendment in 1913 handed their election to "the people." Under Section 1 of Article II, the President is still chosen by Electors, not by citizens or the people.

The original Section 2 of Article I provided that the calculation of the number of representatives from each state would be based on the number of free persons (not just citizens) and three-fifths "of all other Persons," meaning each slave was counted as three-fifths of a person. This Three-Fifths Compromise resulted from the Southern States' desire to add slaves to their population count for the purpose of allocation of seats in Congress and the Northern States' objections to the South's hypocrisy of treating slaves as property in general but as persons to be represented in Congress. As a result, Virginia was awarded ten seats in the House, the most of any State. The Three-Fifths Compromise gave the South enough seats in the House to pass pro-slavery legislation and influence the results of the Electoral College's Presidential vote up to the Civil War.

It wasn't until after slavery was abolished by the 13th Amendment in 1865 and the ratification of the 14th Amendment in 1868, that the Three-Fifths Compromise was effectively rescinded. Section 1 of the 14th Amendment provides that "[a]ll persons born or naturalized in the United States and subject to the jurisdiction thereof, are citizens of the United States and of the State wherein they reside." This Section meant that the slaves freed by the 13th Amendment were now citizens because they had been either born in the United States or naturalized in the course of enslavement after importation.

This Section of the Restated Constitution borrows that language from the 14th Amendment and makes it clear that it extends as well to people born or later naturalized in U.S. possessions and territories, such as Puerto Rico and the U.S. Virgin Islands. This express statement and definition of citizenship should have been in the original Constitution and needs to be carried over from the 14th Amendment.

This Section also makes it clear that "[a]ll persons born outside the United States or its possessions or territories to at least one parent who was a citizen at the time of their birth and who previously resided in the United States are citizens of the United States." This covers the simplest of multiple scenarios in 8 U.S.C. § 1401 creating U.S. citizenship at birth to foreign-born babies, leaving other situations to that statute or future ones.

Immigration

America is the greatest country in the world. No other country comes close. If determining the greatness of countries were an Olympic event, the USA would win gold and no silver or bronze would be awarded.

What makes a country, and the U.S., in particular, great? Let's start with freedom. Freedom of speech, freedom of religion and worship, freedom of travel, freedom of privacy, freedom to do what you want to do so long as you don't harm or impose on others. Freedom to vote for representatives in a democracy. Freedom from monarchs, dictators, tyrants. Protections from abuse and discrimination, although not always respected and implemented.

Opportunities for gainful employment, education, and decent housing. An abundance of food, consumer products, and creature comforts. Premier arts, culture, sports, and entertainment. Advanced technology and medical treatment. Infrastructure and engineering. Natural resources and national parks.

Yes, America has severe drug addiction, alcoholism, and homelessness. Yes, America has gang violence and slums that are hard to escape from. Yes, America has a huge disparity between some of the wealthiest people in the world and some of the poorest.

But since America began, people have striven desperately to enter this country, legally or illegally, with the goal of becoming U.S. citizens. Compared to their native countries, America's streets have appeared paved in gold.

At first, America welcomed immigrants, recognizing that there was plenty of land to accommodate them, especially as the country kept expanding westward. America simply needed lots of bodies to settle the West. Around the middle of the 19th Century, however, the xenophobic American Party, referred to as the Know Nothings, advocated nativist and nationalistic themes and protested against immigrants from Ireland and Germany, wildly warning of a Roman Catholic overthrow of America's Protestant sensibilities.[5]

Since then, there have been recurring waves of nationalism and anti-immigrant hostility. Many times, as one group of immigrants gradually gains acceptance in American society, it has joined the anti-immigrant clamor of longer entrenched Americans in vilifying and persecuting the next group of immigrants. The Germans and Irish looked down upon subsequent immigrants from Italy and Jews from Eastern Europe, who, in turn, looked down upon Latinos and Asians.

The first- and second-generation Americans tend to view themselves as true Americans and forget the subservient status of their immigrant parents and grandparents. Only lip service is paid to the notion that America is a land of immigrants. Heck, even the so-called Native Americans came from Asia over an ancient land bridge into Alaska. So, all Americans are descended from immigrants, and the notion of superiority based on the number of generations removed from immigration is nonsense. After all, the highest assertion of nobility in America is to claim an ancestor came over on the Mayflower, despite the fact that the Puritans were, themselves, refugees and were tyrannical and not tolerant of others.

As stated above, immigration was encouraged as the country grew in size. In 1875, however, as a result of growing animosity against Chinese, Congress passed the Chinese Exclusion Act, which, as the name suggests, prohibited the immigration of Chinese for ten years. The time period was extended once and became permanent in 1902 until it was repealed in 1943. After the Chinese Exclusion Act, Congress periodically enacted laws restricting different categories of immigrants, culminating in the 1920s with the establishment of national origin quotas that severely constricted immigration until the Immigration and Nationality Act of 1965, which replaced quotas based on national origins with quotas based on the Eastern and Western Hemispheres. Thereafter, Congress has repeatedly tinkered with immigration laws.

Nowadays, immigration policy is a constant political hot potato. Republicans want to build walls and spurn refugees and asylum seekers. They want to expel the Dreamers, children brought here illegally by their parents who have been raised and educated here and many of whom serve in the military, are employed, or are otherwise contributing to our society. Democrats want to loosen immigration restrictions and make the Dreamers citizens.

What a flip-flop between the parties. In 1986, President Reagan and the Republicans passed the Immigration Reform and Control Act that granted amnesty to aliens who had resided illegally in the United States since 1982. At that time, Republicans favored open immigration policies to provide cheap labor for businesses, particularly in agricultural work. For some reason, Democrats favored stricter immigration policy.

This Section grants a similar amnesty to anyone who entered and has remained illegally in the U.S. as of the Effective Date of the Restated Constitution: **"All persons domiciled or residing in the United States or its possessions or territories on the Effective Date of this Restated Constitution who entered or have remained in the United States illegally shall be deemed citizens of the United States."**

In September 2021, Secretary of Homeland Security Alejandro Mayorkas estimated that there were over 11 million undocumented aliens in America and that it was not possible to round them all up for deportation.[6] We are wasting too much time and resources on tracking down and expelling illegal aliens. We are trying to fix a problem that is not broken. Contrary to conservative assumptions that immigrants from Central and South America are criminals and rapists or come here to go on welfare, most immigrants contribute to our society by holding down two or three jobs and are willing to do work that many lower-class Americans deem beneath their dignity, such as cleaning houses, mowing lawns, working at fast-food restaurants, and other minimum wage jobs.

Accordingly, it is time to reset the immigration situation by granting another amnesty to illegal aliens 40 years after the last amnesty. Future immigration policy is left to Congress.

Protection of U.S. Citizens' Rights

The end of this Section declares, "No State shall make or enforce any law that abridges the privileges, **rights, liberties, freedoms,** or immunities of citizens of the United States." This language comes from Section 1 of the 14th Amendment and adds "rights," "liberties," and "freedoms" to expand on the original "privileges" and "immunities" to ensure that the full panoply of rights is protected.

As mentioned at the beginning of this section, Section 2 of Article IV of the Constitution states that the "Citizens of each State shall be entitled to all Privileges and Immunities of Citizens in the several States." That provision required States to provide to citizens of other States the same rights as it provided its own citizens.

The corollary to that provision is the one borrowed at the end of this Section from the 14th Amendment, which prohibits States from making or enforcing laws that deprive any citizens, regardless of the States they live in, of their rights as U.S. citizens. This provision was enacted in 1868 in the aftermath of the Civil War and was primarily designed to protect the freed slaves from mistreatment during Reconstruction. Unfortunately, it was honored more in the breach during the Jim Crow era.

Eventually, the Supreme Court read this provision to extend most of the Bill of Rights that applied only to the federal government to conduct by the States, as well.

VOTING

4.   The right of United States citizens who are 18 years of age or older to vote **in any election or primary** shall not be denied or abridged by the Government on account of age, race, color, sex, **sexual orientation, gender identity, literacy, payment of a fee or tax of any kind, conviction of or imprisonment for any crime, homelessness, or lack of any Government issued identification. Notwithstanding the foregoing, election officials may require that voters provide proof of identity and domicile.** [15th, 19th, 24th and 26th Amend.]

A truly direct democracy would be a government operated by its entire citizenry, and all citizens would have the opportunity to be heard on each issue and to participate in each decision. Even the ancient Athenians, the closest practitioners of direct democracy, fell short of a truly direct democracy by limiting their governing body, the *Ekklesia*, or Assembly, to free, male citizens.

Perhaps recognizing that the distance along the East Coast from New England to Georgia and a population of close to 4 million, as counted in the first census in 1790 and a hundred times larger than ancient Athens, militated against a true democracy, the Framers developed a democracy by proxy in which representatives of the citizens met, debated, and voted on issues. In this form of democracy known as a republic, the constituents vote for the people who represent them in the legislative and executive branches.

That was the theory, but the Framers further diluted the democracy by limiting the popular vote to the House of Representatives and designating Senators to be chosen by State legislatures and the President and Vice President to be chosen by Electors. They further eroded the "representative" aspect of the democracy by failing to define eligibility for voters and leaving that to the States, which tended to permit only free, male landowning citizens to vote. Thus, a large segment of the citizenry had no say even in electing the House of Representatives.

The right to vote is the fundamental foundation of a democracy, and the natural extension of that concept in a representative democracy is the right to vote for the representatives. Thus, the right to vote evolved and expanded through multiple Constitutional amendments over time. In 1870, the 15th Amendment granted people of color and former slaves the right to vote. In 1920, the 19th Amendment granted women the right to vote. In 1964, because Southern States devised ways to get around the 15th Amendment and deny Blacks the right to vote, the 24th Amendment prohibited the practice of imposing poll taxes that served to discourage poor Blacks from voting. In 1971, in response to protests arguing that it was unfair to deem 18-year olds old enough to be drafted to fight in the Vietnam War but not old enough to vote, the 26th Amendment lowered the voting age universally to 18.

Despite these four amendments, some States continue to make it harder to vote. How many more times will voters in Ohio and some Southern States have to wait in lines for hours to vote? How many legal battles have to be fought over Election Day registrations? Congress' refusal to renew the Voting Rights Act of 1965 was based on the false premise that all voter intimidation and discrimination have been cured now. On the contrary, we need to make stronger efforts to encourage and facilitate greater voter participation.

We claim to have a representative democracy, but the percentage of eligible voters who actually register and vote is pretty low. Aside from Presidential elections, many State and local elections draw only a third or fewer of the eligible voters. Even in 2020, when mail ballots prompted by the pandemic and vitriol stoked by the Presidential candidates fueled a surge in voter participation, only two-thirds of eligible voters voted.

The old Soviet Union forced its citizens to vote by making it a crime **not** to vote. Perhaps, they thought a 100% voter participation rate would demonstrate to the world that communism was superior to democracy and capitalism. In any event, whatever point they were trying to make was severely undermined by the fact that there was only one candidate for each office because there was only one party. So, the irony is that every citizen in the Soviet Union voted for the single candidate for each office, while in the United States only a fraction of citizens vote even though they could choose among two or more candidates for all offices and could also write in their own candidates. Freedom is often taken for granted.

One of the few good things to come out of the pandemic was the emergency employment of voting by mail or public ballot boxes that most States instituted. While absentee ballots have been around for a long time, very few States allowed early voting without an excuse that the voter was infirm or would be out of town on Election Day. It is time we give up the notion that Election Day should replicate a Town Hall meeting where everyone votes on the same day. We can avoid all the hassles of long lines, travel, bad weather, and bad tempers by moving to mail or early ballots or, better yet, electronic voting as in Oregon. We can also move national and Presidential elections from the first Tuesday following the first Monday of November to the first Saturday *and* Sunday following the first Monday of November, as set forth in Article II of the Restated Constitution, to give people two days to vote on the weekend, which should be more convenient.

As to concerns about the reliability of remote voting, we conduct business, in general, and governmental business, such as car registration, filing of income tax returns, Social Security, and Medicare, by mail or electronically without fear of widespread fraud. We need to remove barriers to voting, and we now have the technology to do so. Not only will mail and electronic voting speed up the counting of votes, but it will considerably reduce the costs incurred in staffing polling places.

So, instead of maintaining the incremental steps in formulating voting rights spread over four nonsequential amendments over a century, they are all consolidated in a single Section. Sexual orientation and gender identity are added to form the litany of protected classifications that appear in Sections 1 and 13 of Article I for consistency. While there do not seem to have been attempts to deny voting rights based on sexual orientation or gender identity, such discrimination would be wrong and we may as well nip that potential problem in the bud now.

Literacy tests went hand in hand with poll taxes as a way to prevent poor, uneducated Blacks from voting in the South, so those are prohibited along with poll taxes. Illiteracy is not the same thing as mental incompetence. For example, people with dyslexia do not have low IQs. People who cannot read English because they don't speak English can still make informed decisions.

Surely, there are ways to help people who are illiterate or can't read English to vote, such as allowing them to vote orally, with a translator if necessary, and having the town clerk mark their ballots or otherwise attest to their choices. There are Braille ballots for blind voters, and we can similarly accommodate voters who cannot read. Ballots in foreign languages are not burdensome to produce because they consist mostly of the candidates' names with very little instruction, such as "vote for one of the following." Heck, in New York, you can take a written learner driving permit test in Albanian, Arabic, Bengali, Bosnian, Chinese, French, Greek, Hebrew, Italian, Japanese, Korean, Nepali, Polish, Russian, and Spanish.[7]

In any event, the ability to make wise decisions has never been a criterion for voting, and we have had many elections whose results prove that point.

Felons

There is no federal statute and no provision in the Constitution addressing the issue of whether persons convicted of felonies are eligible to vote. About half of the States allow felons to vote upon completion of their sentences, and other States allow them to vote upon fulfillment of certain conditions related to parole, probation, time, and the nature of the crimes. The right to vote is automatically restored in some States, but, in others, felons must apply to restore their rights to vote. A few States make it almost impossible for felons to vote. On the other hand, convicts never lose their right to vote and may vote even while incarcerated in Maine, Vermont, and the District of Columbia.[8]

The trend is toward allowing felons who have completed their sentences to vote. The argument is that they have served their punishment, have reentered society, and should be assisted in successfully assimilating back into the community in every way possible to reduce recidivism. Attaching stigmas and conditions to their everyday lives creates frustration, feelings of futility, and depression that understandably lead them back to inappropriate and illegal conduct and, as a result, prison.

With respect to the approximately 2 million felons who are still serving time in prison, the argument has been that they have been isolated from society due to their illegal and harmful conduct and, therefore, have forfeited any rights to participate in society's democracy. That argument, however, has no logical basis.

First, unless the felon has committed a crime undermining the integrity of the voting system such as voter fraud, the removal of voting rights has no relationship to the crime and is cruel and unusual punishment in violation of the 8th Amendment. Second, prisoners retain other rights while incarcerated, such as the right to bring lawsuits, which they exercise quite frequently, especially through claims against the prison system and corrections officers.

Third, in some States, the prisoners are counted as residents of the locale in which the prison is sited for purposes of drawing district boundaries for local and national elections. If they are counted as residents for representative purposes, they should be permitted to have a say in electing their representatives. Furthermore, just like recourse to the courts, prisoners should be permitted to seek redress from their local, State, and federal representatives about any matters that constituents raise, not only concerning their prison conditions but other personal issues such as Social Security or veteran benefits or general political issues. Needless to say, these representatives will pay more attention if they know the prisoners have the right to vote. Denying prisoners the right to vote is the same thing as the Three-Fifths Compromise that counted a slave as three-fifths of a person for purposes of determining the number of representatives in Congress but did not permit the slave to vote.

Accordingly, this Section provides that anyone who is otherwise eligible to vote by virtue of citizenship and age cannot be denied the right to vote due to conviction or imprisonment.

Homelessness and Lack of IDs

It is estimated that there are over half a million homeless people in America, many of whom are veterans. If they are over 18 and are citizens, they have a right to vote. Most polling sites, however, require proof of residence. How does a homeless person prove that he or she lives under a bridge? They don't have a mortgage or lease and can't produce recently post-marked mail addressed to an interstate overpass. Very few have unexpired driver's licenses, and the addresses indicated in those have been abandoned.

Aside from vagabonds hopping freight cars, most homeless people tend to stay in the same locale. So, any concern that a homeless person may be simply passing through on Election Day is exaggerated.

A different concern that a candidate's campaign may be rounding up homeless people to vote multiple times under different names at different polling grounds sounds more legitimate. That's the story of how Edgar Allan Poe died on Election Day in Baltimore in 1849 after being plied with liquor and trotted around to multiple polling places.

In addition to homeless people, there are other citizens, particularly in cities, who do not have driver's licenses or any other government-issued photo ID. Many of these people do not speak English, fly under the Government's radar, and/or are fearful of the Government.

How do we open up voting for homeless people or people lacking acceptable photo IDs while at the same time verifying their eligibility and preventing voter fraud? Since they have the Constitutional right to vote, however, we need to figure out how to protect the integrity of the vote. Consequently, this Section provides, "**Notwithstanding the foregoing, election officials may require that voters provide proof of identity and domicile.**" In other words, officials need to explore ways to verify the identity of the voters and the town or city in which they live, even if they do not reside at a specific address.

FREEDOM OF SPEECH AND OF THE PRESS

5.   All persons shall have the right to exercise freedom of speech, freedom to assemble peacefully, and freedom to petition the Government for a redress of grievances. The media shall likewise enjoy freedom of expression. **Notwithstanding the foregoing, the Government may restrict or punish hate speech, hate crimes, and speech advocating the overthrow of the Government by force. Similarly, targets and victims of hate speech or hate crimes shall have the right to sue civilly the perpetrators of such hate speech or hate crimes. This Section shall not affect common law claims such as infliction of emotional distress, defamation, and invasion of privacy.** [1ˢᵗ Amend.]

While the wording of the free speech aspects of the 1ˢᵗ Amendment is being changed, the first two sentences are not bolded because the gist of the 1ˢᵗ Amendment is not changing. Rather, as discussed in the case of the freedom of worship and religion in Section 1, freedom of speech and freedom of the press are being expressed as affirmative rights rather than as principles that Congress should not abridge. As also discussed above, these rights are being protected not only from Congress but from State and local governments, as well, by defining the rights here and separately providing in Section 16 that "the Government shall respect, shall be bound by, and shall not violate, infringe, or abridge the personal rights, liberties, and freedoms in this Article."

Hate Crimes

The language added in bold summarizes two of the exceptions to freedom of speech and freedom of the press. While we can leave the other exceptions, such as regulation of commercial speech, to the case law that has developed over the centuries, the accelerating toxic climate of hate speech, hate crimes, and insurrection that has been festering for decades and that social media has fostered demands addressing expressly in this Section.

In the late 1970s, the National Socialist Party of America, a neo-Nazi organization, applied for a permit to march in Skokie, Illinois, a location it deliberately picked because of the high number of Jewish Holocaust survivors in that town north of Chicago. Not surprisingly, the permit was denied, and the American Civil Liberties Union, always an ardent advocate for freedom of speech, sued on the neo-Nazis' behalf to allow them to march. The Illinois state courts refused to overturn the denial of the permit. The U.S. Supreme Court, however, sent the case back to the Illinois courts on procedural grounds. Eventually, the Illinois courts allowed the march to proceed. Despite that victory, the neo-Nazis decided to move the march from Skokie to Chicago due to the furor the followers of the Fuehrer had provoked and to dissension among their ranks. Ultimately, the two dozen neo-Nazis who marched were drowned out by the thousands of counter-protesters.[9]

At the time, it seemed more important to preserve the ideal of freedom of speech than to protect the understandable sensitivities of not only the Holocaust survivors but also all Jews as well as gentile World War II veterans and their families. After all, it is easy to proclaim and espouse freedom of speech when people are debating a big box store development proposal at a sleepy Town Council meeting. The true test of freedom of speech occurs only when the question is whether to allow loathsome, offensive, and odious speech.

Forty years later in 2017, the neo-Nazi/white supremacist group Unite the Right marched in Charlottesville, Virginia, ostensibly to protest the removal of an equestrian statue of General Robert E. Lee from Lee Park. The march devolved into violence and chants of "Jews will not replace us," which obviously had nothing to do with General Lee. Commenting on the incident, President Trump said, there were "very fine people on both sides."

The proliferation of hate speech has reached new heights in recent years, boosted by easy access for millions of people to social media platforms from which they can launch their vitriol to the millions of receptive ears.

In the second half of the 20th Century, the print and TV press strove to present objective and accurate reporting of facts. Those days are gone.

Shortly after the horrific massacre of Sandy Hook Elementary School children and staff in Newtown, Connecticut in 2012, Alex Jones spouted groundless, insane accusations on his Infowars radio show that the entire incident had been a hoax staged with actors in a plot by the government to take guns away from the people. Parents of the victims sued him for infliction of emotional distress and in 2022 were awarded billions of dollars in damages. They proved that he knew his accusations were false but that he continued to spew them out because they drove up his ratings and sales of his merchandise. The worst part of his malicious rants and ravings was that a lot of people believed him and they, in turn, sent messages taunting the parents.

What has happened to America? How could anyone hear about the shattered, mutilated bodies of seven-year old boys and girls, listen to police press conferences, and watch the suffering of grieving parents and yet callously believe that it was all faked? No Hollywood production could ever replicate the true horror of what happened at Sandy Hook. No actor could perform so convincingly.

So, the Government should be permitted to define and punish hate crimes, and victims of hate speech should have recourse to compensation and protection through the courts.

Advocating Rebellion

Advocating the overthrow of the Government by force has long been an exception to freedom of speech. You can say just about anything critical of the Government, and you can advocate ousting elected officials through the election system and changing the laws and forms of the Government peacefully. You just can't incite insurrection by force and violence, which is the way most governments changed before the ratification of the Constitution supplanted the Articles of Confederation in 1788.

In fact, this book is a prime example of permissible freedom of speech. Although advocating for dramatic changes in the structure of our Government, implementation of those changes is proposed through the very process of amendment as provided in the Constitution, itself, and not by overthrowing the Government through the use of force or violence.

Before January 6, 2021, America had become complacent in its assumption that election results would be respected and power would be transferred peacefully. George Washington set the stage by voluntarily stepping down after two terms as President. John Adams set the standard when he simply left Washington, D.C. on the morning of Thomas Jefferson's inauguration after a bitter campaign.

Consequently, it was appalling to witness the storming of Congress by insurrectionists on January 6, 2021. It seemed that time-honored American traditions and morality had been tossed out the window as the mob crashed through the Capitol's windows. All hell broke loose, and, due to the pandemic, most of America was at home watching it live.

Many of the insurrectionists have been caught, prosecuted, and sentenced. Time will tell whether the true culprits, who incited the intruders but did not approach the Capitol, will be punished.

So, however broad we may wish our cherished freedom of speech and freedom of the press to remain, there are reasonable limits that the Government should be able to draw to protect the country from violent rebellion, insurrection, and coups.

The final sentence in this Section makes it clear that the Section does not affect civil claims like infliction of emotional distress, defamation, and invasion of privacy developed over the years in the common law.

Free Speech in the Private Sector

As noted before, the 1st Amendment only prohibited Congress from interfering with freedom of speech and freedom of the press. The 14th Amendment extended that prohibition to the States.

Neither the 1st nor the 14th Amendment, however, prohibits private actors from restricting or punishing speech. To that point, nowadays, it is almost expected that private employers will discipline, if not summarily terminate, employees for saying something that is not politically correct. The exposé of racist and misogynist statements, even if uttered many years ago, is often met with public clamoring for immediate discharge. Employers, eager to cater to their customers lest they lose sales, dismiss employees or spokespersons as soon as their blunders surface.

An egregious example of this zero-tolerance attitude is the pressure to resign exerted on Senator Al Franken by other politicians after pictures came to light of his goofing around at the expense of a female comedian when he was still a comedian years before his election to the Senate. While such conduct may have been unbecoming of a U.S. Senator, it is expected of comedians.

Elon Musk is such a fierce advocate of free speech in the private sector that he acquired Twitter, which he renamed "X," as part of his mission to remove censorship of content and has lifted the ban on Trump's account that had been imposed for his persistent lies and twisted versions of facts.

Of course, legal claims for defamation and invasion of privacy provide some curb on private freedom of speech, unless the subject of the speech is a public figure, in which case the law developed under the 1st Amendment requires that the plaintiff subject prove that the defendant speaker made the statement with malice and in reckless disregard of its truth. Plus, while truth is a defense to a defamation claim, the burden is on the defendant speaker to prove the truth of the statement, unlike in England where the burden is on the plaintiff to prove the falsity of the statement.

Free Speech in the Land of the Free and the Home of the Brave

We need to be vigilant about preserving the guaranty of free speech. For instance, it can be argued that the Government subtly infringes the right of free speech through the time-honored Pledge of Allegiance and the *Start-Spangled Banner*.

Most kids learn the Pledge of Allegiance in kindergarten, if not earlier, and recite it each day of primary and secondary education up through their high school graduation. When they first learn it, they understand barely half the words.

As kids grow older, they learn the meaning of the words but have said them so many times by rote that they never really pay much attention to what they are saying. At most, they experience and accept the Pledge as a morning ritual with some vague notion of performing a civic duty.

Making little kids spout back words of commitment that they don't understand while imprinting on them a sense they are performing a mandatory civic duty is the very definition of indoctrination and brain-washing. After all, don't we abhor it when we see a newsreel of German children in the Thirties and Forties stiff-arming while chanting their undying love for Adolph Hitler?

No one is required in the Constitution to pledge loyalty to America. No pledge is required by any federal statute, and statutes requiring school children to salute and pledge allegiance to the flag were held unconstitutional by the Supreme Court in 1943. The only expressly prescribed pledge in the Constitution appears at the end of Section 1 of Article II as the oath of office that the President takes when being sworn in: "I do solemnly swear (or affirm) that I will faithfully execute the Office of the President of the United States, and will to the best of my Ability, preserve, protect and defend the Constitution of the United States."

Think about the first words of the Pledge: "I pledge allegiance to the flag of the United States of America . . . ." Really? Should anyone really pledge allegiance to a flag, a piece of cloth? Doesn't pledging allegiance to a piece of cloth smack of idolatry? What's the difference between pledging allegiance to a piece of cloth with a distinct three-color, symbolic design and praying to graven images, which is prohibited by the second of the Ten Commandments? Many rah-rah cheerleaders of the Pledge also claim to be God-fearing Christians but fail to see that pledging allegiance to the flag necessarily violates the Second Commandment. After all, they wouldn't worship a golden calf.

Flag-wavers hold the flag up as an icon, something sacrosanct to be respected to the point of worship. In fact, we have a special holiday every June 14th to honor the flag, although not many people really observe Flag Day as a holiday and it hasn't yet been moved to a Monday to provide a three-day weekend.

In the late Sixties, college radicals would get arrested for wearing the flag as clothing in some manner or burning it in protest. Nowadays, in their fervor, flag supporters do not merely salute the flag with hats off and hands over heart, but they literally wrap themselves in the flag by wearing its design in ties, hats, t-shirts, and even bathing suits, meaning they inevitably will soil the flag with food, beer, and sweat and sit on it as it covers their patriotic butts. They believe self-righteously they are honoring the flag by wearing their hearts on their sleeves, even though wearing the flag contravenes 4 U.S.C. § 8(d). Try finding a politician without a flag pin in his or her jacket lapel.

So, why do the American flag, the Pledge, and the national anthem have so many devotees in the country that invented freedom of speech? Why is "Mom, the flag, and apple pie" the epitome of patriotism?

The Pledge is recited mostly in school where half-asleep kids mutter it with no thought to its meaning and in legislative sessions populated by politicians competing with one another to show off their undying love of God and country. Flag rituals opening government events and functions are understandable. After all, the Pledge states, "I pledge allegiance to the flag of the United States of America and to the republic for which it stands . . . ."

So, now the Pledge moves off of idolatry and gets to the point of showing loyalty to the country. In other words, the grand old flag is the "emblem of the land I love," to quote George M. Cohan's *You're a Grand Old Flag*. As a result, it makes sense to open a session of Congress, for example, with the Pledge, although it is not appropriate to require citizens to repeatedly vow their fealty to the country. Other instances where the Pledge at least relates to the occasion include swearing-in ceremonies for judges and Presidential and gubernatorial inaugurations, as well as parades on holidays such as Memorial Day, July 4th, and Veterans Day. Perhaps, the most and only important time to require the Pledge is during a naturalization ceremony when an immigrant becomes a citizen.

But how come we play *The Star-Spangled Banner* and salute the flag before sports games? Why do jet fighters fly over before kick-off at the Super Bowl? Why, after 9/11, do we sing *God Bless America* during the seventh-inning stretch and parade military officers in uniform on top of dugouts? We don't do any of these rituals before other forms of entertainment such as Broadway musicals, movies, rock concerts, or comedy acts.

The Star-Spangled Banner was not played before baseball games prior to the World Series between the Chicago Cubs and Boston Red Sox in 1918.[10] In fact, the national anthem did not become the official national anthem until an act of Congress in 1931. While people generally observe the playing of the national anthem by what they believe is custom, they probably don't realize that their conduct is prescribed by law requiring military members to salute and all others to "face the flag and stand at attention with their right hand over the heart, and men not in uniform, if applicable, should remove their headdress with their right hand and hold it at the left shoulder, the hand being over the heart." 36 U.S.C. § 301(b)(1)(C). Failure to stand, remove headgear, or place the right hand over the heart is, therefore, a technical violation of law, although not punishable as a criminal offense.

While Europe was immersed in the horrors of World War I, President Wilson tried his best to satisfy the isolationists and keep America out of the war. When Germany made the mistake of attacking U.S. ships, however, he had no choice but to enter the war. War protests, however, were just as vigorous then as they were against the Vietnam War 50 years later, and riots erupted in response to military drafts.

Presumably in an effort to change the national temper, Wilson reportedly asked Major League Baseball to play *The Star-Spangled Banner* at a ballgame as early as 1916.[11] Although not yet officially the national anthem, *The Star-Spangled Banner* was popularly thought of as such, along with, at various times, *Hail, Columbia*; *My Country, 'Tis of*

Thee; and *America the Beautiful*. As a war song of survival, it fit Wilson's agenda of propaganda to play before playing the national pastime. After the war, teams continued to play the song out of habit, which spread to other sports.

So, why do we continue to play *The Star-Spangled Banner* before games? After all, it has nothing to do with the game itself, unlike *Take Me Out to the Ballgame* sung during the seventh-inning stretch. The national anthem is played while fans are still streaming into the park, buying beer and hot dogs, looking for their seats, and taking selfies. In fact, television broadcasts rarely show the playing of the national anthem, preferring to show commercials or interviews with managers about the blister on their ace's pitching finger.

One reason to play it may be that sports events are the few times we assemble en masse in person. Sports stadiums in America serve the function of piazzas in Europe as a forum in which to assemble the citizenry. Major League Baseball games average between 10,000 and 45,000 in attendance, depending on the stadium and popularity of the teams. National Football League games average about 69,000, and the Dallas Cowboys at times break 90,000. When full, Memorial Stadium at the University of Nebraska holds more people than all but two cities in the state.

Thus, sports events present the best opportunity to impose the national anthem on the most people. Playing the national anthem today is not simply an historic relic, like the seventh inning stretch, that we perform perfunctorily out of tradition. Rather, the military honor guards and choirs that present the national anthem and other military activities, such as unfurling enormous flags across the outfield, singing *God Bless America* during the seventh-inning stretch, and jet fighter fly-overs, are, in fact, advertisements paid for by the Department of Defense to promote the military's image and increase enlistment.

It's clear, then, that playing the national anthem and other related activities are pro-governmental statements intended to impart and inculcate patriotic sentiment.

For several years starting with Colin Kaepernick in 2016, Black NFL players staged protests during the playing of the national anthem against America's treatment of Blacks, particularly white police officers' killing of unarmed black men, by kneeling, raising fists, or other forms of behavior not conforming to the statutory and traditional pose of standing with hand over heart. They have been criticized and cursed by President Trump, NFL owners, the media, and conservative politicians.

Of course, none of these hypocrites vilified Tim Tebow when, in his short football career, he would take a knee and pray on the field because they supported his exercise of free speech and free worship, although totally unrelated to the game of football and, therefore, inappropriate. Similarly, some baseball players cross themselves before every at-bat or point to heaven as they cross the plate after hitting a home run. Furthermore, a lot of athletes and coaches across many sports thank Jesus in interviews after their victories. No one objects to these personal statements even though it is not the time or place to express them.

Consequently, the outrage over NFL players kneeling is based solely on the content of the statements they are making. Our notion of free speech, however, is supposed to be content-neutral, meaning that if someone has the right to speak, the content cannot be regulated depending on what is considered disagreeable, with some exceptions, of course.

Technically, the 1st Amendment only prohibits the Government from restricting the freedom of speech and, as a result, does not prohibit a private party like the NFL from restricting its players from expressing themselves. Nevertheless, Americans view the First Amendment as so ingrained in our values that we tend to extend its policy into the private sector when assessing individual rights.

Kaepernick was not the first athlete to seize the public stage of the playing field to make a political point. After receiving their gold and bronze medals in the 200-meter sprint at the Summer Olympics in Mexico City in 1968, Tommie Smith and John Carlos removed their shoes to represent poverty and lowered their heads and raised a fist covered in a black glove in a Black Power salute while standing on the platform as the national anthem played. They also wore beads and a scarf around their necks to symbolize lynchings. In winning the race, Smith set a new world record, but International Olympic Committee President Avery Brundage immediately suspended both of them from the U.S. team and ordered them to leave the Olympic Village.[12] Brundage was no stranger to quelling controversy, as he successfully fought against a proposed U.S. boycott of the 1936 Olympics in Berlin and was rumored to have prevented Jews from competing for the U.S. team to avoid offending Hitler.[13]

Kaepernick has paid dearly for his protests. After the 2016-17 season, he became a free agent, but no NFL team ever signed him—even as a back-up—despite the fact that he was better than at least half of the starting quarterbacks. Thus, collusion among the NFL owners is obvious. Perhaps, they fear backlash from their fan base who will boo him or, worse, stop buying tickets or team merchandise. The owners are similarly jointly refusing to sign players accused of violence against women, probably for the same reasons. They don't seem to have a problem, however, with players who fail drug and alcohol tests or who have been accused of or arrested for gun infractions, driving while intoxicated, assault (so long as it was against another man), whipping a son, and even murder.

Kaepernick could still be playing in the NFL if he had taken the easy way out and confined his political statements to the media. After all, professional athletes have so many platforms from which to speak nowadays, such as local and national sports shows on television and radio, Derek Jeter's *The Players' Tribune*, *The Athletic*, and all sorts of social media.

None of those stages, however, present the head-to-head confrontation that made his protests so powerful. In essence, he was saying that the American establishment was forcing its brand of patriotism on athletes and fans by insinuating itself into a private activity having nothing to do with democracy, civics, or public service. He was saying that if the American establishment wished to assert its view before a football game, then he was going to express his views about the American establishment as a counterstatement at the same time. Accordingly, it was the best and most appropriate forum, the right time and place, for him to take a knee.

It is unfair for NFL owners and fans to criticize Kaepernick or any other player who cringes at their attempts to force an establishment view of patriotism on them. It is also wrong to accuse them of disrespecting the military, for that assumes that the flag, national anthem, and patriotism are the sole dominion of the military. In the unique experiment devised by our Founders, the Government of the people, by the people, for the people is served not only by people who fight and die in wars but also by people who fight racism, sexism, bigotry, poverty, illiteracy, ignorance, hatred, and injustice. Martin Luther King, Jr. wasn't in the military, nor were John Adams and Benjamin Franklin, but who would claim they weren't patriots?

So, we shouldn't be asking whether it's right for players to protest before a game or to punish players for protesting before a game. We should be asking whether a game is the right time and place to ask people to stand at attention and permit the Government to intrude into their enjoyment of a non-governmental activity with a call to allegiance and at least a tacit acknowledgment of its pervasive power over our lives.

There does not seem to be any good reason for continuing to play the national anthem before a game. If it's so important to our national security and patriotic duty, then why do we so often have soloists performing the national anthem instead of asking 50,000 voices to sing it in unison?

FREEDOM OF SAFETY AND FREEDOM FROM VIOLENCE

6.   **All persons shall enjoy freedom of safety and freedom from violence. In furtherance of such rights, after the Effective Date of this Restated Constitution, no civilian shall have the right to carry any firearm in any area reasonably declared by the Government to be gun-free and off-limits to firearms. Moreover, commencing one year after the Effective Date of this Restated Constitution, no civilian shall have the right to use, carry, or possess any weapon of war, including assault weapons and high-capacity magazines or ammunition. The two preceding sentences shall not apply to the military, the National Guard, or**

Government law enforcement personnel acting in their official capacities.

When early humans were hunters and gatherers, they lived in small, nomadic tribes. As cultivation of crops developed, they became less dependent on foraging and built permanent habitats. Agriculture, domestication of animals, and construction of settlements required more labor and, thus, more people. The resulting communities provided safety in numbers against wild animals and other humans. With the increase in population living permanently in close proximity, internal conflict naturally arose, necessitating the creation of rules to maintain an ordered society.

Nowadays, most people grow up learning how to behave and interact with others from their parents, teachers, leaders, and even their peers. They develop an ingrained sense of right and wrong and respect laws that forbid and punish bad conduct. They do not steal, lie, cheat, or physically harm other people. Most people are innately good, kind, and considerate, and laws deterring bad acts through punishment simply reinforce their natural personal makeup. For instance, even if there were no laws prohibiting murder, it is doubtful that most people would kill another human being.

On the other hand, there are other people whose passions, hatred, and warped beliefs impel them to commit atrocities. No laws and no threats of harsh punishment can deter them.

America has become a battlefield of daily massacres fueled by easy access to guns. Criminologists and psychologists come up with various hypotheses in an attempt to explain the surge in shootings. They attribute these attacks to mental illness, stress, video games, violence in movies and TV shows, drugs, alcohol, troubled upbringings, school, the internet, bullying, and so on.

There are more guns in America than there are people. Gun advocates say, "Guns don't kill people. People kill people." Well, they can't deny that "People *with guns* kill people."

Gun violence has invaded every aspect of our lives on a daily basis. In the last 30 years, there have been thousands of mass shootings and killings at churches (Emanuel African Methodist Episcopal Church in Charleston and First Baptist Church in Sutherland Springs, Texas), synagogues (Tree of Life in Pittsburgh), other places of worship (Sikh temple in Oak Creek, Wisconsin), movie theaters (Aurora, Colorado), nightclubs (Pulse in Orlando), concerts (Las Vegas), malls (Westroads Mall in Omaha), retail stores (Walmart in El Paso), grocery stores (King Soopers in Boulder and Tops Supermarket in Buffalo), restaurants (IHOP, Chuck E. Cheese), abortion clinics (Colorado Springs Planned Parenthood), tourist sites (Empire State Building), dance studios (Monterey Park, California), gyms (Tallahassee), bowling alleys (Rockford, Illinois), massage parlors (Atlanta), parades (Highland Park, Illinois), civic centers (Binghamton, New York), town meetings (Kirkwood, Missouri), workplaces (San Bernardino, California), airports (LAX, Fort Lauderdale), trains and subways (New York), military sites (Washington Navy Yard and Fort Hood), and, saddest of all, every level of education (Sandy Hook Elementary School, Robb Elementary School, Frontier Middle School, Marjory Stoneman Douglas High School, Columbine High School, Virginia Tech).[14]

These are just a handful of examples of mass shootings. They occur every day throughout the country and in every location where people gather or visit.

Obvious motivations for many of these mass shootings appear to include racism, antisemitism, white supremacy, anti-gay animus, politics, and revenge against family members, employers, co-workers, teachers, and fellow students. Other shootings are delusions of grandeur, hoping for 15 minutes of fame. Some are attempts to complete suicide by cop, baiting the police to gun down the gunman. I say "gunman" because virtually all mass shootings are perpetrated by males. Some shootings are simply senseless, random attacks whose purpose will never be known.

Regardless of the reasons, no place in America is safe anymore.

With every passing year, the number and intensity of mass shootings increase. While the motivations for mass shootings may vary widely, the prime common element in the murders is the use of a firearm. After all, it is hard to go on a rampage and kill more than a few people with only a knife or baseball bat. Moreover, it is hard to kill dozens of people in minutes without an assault weapon.

It's not just mass shootings that are turning America into a daily battlefield. People are firing handguns at strangers who innocently knock on their doors, approach their cars, or turn around in their driveways. They are emboldened by "stand your ground" laws that shield them from criminal and civil liability for defending themselves. The problem is that they are too trigger-happy with a "shoot first, ask questions later" attitude that fails to objectively assess whether they are in imminent danger. Even worse, they are often shooting victims who are fleeing. The justification of self-defense does not apply when a perceived attacker is running away because the shooter is no longer in danger.

In response to this explosion of mass shootings and random attacks, our elected officials—our supposed leaders—have completely failed to protect us. They offer the victims and their families and friends only their self-righteous "thoughts and prayers." While some States have enacted stricter gun laws, others have made it easier to obtain guns. Any proposed legislation with real teeth from Democratic Congressmen and Senators is quickly shot down by Republicans.

The preamble to the Constitution proclaims that two of its purposes are to "insure domestic Tranquility" and "promote the general Welfare." Who, nowadays, feels tranquil when going anywhere at any time of the day? Who believes we are faring well?

As stated above in the context of abortion, the *parens patriae* doctrine empowers the Government to act as a parent and safeguard all within its borders. *Parens patriae* is not just a power but a responsibility to protect.

While about a third of adults own a gun and many of them own multiple guns, almost a half of households with children have at least one firearm.[15] No matter how many locks parents use to try to keep guns away from kids, nothing is foolproof and kids can be ingenious.

Politicians and citizen groups clamor for better access to mental health resources. Expanded mental health services in general would be great, as anyone who has tried to find a child psychiatrist will agree. As a preventative measure, however, that will not put much of a dent in mass shootings because only a small fraction of the people suffering from mental health issues commit mass shootings, regardless of whether they are receiving treatment. Plus, we can't expect mental health providers to be able to detect and deter all mass shooters.

So, increasing mental health resources is a great idea for the wellbeing of the public in general but not a cure for mass shootings. Disarming people suffering from mental illness is a better idea.

The only way to make America safer from gun shootings is to take aim at guns. Mayors of cities of all sizes and police departments throughout the country have been pleading for greater gun control for decades.

Instead, Congress' most significant action in this area in the past 20 years has been to give greater protection from liability to gun manufacturers in civil actions by enacting The Protection of Lawful Commerce in Arms Act of 2005, clearly a step in the wrong direction.

When States enact red flag laws allowing courts to order people who pose a danger to others or to themselves to surrender their guns, some courts rule the laws unconstitutional as violative of the 2nd Amendment.

When States contemplate enacting tougher gun laws, gun sales go up, presumably a result of consumer hoarding of products that they fear may become harder to get.

When the Supreme Court has addressed gun control laws in this century, it has sided with gun owners under a new, warped interpretation of the 2nd Amendment. For two centuries, the Supreme Court viewed the 2nd Amendment as empowering a "militia," which became the National Guard. Starting with *District of Columbia v. Heller*, 554 U.S. 570 (2008), and then *New York State Rifle & Pistol Association, Inc. v. Bruen*, 597 U.S. 1 (2022), however, the Supreme Court has held that the 2nd Amendment is a proclamation of the rights of individuals to own guns. A slight retrenchment has occurred, however, with the Supreme Court's decision in *United States v. Rahimi*, 602 U.S. ___ (June 21, 2024), upholding a section of the Bipartisan Safer Communities Act, one of the few recent Congressional gun control statutes, that authorizes the removal of guns from people who are the subject of domestic violence restraining orders.

The 2nd Amendment provides in its entirety that "[a] well regulated Militia, being necessary to the security of a free State, the right of the people to keep and bear Arms, shall not be infringed." What the heck does that mean? It is difficult to parse this sentence, partially because it appears to use a construction akin to the Latin ablative absolute. How does the phrase, "well regulated Militia," relate to "the right of the people to keep and bear Arms"? Is one phrase the cause or premise for the other?

What is clear from the legislative history of the 2nd Amendment is that it was intended to counterbalance the right given to Congress to establish an army and a navy in Section 8 of Article I. The anti-Federalists feared a standing national armed force and wanted to give more power to individual State militias as a curb on tyranny. A review of the various proposals for what became the 2nd Amendment, however, reveals the epitome of legislative sausage-making, as phrases were rearranged, reworded, or dropped.[16] The result is an unintelligible mess.

In the ensuing century, the gun industry grew, fueled by the demand of pioneers moving westward for protection against animals and Native Americans and supplied by New England manufacturers inventing new and better firearms during the Industrial Revolution. America created a Wild West mentality that persists today. Americans own way more guns than any other nation, and we have many more mass shootings, gun fatalities and injuries, suicides, and gun accidents, as a result.

Clearly, State legislatures, Congress, and the courts have proven reluctant to solve or incapable of solving the problem of how to ensure safety from gun violence. Consequently, **"freedom of safety"** and **"freedom from violence"** are introduced as affirmative rights in the Restated Constitution. Now, Congress and the States will be obligated to enact laws that make our schools, places of worship, workplaces, and all public and private areas safe. By stating that **"no civilian shall have the right to carry any firearm in any area reasonably declared by the Government to be gun-free and off-limits to firearms,"** these new freedoms overrule the Supreme Court's recent decision in *Bruen*, which held that a hundred-year old New York law prohibiting the carrying of weapons in public without a permit violated the 2nd Amendment.

While the 2nd Amendment is not expressly repealed, "the right of the people to keep and bear Arms" or words to that effect do not appear in the Restated Constitution. The effect, however, is the same as repeal because Section 1 of Article IX of the Restated Constitution provides that the Restated Constitution **"shall supersede and replace the original Constitution and its amendments in their entirety."** Thus, the 2nd Amendment is effectively repealed without the need to state so expressly.

Now, we don't have to listen to more nonsense from the Supreme Court trying to make sense of the gibberish appearing in the 2nd Amendment. Now, we don't have to listen to more nonsense from the National Rifle Association, whose mission has been perverted from teaching gun safety, especially to kids, to preserving at all costs the right to possess and use weapons of war.

The Restated Constitution does not tackle the problem of how to deal with the 400 million or more guns in the U.S. Many are held by responsible people for arguably legitimate purposes, such as hunting, self-defense, sport (target practice, skeet shooting), and antique collecting. The problem of balancing these interests against the new freedom of safety and freedom from violence is left to Congress and the States. Good luck. Now that gun advocates will no longer have the 2nd Amendment to rely on, the Government should be able to make strict gun control stick. There is a concern, however, that some gun enthusiasts could argue that Section 16 of Article I of the Restated Constitution might be construed as creating a residual right in the People to bear arms.

A much simpler subset of firearms that can be more readily tackled in this Restated Constitution is assault weapons. There simply is no legitimate purpose for civilians to own assault weapons. None. The argument that individuals need to own assault weapons to protect our liberties in the event that our democracy becomes a dictatorship or comes under martial law is ridiculous. If the U.S. military, which is the largest and best equipped military in the world, decides to take over the country, scattered pockets of wacko, over-weight, and out-of-shape self-proclaimed militiamen with a few dozen assault weapons will be easily blown away. Also, if the U.S. military is conquered by a foreign army, these militiamen will not stand a chance.

So, "**commencing one year after the Effective Date of this Restated Constitution, no civilian shall have the right to use, carry, or possess any weapon of war, including assault weapons and high-capacity magazines or ammunition.**" This provision will require institution of a buy-back program under which the Government will have to pay just compensation to owners turning in assault weapons, as required by the present 5th and 14th Amendments and Section 13 of Article I of the Restated Constitution. It will be up to Congress and the States to enact appropriate legislation to set up the buy-back programs.

Recognizing the difficulty in accomplishing a successful buy-back program, a deadline is set for one year after the Effective Date of the Restated Constitution. Since the Effective Date is defined in Article IX as two years after ratification of the Restated Constitution, the Government will have three years to institute the program and complete the divestiture of the most dangerous weapons threatening the public every day and everywhere.

To avoid any confusion or ambiguity, the ban on assault weapons and the right of the Government to declare gun-free zones do not apply to "**the military, the National Guard, or Government law enforcement personnel acting in their official capacities.**" Disarming the military or police would undermine the "**freedom of safety**" and "**freedom from violence**" created by this Section. Of course, that's assuming they abide by their duty to protect and not attack us.

Finally, in light of the atrocities committed by some police against individuals particularly in recent years, the guarantees of freedom of safety and freedom from violence compel Congress and the States to enact statutes and establish practices, procedures, and programs to eliminate police brutality. Section 15 of Article III of the Restated Constitution, which states that "Congress shall have power to enforce **and implement Articles I and II** by appropriate legislation," provides not only the power of Congress to act but also implies the duty to act to protect the rights, liberties, and freedoms of Article I.

SEARCHES AND SEIZURES

7.   The right of the people to be secure in their persons, houses, **places of business, automobiles,** papers, **electronically stored information,** and effects against unreasonable searches and seizures shall not be violated, and no warrants shall issue but upon probable cause supported by oath or affirmation and particularly describing the place to be searched and the persons or things to be seized. [4th Amend.]

We now proceed with several sections reaffirming fundamental rights regarding criminal prosecutions and with less dramatic changes. Sections 7 through 11 follow somewhat the progression of a criminal case through a reorganization of the 4th, 5th, 6th, and 8th Amendments.

This Section proposes no novel ideas on how to improve the law of searches and seizures that has developed under the 4th Amendment. Originally, the 4th Amendment focused on protecting people from the forceful searches of their homes through the use of general writs of assistance authorizing the British authorities to enter any house of American colonialists to search for and seize smuggled goods.

Over the years, the courts interpreted the 4th Amendment to protect from unreasonable searches and seizures not only homes and one's body but places of business and automobiles, locations where there are expectations of privacy. So, "**places of business**" and "**automobiles**" are added to continue the list starting with "persons" and "houses" of places that are protected from unreasonable searches.

To protect information on our computers and smart phones, **"electronically stored information"** is added to "papers" and "effects" as objects protected from unreasonable searches and seizures. Electronically stored information is to us what "papers" were to 18th Century Americans.

While on the subject of homes, there appears no need to preserve the 3rd Amendment's prohibition against the forced quartering of soldiers in civilians' homes during peacetime. That practice during colonial times doesn't seem to be a concern nowadays. On the other hand, maybe it's not a concern now because the 3rd Amendment prohibits it. In any event, part of the purpose in updating the Constitution is to discard anachronisms, and, therefore, the 3rd Amendment has been jettisoned.

PRESUMPTION OF INNOCENCE AND BAIL

8.   **All persons charged with a crime shall be deemed innocent until proven guilty beyond a reasonable doubt. Accordingly,** excessive bail shall not be required. **Bail shall be set within defendants' reasonable ability to pay, unless they are flight risks or pose a danger to the public. No bail shall be required for misdemeanor charges.** [8th Amend.]

The presumption of innocence in a criminal case has a long history running from Deuteronomy through Roman law, English and American common law, and several Supreme Court pronouncements. For instance, the Supreme Court has stated that the "presumption of innocence, although not articulated in the Constitution, is a basic component of a fair trial under our system of criminal justice." *Estelle v. Williams*, 425 U.S. 501, 503 (1976).

Similarly, American common law followed English common law in requiring proof of guilt beyond a reasonable doubt. *See, e.g., Leland v. Oregon,* 343 U.S. 790, 794 (1952).

The presumption of innocence and proof of guilt beyond a reasonable doubt are two of the legal principles most recognized by nonlawyers, and they deserve to be enshrined in the Restated Constitution.

Not only is the presumption of innocence fundamental to the requirement that the Government must prove guilt beyond a reasonable doubt to get a conviction, but it provides the basis for assuming that persons arrested and charged with a crime should not be imprisoned while awaiting trial. Since we well know that many innocent people have been mistakenly arrested, let alone convicted, the presumption of innocence logically requires that arrestees not be held in jail before a conviction.

The purpose of bail is to ensure that criminal defendants return to court for trial. While the 8th Amendment prohibited excessive bail, bail has been abused over the years to the point where currently it causes the imprisonment of defend-ants for lengthy times before trial simply because they lack the financial resources to post bail.

To correct this abuse, this Section provides that "[b]ail **shall be set within defendants' reasonable ability to pay,**" which would require judges to take not only the seriousness of the charges into consideration when setting the amount of bail but also the financial ability of the defendant to post the amount.

Nevertheless, bail need not be set within defendants' reasonable ability to pay if "**they are flight risks or pose a danger to the public,**" which is the traditional standard for denying bail. If prosecutors show that there is a strong possibility that defendants will not return for trial or will likely commit more crimes while free and awaiting trial, judges may set bail beyond the defendants' ability to pay or deny bail altogether.

The most egregious instances of excessive bail occur in misdemeanor cases, where the charges are not as serious and the potential sentences do not exceed one year. Nevertheless, accused who are not able to make bail often end up serving almost as much time in jail before trial as the maximum allowable sentence, if not more. In other words, they serve the full sentence in pretrial detention although they have not been convicted of any crime. Clearly, that is not right. Consequently, this Section provides that "[n]**o bail shall be required for misdemeanor charges**." The Government can utilize other means of ensuring that defendants charged with misdemeanors appear at the trial, such as periodic reporting to parole or probation officers.

INDICTMENT, DOUBLE JEOPARDY, AND SELF-INCRIMINATION

9.   No person shall be held to answer for a **felony**, unless on a presentment or indictment of a grand jury, except in cases arising in the land or naval forces or in the **National Guard** when in actual service in time of War or public danger. No persons shall be subject for the same offense to be twice put in jeopardy of life or limb, nor shall be compelled in any criminal case to be a witness against themselves, nor be deprived of life or liberty without due process of law. [5th Amend.; 14th Amend., Sect. 1]

This Section replaces the phrase "capital, or otherwise infamous crime," with the more precise "**felony**," with no intention to alter the meaning of the 5th Amendment. Likewise, "Militia" is replaced with **"National Guard,"** which replaced state militias in the Dick Act of 1903 and the National Defense Act of 1916.

Otherwise, the criminal law aspects of the 5th Amendment remain intact. The 14th Amendment is referenced as a source for this Section because the phrase banning deprivation of life or liberty without due process of law is repeated in the 14th Amendment. The 5th and 14th Amendments' inclusion of "property" in the phrase and the 5th Amendment's requirement of just compensation for public takings of property are cut from this Section because they seem out of place in a provision devoted to criminal law protections. Instead, these principles are joined with the 14th Amendment's equal protection of laws provision in new Section 13 of Article I.

The upshot of this Section 9 is that one can be charged with a felony only by presentment or a grand jury indictment, except in the military.

No one can be charged twice for the same crime within the same judicial system. This protects acquitted defendants from prosecutors who don't like the result and seek a do-over. This phrase, however, has been interpreted to permit separate prosecutions for the same crime in the federal and State systems.

No defendants can be forced to testify against themselves. Long ago, we recognized that medieval tortures produced many false confessions simply to stop the excruciating pain and suffering. Presently, suspects sometimes confess to crimes they didn't commit as a result of prolonged and excessive interrogation, even in the absence of physical coercion. Under the 5th Amendment, prosecutors may not call defendants to testify against themselves and must prove their cases without any evidence from defendants who invoke their 5th Amendment rights to remain silent. Police give Miranda warnings to people they arrest, advising them that they have the right to remain silent. Thanks to movies and TV shows, the Miranda warnings are probably the most widely-known rights in America.

The overarching principle in the 5th Amendment is that defendants are entitled to "due process of law" throughout the criminal justice system. The meaning of that phrase continues to develop on a case-by-case basis, usually in favor of granting more protections. In general, it means that criminal defendants will be given a fair trial.

SPEEDY PUBLIC TRIAL, CROSS-EXAMINATION, AND REPRESENTATION

10.   In all criminal prosecutions, the accused shall enjoy the right to a speedy and public trial by an impartial jury of the State and district wherein the crime shall have been committed, which district shall have been previously ascertained by law, and to be informed of the nature and cause of the accusation. Accused persons shall have the right to be confronted with the witnesses against them, to have compulsory process for obtaining witnesses in their favor, and to have the assistance of counsel for their defense. [6th Amend.]

Another complaint the colonialists had with the British criminal justice system was the custom of shipping some defendants back to England to stand trial. The Declaration of Independence rails against King George III and Parliament "[f]or transporting us beyond Seas to be tried for pretended Offences." Not only did deportation cause delay in the trial, but it also deprived the accused of a jury of local peers and the ability to call local witnesses.

The 6th Amendment changed all that by requiring a speedy trial, a public trial, and trial by jury, all in the locale of where the alleged crime was committed. Plus, it requires that prosecutors sufficiently inform defendants of the charges, that the Government's witnesses testify in the defendants' presence, and that defendants have the right to cross-examine adverse witnesses, to call their own witnesses by subpoena, if necessary, and to counsel.

The reference in this Section to the "district wherein the crime shall have been committed" refers to the geographic areas where the district courts are located and not to the Districts into which the Commission on National Elections and Compensation will divide the country according to population for voting purposes. Small States have a single district court while States with larger populations, like California, New York, and Texas, have up to four district courts.

The 6th Amendment covers a lot of ground and provides many fundamental rights. Since it ain't broke, we don't fix it.

CRUEL AND UNUSUAL PUNISHMENT

11.   **In criminal cases,** excessive fines **shall not be** imposed, nor cruel and unusual punishments inflicted. **No Government shall impose on any incarcerated person a fee related to the cost of housing, feeding, or providing medical care to such person during or arising out of the incarceration. No Government shall execute any person as punishment for any crime.** [8th Amend.]

Excessive Fines

The 8th Amendment prohibits excessive fines. The wording gives discretion to State legislatures, Congress, and courts in determining reasonable fines as a form of punishment. Such determinations will be case-specific, and that is why many statutes set forth ranges with floors and ceilings to allow courts flexibility in gauging appropriate fines under the circumstances.

Many State criminal justice systems follow a practice that skirts the 8th Amendment by imposing court fees that, while not fines by name, accomplish the same monetary punishment as fines.

The legislatures in some States permit their Department of Corrections to charge prisoners after their release with the costs incurred in housing, feeding, and providing medical care to them while incarcerated. While the Departments of Corrections primarily use this authority to go after former prisoners only if they come into a windfall of large sums of money, such as through inheritance or winning a lottery, the effect of such policies undermines successful rehabilitation of prisoners and their re-entry into society. Upon completion of a sentence and probation, prisoners have fulfilled the terms of their punishment, and reaching back and forcing them to reimburse the Government for the "privilege" of the fine lodgings and cuisine of imprisonment is simply imposing on them fines that were not part of their sentences.

Besides imposing fines beyond the terms of sentences, such indirect fines are excessive because the charges usually are well above what the free market would pay for these often substandard services. How much would you pay for a bunk bed in a small room shared with one or more strangers and an unenclosed toilet bowl next to your bed with mandatory lights out and early wake-up calls? Add to that, lack of proper heat in the winter and air conditioning in the summer. As to board, the food is of low quality in small portions with dinner often served at 3:00 p.m. and no more food until 15 hours later. Most people have no idea how deplorable the conditions are in our prisons.

True, prisoners with financial resources or friends and families with money can supplement the poor quality and quantity of food, clothing, and supplies by purchasing items on private services that contract with prisons. These services charge premiums because they have monopolies. This bone of contention, however, is not a subject for the Restated Constitution and should be addressed in a long overdue overhaul of this country's antiquated and poorly staffed prison systems.

Consequently, this Section prohibits the Government from charging prisoners for room, board, and medical services. We have more people in prison as an absolute number and as a percentage of our population than any other nation. If we want to keep locking people up, it is immoral to charge them for the costs of locking them up.

The Death Penalty

Let's play God. Let's decide who shall die and when and how and why.

"Thou shalt not kill," decrees the Sixth Commandment. Yet, killing occurs all the time. Soldiers kill soldiers and civilians in conflicts sanctioned and directed by nations. In fact, soldiers who are drafted into the military are compelled to kill in wars they want no part of. Gang members kill rival gang members and bystanders. Automobile drivers kill deer, dogs, racoons, possums, pedestrians, cyclists, passengers, and other drivers. Hunters kill game and other hunters. Doctors kill patients. Spouses kill spouses. Children kill parents, and parents kill children. Terrorists kill indiscriminately and randomly, as do mass shooters. Many people kill insects, bugs, and rodents. Nations commit genocide. Life is precious, and life is cheap.

Some governments kill their own people. America is one of the few industrialized nations that impose the death penalty and execute convicts. Our friends include such progressive places as North Korea, China, Iran, Saudi Arabia, and Indonesia—what lovely company.

Politicians in Congress and State legislatures often promote capital punishment to show they are tough on crime. Proponents of capital punishment argue that murderers, mobsters, and career criminals have forfeited their right to live and that executing them would save law-abiding taxpayers the expense of providing them with shelter, food, and clothing and all the other wonderful amenities of prison.

Criminologists cite four purposes and functions of punishment in an ordered society: deterrence, isolation, re-habilitation, and retribution. The first three have superficial appeal, but retribution has no merit or justification what-soever.

Deterrence. We want to discourage people from committing crimes. Many people don't even think of committing crimes due to their upbringing and the morals imparted to them by their parents, teachers, mentors, and peers. For such people, criminal sanctions don't serve as a deterrent because they wouldn't commit the acts even if they were not illegal.

For other people lacking a strong moral fiber, letting them know that they will be punished if they commit a crime and how severely they will be punished is one way to deter them from committing a crime. We inform them of the consequences of crime through public laws (which most are unaware of) and through media publicity of the actual sentences imposed on people who are found guilty of or plead guilty to crimes. This is called, "general deterrence."

For people who are convicted of a crime, the sentence imposed is supposed to serve as, among other things, a deterrent to them of what will happen to them if they commit further crimes while in prison or after their release. This is called, "specific deterrence."

How well does the death penalty serve as either a general or specific deterrent? Not well at all. Highly moral people are not deterred from committing murder simply out of a fear of the death penalty. People who kill out of a sudden, uncontrollable anger or temporary insanity are so overwhelmed by emotion that they cannot act rationally and certainly aren't considering the consequences of their actions. In contrast, people who plan a murder or a crime that involves a high risk of violence clearly think the benefit of the crime outweighs the possibility of getting caught and executed, if they think at all about the consequences.

So, the death penalty fails as a general or specific deterrent.

Isolation. Criminal laws are designed to protect people from physical, mental, and financial harm. Accordingly, it makes sense to keep someone who inflicts such harm on others away from society so he or she cannot harm more people. The death penalty is clearly the best solution for isolating someone from society and on a permanent basis. An extended term in prison, however, will also keep someone from harming society.

So, while the death penalty succeeds in isolating convicted persons from society, there is a less drastic measure available that is virtually as effective.

Rehabilitation. The death penalty has absolutely no rehabilitative effect. Executing prisoners doesn't make them better persons or enable them to rejoin and contribute to society. It doesn't provide them with the education or vocational training they never had. It doesn't give them tools to cope with psychological problems, emotions, anxiety, and stress.

The death penalty, by its very nature, fails to rehabilitate anyone.

Retribution. Retribution is revenge. One of the oldest recorded laws is the Code of Hammurabi dating back to Babylonia circa 1754 B.C.E., proclaiming, "an eye for an eye, a tooth for a tooth." Under the death penalty, a killer is killed. No other criminal punishment in modern day America makes the convicted person suffer the same act he or she committed against another. We don't place a hit-and-run driver in the middle of a street and then run him over with a car. We don't stab someone who slashed someone else with a knife. We don't rape a rapist. But we kill a killer.

The death penalty is the only form of punishment in which the Government commits an act that is itself a crime, unless incarceration is deemed a type of kidnapping. It seems perverse that some people who oppose abortion at any time and for any reason, claiming that life is sacred, believe in the death penalty. Obviously, not all life is sacred to them.

The death penalty certainly fulfills the purpose of retribution, but that is the most reprehensible and least justifiable purpose of punishment.

Tallying up the four purposes of punishment, the death penalty succeeds in permanent isolation and retribution but fails as deterrence and rehabilitation. Since a long term or life in prison would effectively accomplish isolation and since retribution is not a moral ground for punishment, the death penalty on the whole fails to fulfill a modern view of the purposes of punishment.

Death penalty supporters contend that taxpayers shouldn't bear the burden and expense of keeping someone in prison for life. They don't recognize, however, that life imprisonment costs less than providing counsel for the condemned, as required by the 6th Amendment, for all the mandatory appeals when the death sentence is imposed, plus the costs of prosecutors and judges.

When confronted with that point, they argue for elimination of appeals or, perhaps, allowing no more than a single appeal. The Innocence Project, however, has demonstrated over the last 25 years through DNA tests and other evidence that many people on Death Row have been convicted of crimes they did not commit. Thus, maintaining mandatory appeals of death sentences is crucial to ensuring no innocent person is executed. Needless to say, exoneration after execution is too little, too late.

If death penalty advocates were truly concerned about costs, they would press for the elimination of the death penalty.

Finally, there is no humane way to execute someone. It's safe to assume we can all agree that burning at the stake, submersion in boiling water, drawing and quartering, and other similar techniques employed throughout history are not acceptable today. For many years, hanging was seen as a more humane method. Hanging can be swift and painless if done perfectly and the neck is snapped instantaneously. If not, the person will slowly asphyxiate, kicking and screaming in his or her last moments.

The electric chair, developed in the late 19th Century and the most prevalent form of execution in the United States in the 20th Century, was supposed to eliminate problems with hanging. By the 1980s, however, the electric chair fell into disfavor due to many malfunctions resulting in prolonged and painful executions accompanied with burning hair and body parts.

Then, lethal injection became the rage, but that method also inflicts excruciating pain and often fails to cause death instantly. Furthermore, because no licensed medical professionals are willing to administer the injections, lay executioners often botch the series of injections, thereby compounding the problems, and now pharmaceutical companies are no longer willing to furnish the necessary drugs.

Probably the most effective method of execution is the Guillotine, but chopping off a person's head is a gruesome spectacle. Another horrific approach is the firing squad, which tends to blow body parts apart.

So, even if the Government can find a way to justify execution as a means of punishment, it has yet to find a way to kill humanely and comply with the 8th Amendment's proscription against cruel and unusual punishment.

In 1972, the Supreme Court held that the death penalty was cruel and unusual punishment in violation of the 8th Amendment. Four years later, it pulled a 180 and held that the death penalty was okay.

Nevertheless, since reinstatement of the death penalty in 1976, the federal government had performed only two executions, the last of which was in 2003, until Trump pushed for 13 executions in the final six months of his term in 2020 and January 2021. The federal government rarely seeks the death penalty now, reserving it for the most monstrous cases such as the 2013 Boston Marathon bombing, the 2015 Emanuel African Methodist Episcopal Church massacre in Charleston, and the 2018 Tree of Life synagogue slayings in Pittsburgh. Even in such horrible political, racist, and antisemitic travesties, some family members of the victims have voiced their opposition to seeking the death penalty.

Currently, almost half of the States have abolished the death penalty.[17] The number of State executions has been dropping year after year, primarily due to the difficulties in performing executions, which has prompted even Republican governors to stop executions. Due to the legal hurdles and years of appeals, prosecutors are opting to seek life in prison without parole rather than the death penalty, and fewer defendants are being sentenced to death.

A handful of States, however, continue to seek the death penalty and to carry out executions. In the last ten years, Texas has been far and away the league leader, followed distantly by Florida and Georgia.

Let's take the death penalty out of the hands of whoever happens to control State legislatures, Governors' offices, Congress, and the Supreme Court. Let's bury it once and for all by banning it in the Restated Constitution.

CIVIL JURY TRIALS

12.   In suits at common law, where the value in controversy shall exceed **$5,000**, the right of trial by jury shall be preserved, and no fact tried by a jury shall be otherwise re-examined in any court of the United States,

other than according to the rules of the common law. [7th Amend.]

In 1791, the 7th Amendment set the threshold for juries in civil trials at a minimum of $20 at stake. In the mid-20th Century, States began instituting small claims courts in which parties could sue for small amounts in a streamlined procedure without the need for attorneys. The purpose was to remove these cases from the increasingly heavy caseload in trial courts and to expedite resolution of cases where not much money was at issue. Due to the 7th Amendment's right to trial by jury for cases involving more than $20, however, it was necessary to require the parties to formally waive their rights to a jury.

Many small claims courts have a jurisdictional maximum of around $5,000 at issue. Modifying the 7th Amendment's threshold to preserve the right to jury trials only for claims exceeding $5,000 will simply recognize the legitimacy of small claims courts and remove the need to waive jury trials for claims between $20 and $5,000. So, this Section increases the threshold from $20 to $5,000 for a jury trial.

DUE PROCESS AND EQUAL PROTECTION

13. No person shall be deprived of property without due process of law. No private property shall be taken for public use without just compensation. **All persons are entitled to** equal protection of the laws **regardless of sex, sexual orientation, gender identity, race, or religion, and all persons are entitled to freedom from discrimination based on sex, sexual orientation, gender identity, race, or religion. For purposes of this Section, corporate entities, such as companies and**

partnerships, shall be considered "persons" solely with respect to laws regarding property and criminal liability and not with respect to individual civil rights, liberties, and freedoms. [5th Amend.; 14th Amend., Sect. 1]

The concept of due process of law appeared initially in the 5th Amendment and reappeared 77 years later in the 14th Amendment after the Civil War. The 14th Amendment also introduced equal protection of the laws. Since these two concepts seem related and appear side by side in the 14th Amendment, they appear together in the same Section here.

Due Process of Law

The first two sentences are taken from similar language in the 5th and 14th Amendments. As mentioned in Section 9, above, due process rights regarding property are carved out from those regarding life and liberty. This principle requires courts to afford due process of law before entering any judgments that affect a person's property, whether in a suit with another person or company or in an eminent domain proceeding where the Government must pay just compensation for taking private property, for example, to build a highway. The determination of what due process constitutes develops over time and is based on the particular situations. Basically, due process is fair treatment.

Equal Protection of the Laws

The notion that all persons shall be entitled to equal protection of the laws seems inherent in the original Constitution and the Bill of Rights. Except for the Three-Fifths Compromise, where slaves were counted as three-fifths of a person for purposes of determining the number of Representatives from a State, and aside from the requirement that only natural born citizens are eligible to serve as President, there are no provisions that expressly apply to only a subset of the People. Even aliens living in the U.S. are entitled to protections under the Constitution.

Despite the repeal of slavery by the 13th Amendment in 1865, Southern States were slow to afford former slaves all the rights and protections of the laws. Hence, in 1868, the 14th Amendment more pointedly provided that "[n]o State shall . . . deny to any person within its jurisdiction the equal protection of the laws." When that wasn't enough, the 15th Amendment was enacted two years later to prohibit States from denying any person the right to vote "on account of race, color, or previous condition of servitude."

So, the 14th Amendment's promise of equal protection and application of the laws seems to be a redundant approach to the obvious and inherent structure of the Constitution. Yet, even that belt-and-suspenders approach proved not to be enough because 28 years later in *Plessy v. Ferguson*, 163 U.S. 537 (1896), the Supreme Court upheld segregationist Jim Crow laws in the South by declaring that separate but equal facilities satisfied the 14th Amendment's requirement of equal protection of the laws.

This case demonstrates the danger that the Supreme Court poses when it mangles and manipulates the meaning and purpose of statutes or Constitutional passages. How the *Plessy* Court could read "separate" into the 14th Amendment is inexplicable, and it took 58 more years for the Supreme Court to reverse *Plessy* with the phrase that "separate educational facilities are inherently unequal." *Brown v. Board of Education of Topeka*, 347 U.S. 483, 495 (1954).

The Equal Rights Amendment, or ERA as it was referred to, was proposed to Congress in 1923 to guarantee equal rights for women in addition to the right to vote secured by the 19th Amendment in 1920. It died in Congress but was reintroduced in 1971, providing that "[e]quality of rights under the law shall not be denied or abridged by the United States or by any State on account of sex." It was passed by Congress and submitted to the States for ratification in 1972. Thirty-five of the necessary 38 States soon ratified the ERA by the initial deadline, which was then extended. Three more States eventually ratified it, but five States have rescinded their ratifications.[18] It is currently in limbo.

Do we really need the ERA? Doesn't it just cover a specific subset of the 14th Amendment's equal protection of "any person"? Moreover, the number of federal and State laws, along with Supreme Court decisions in the 1970s, prohibiting discrimination based on sex also seem to obviate the need for the ERA.

In any event, sometimes it can't hurt to wear both a belt and suspenders. This Section adds, therefore, to the 14th Amendment's language of equal protection of the laws: "**regardless of sex, sexual orientation, gender identity, race, or religion, and all persons are entitled to freedom from discrimination based on sex, sexual orientation, gender identity, race, or religion.**" This is the same litany of classifications specified in Section 1 (privacy) and Section 4 (voting). That pretty much covers the primary, different classifications or subsets of individual "persons" who have sought inclusion in the 14th Amendment's equal protection of the laws in the last 50 years.

Corporations have also sought to be considered "persons" under the 14th Amendment. The Supreme Court assumed shortly after ratification of the 14th Amendment that corporations were covered within the meaning of "persons." That seems fine for granting corporations equal protection and due process regarding property laws and regulations, such as contract laws and zoning ordinances, as well as criminal laws.

But does it make sense to grant corporations what we consider to be personal rights, liberties, and freedoms, such as those in Sections 1 (privacy), 2 (abortions), 3 (citizenship), 4 (voting), 5 (free speech and religion), and 15 (basic human necessities)? In *Citizens United v. Federal Election Commission*, 558 U.S. 310 (2010), the Supreme Court held that corporations have free speech rights. The upshot of that case has been that corporations are deemed persons that can exercise free speech rights by contributing to political Super PACs, thereby inordinately impacting elections. In *Burwell v. Hobby Lobby Stores, Inc.*, 573 U.S. 682 (2014), the Supreme Court held that closely held private corporations can exercise the freedom of religion rights of their principals and refuse to provide their employees insurance coverage for contraceptives mandated by the Affordable Care Act, commonly referred to as Obamacare.

To correct these decisions, this Section specifies that **"[f]or purposes of this Section, corporate entities, such as companies and partnerships, shall be considered 'persons' solely with respect to laws regarding property and criminal liability and not with respect to individual civil rights, liberties, and freedoms."**

ABOLITION OF SLAVERY

14.   Slavery is banned, including involuntary servitude as punishment for a crime. Consequently, the Government must pay prisoners at least minimum wage for work they perform. [13th Amend.]

One would think it unnecessary to keep the 13th Amendment's abolition of slavery, believing that the inhumane practice has died out and stands no chance of revival. On the other hand, the rise of white supremacy, the subjugation of illegal immigrants for cheap labor, the abuse of women and children as unwilling sex workers, and the unpredictability of the Supreme Court requires reaffirmation of abolition of slavery. Plus, it couldn't hurt.

Most people understand that slavery in general has been banned but don't recognize that the 13th Amendment carves out from the prohibition "punishment for crime whereof the party shall have been duly convicted." Thus, prisons are free to exploit prisoner for cheap or free labor, like old time chain gangs. Prison jobs, if they pay at all, pay a nominal amount, such as 30 cents an hour, way below the federal and State minimum wages. As a result, prisoners often complete their sentences and leave prison with little or no savings to begin a new life. No wonder such a large percentage return to prison shortly after release.

This Section, therefore, abolishes not only slavery but also the exception permitting prisons to treat prisoners as slaves. It requires payment of minimum wage for work performed by prisoners. Not only will this provide prisoners with the incentive to work hard in prison and save for their future release into this expensive world, but it will give them a sense of dignity and self-worth that will enhance their chances for successful rehabilitation and contribution to society upon re-entry.

Removing the exception to the 13th Amendment does not mean the Government cannot incarcerate persons convicted of crimes. "Involuntary servitude" means working for free or a pittance against one's will. Incarceration is forced isolation from society, not forced labor.

BASIC HUMAN NEEDS

15.   **All persons are entitled to basic human necessities, including healthcare, housing, food, clothing, and education.**

This Section derives from Articles 25 and 26 of the United Nation's Universal Declaration of Human Rights adopted in 1948. This was the brainchild of Eleanor Roosevelt, who chaired the U.N. commission tasked with the drafting. The Declaration spells out basic human rights and fundamental freedoms.

Many people may think this Section pushes America to socialism, but how can they maintain that this is the greatest country in the world when we have so many people living below the poverty line and lacking the resources to pull themselves up and out of poverty? "The measure of society is how it treats the weakest members" is a saying that has been attributed in various forms to Thomas Jefferson, Fyodor Dostoevsky, Winston Churchill, Pope John Paul II, and many other luminaries.

It is estimated there are over half a million homeless people in the U.S., including a significant number of military veterans and children.[19] While cities and charitable organizations do their best to care for the homeless, the need far exceeds the means to provide shelter, food, and medical care. Most have mental health issues, but many simply can't earn enough to care for themselves and their families. As a result, children are growing up with little chance of upward mobility, and the homeless pattern perpetuates.

There are no simple and expedient solutions to these problems. Sociologists, psychologists, and public health and housing officials haven't solved these problems. Perhaps, affirmation of these rights of basic human necessities will throw more resources at these problems. Reducing the numbers of homeless people is better for everyone.

RESERVATION OF RIGHTS

16. The enumeration in **this Restated Constitution** of certain rights, **liberties, and freedoms** shall not be construed to deny or disparage others retained by the People, **and the Government shall respect, shall be bound by, and shall not violate, infringe, or abridge the personal rights, liberties, and freedoms in this Article.** [9th Amend.]

As explained in the context of the right to privacy in Section 1, above, the 9th Amendment wisely provided that the rights specified in the Constitution and, in particular, the Bill of Rights, were not meant to be construed as an exhaustive list. After all, who can think of all rights under natural law at the present, let alone predict ones arising in the future? While Article I attempts to include all our traditional personal rights plus ones like privacy, abortion, freedom of safety, and freedom from violence that are not expressly addressed in the Bill of Rights, there surely are additional values we hold that can be viewed as rights now or that may grow in significance over the years. Thus, this Section reserves such rights, along with "liberties" and "freedoms" that have broadened the meaning and scope of "rights."

The second clause prohibits the Government from interfering with rights, liberties, and freedoms. As pointed out earlier, many of the rights, liberties, and freedoms in the Constitution and its amendments are expressed in an indirect manner by stating that Congress or the States shall not infringe the rights. The Restated Constitution prefers to assert them as affirmative rights, liberties, and freedoms. While the implication is that rights, liberties, and freedoms may not be infringed, the final clause makes it perfectly clear that the Government must stay clear of our rights, liberties, and freedoms.

RESTRUCTURING
OF THE NATIONAL
GOVERNMENT

A rticle I expands the Bill of Rights by adding rights, liberties, and freedoms relating to privacy, abortion,
freedom of safety, and freedom from violence. For the most
part, however, it keeps the essence of the Bill of Rights intact,
with some reorganization, updating, and revamping to
cover issues that have arisen in the past 230 years.

We now embark on Articles II, III, IV, and V, in which
the Restated Constitution ventures much more dramatically
from the original structures of our three branches of government, namely, the legislative (Congress), executive (the
Presidency), and the judicial (federal courts) branches.

The initial intention was not to make radical changes but
rather to impose term limits on Congress, switch election of
the President from the Electoral College to a popular vote,
and impose term limits on federal judges. Those goals could
have been achieved with very little revision of Articles I, II,
and III of the Constitution and the various amendments regarding election of the President.

Most lawyers accept and work with the law as it is. It is
much easier to take the facts of a lawsuit and creatively
characterize them in a way to fit within the traditional
elements of a cause of action than to try to persuade a judge
to make new law because the current law does not favor a

client's position. In other words, lawyers tend to think within the box or, at most, just beyond its borders.

Once one starts down the road of tinkering with the structure of the national government, though, more ideas keep popping up, resulting in more expansive thinking. Consequently, the governmental structure of the Restated Constitution ended up way out of the box.

Many modern problems emanate from power that States still exert on the federal system.[20] While it is understandable that in 1788 the States were wary of trusting one another on the one hand and ceding too much authority to the experimental national government on the other hand, it makes no sense that the States continue to control the process of electing national officials today.

Article II of the Restated Constitution, therefore, proposes the creation of a Commission on National Elections and Compensation, which will assume control over every aspect of national elections and compensation of nationally elected officials and the selection and compensation of federal judges.

Article III eliminates the Senate and converts Congress into a more streamlined, single chamber. Article IV places the election of the President directly in the hands of the People and imposes limits on the President. Article V changes the method of appointing judges and their tenure.

ARTICLE II

COMMISSION ON NATIONAL ELECTIONS AND COMPENSATION

As we witnessed in the turbulent 2020 Presidential election, the procedures, methodologies, technologies, and timing of the election were governed by the Secretaries of State of 50 States and the District of Columbia. Many jurisdictions had early voting without excuse due to the pandemic, some had absentee voting with excuse, some had mail-in ballots, Oregon had electronic voting, some had ranked-choice voting, two split Electoral votes rather than apply a winner-take-all approach, some had same-day registration, some provided inadequate resources resulting in lines taking hours to vote, and so on.

While States may wish to retain their own voting customs for their own local and statewide officials, we need to institute a uniform system for the election of all national officials, regardless of whom they will be representing. This means that Congress, the President, and the Vice President will be elected pursuant to procedures followed nationwide. We also need to redraw the boundary lines for Congressional districts to stop flagrant gerrymandering.

If the States can no longer be trusted to conduct fair elections and to draw nonpolitical district lines, who can? Clearly, Congress is a nonstarter. We can't assign the fox to guard the hen house. The President is too partisan. The courts have been historically reluctant to handle political questions and, in any event, lack the resources and capabilities to do so.

Consequently, we need to create and empower an independent agency to conduct and regulate elections for Congress, the President, and the Vice President. Hence, the Commission on National Elections and Compensation.

CREATION OF THE COMMISSION

1.   **Upon ratification of this Restated Constitution, there shall be established a new independent and autonomous agency called, the "Commission on National Elections and Compensation" (the "Commission"), comprised of 20 members who shall be called, "Commissioners." Half of the Commissioners must not be affiliated with or a member of any political party. The initial 20 Commissioners shall be appointed by the House of Representatives within 30 days after ratification of this Restated Constitution in accordance with the requirements of eligibility provided in the following Section of this Article. Because no Regions will have been established at the time of the appointment of the initial Commissioners, the House of Representatives shall appoint two Commissioners to represent each geographical area consisting of approximately one-tenth of the population of the nation based on the most recent national census. Upon appointment, the Commissioners shall divide the United States and its possessions and territories into ten Regions, each consisting of approximately one-tenth of the population of the nation, and ten Districts of approximately equal population within each Region based on locale and not on political affiliation.**

The crucial purpose and goal of the Commission is political neutrality. We have to modulate the power of party politics because they taint and pervert the election process. Political parties influence outcomes by injecting partisanship into what should be an objective process.

For example, was it fair to have Katherine Harris, Florida's Republican Secretary of State, make decisions to purge almost 200,000 people from the voter rolls and make decisions on how to count and recount hanging chads in the 2000 election? Her decisions resulted in Republican George Bush's victory over Democrat Al Gore. The potential for bias has become even worse in Florida since its Secretary of State is now appointed rather than elected.[21]

By design, there is no mention of political parties in the Constitution. James Madison, the primary draftsman of the Constitution, warned about the danger of political parties in *The Federalist*, or the *Federalist Papers*, as it is often called, a collection of essays by Madison, Alexander Hamilton, and John Jay circulated to explain the Constitution and drum up support for its ratification.

George Washington later said in his farewell address, "I have already intimated to you the danger of parties in the state, with particular reference to the founding of them on geographical discriminations. Let me now take a more comprehensive view, and warn you in the most solemn manner against the baneful effects of the spirit of party, generally."[22]

He also said, "However [political parties] may now and then answer popular ends, they are likely in the course of time and things, to become potent engines, by which cunning, ambitious, and unprincipled men will be enabled to subvert the power of the people and to usurp for themselves the reins of government, destroying afterwards the very engines which have lifted them to unjust dominion."

The Presidential election of 2020 has shown how political parties and partisanship can exert undue influence and taint elections with potential corruption. Fortunately, Secretaries of State performed their duties and preserved the integrity of their elections by refusing to kowtow to pressure from not only Trump but also many Republican federal and State elected officials to throw out legitimate ballots voting for Joe Biden and "find" votes for Trump. Such attempts continued even after President Biden's inauguration with the belated recount of votes in Arizona. Consequently, we should attempt to remove any possibility that State election officials may be swayed or bullied by political factions in the future.

Accordingly, half of the Commissioners "**must not be affiliated with or a member of any political party.**" In other words, half of the Commission will be "Independents" or "Unaffiliateds." Since some studies show that over 40% of voters are Independents or Unaffiliateds—more than either the Democrats or Republicans, there should be plenty of intelligent and impartial candidates who would make fine Commissioners.[23] Section 4 of this Article II will implement this allocation by requiring that one of the two Commissioners from each Region must not be affiliated with or a member of any political party.

This dedication of half of the Commission seats will leave the Republicans and Democrats, as well as any smaller party, to vie for the remaining half of Commission seats. As a result, no formal party will be able to assert majority control over the Commission.

Twenty Commissioners is an appropriate number. That number keeps the Commission small enough to work effectively and large enough to prevent abuses.

In creating a new agency like the Commission, we have a chicken-or-the-egg situation. The ultimate plan is to elect two Commissioners representing each Region in the midterm election of every Presidential cycle, but the Commissioners will be the ones to determine the geographic boundaries of each Region and have to do so before the first election. So, the House of Representatives is tasked to roughly carve the country into ten Regions of approximately one-tenth of the population and appoint two Commissioners for each Region. Each initial Commissioner must satisfy the eligibility requirements in Section 2, namely, be 35 years or older, a United States citizen for more than eight years prior to appointment, and domiciled in the Region he or she will be representing at the time of appointment.

The House of Representatives was designated to appoint the initial Commissioners because the House members each represent the smallest constituencies of our elected national officials, for the most part, and, therefore, can best approximate a popular election. Of course, an alternative would be to have the House draw the initial Regions and hold a special election for Commissioners in each Region, but it is more important to have the Commissioners quickly chosen by appointment so that they can set up the Regions and Districts for the first national election under the Restated Constitution without the delay of campaigns and elections.

To avoid delays in the appointment process, a deadline is set of 30 days from ratification of the Restated Constitution for the House to establish initial Regions and appoint the first Commissioners. The Senate and the President have been deliberately excluded from the process because they would prolong it.

The Commission is charged with drawing up the Regions and Districts to eradicate gerrymandering from elections. The term "gerrymander" is a portmanteau or, in current jargon, "mashup," of "Elbridge Gerry" and "salamander." In 1812, Governor Elbridge Gerry of Massachusetts signed a bill splicing and dicing voting districts to favor his party, the Democratic-Republican Party. A cartoonist illustration of a resulting district in Boston looked like a salamander. Hence, the combination of "Gerry" and "mander." As a side note, Gerry was one of the few delegates to the Federal Convention of 1787 who stayed to the end but refused to sign the Constitution, believing it gave too much power to a central government. Also, he became Vice President in James Madison's administration.[24]

Gerrymandering is considered political manipulation of elections and has been used by both parties to dilute the power of voters of the opposite party in a district and to con-centrate voters of the opposite party in as few districts as possible to limit their total number of elected officials. It continues to this day because it works, especially in reducing the voting power of minorities. Since State voting districts are usually drawn by State legislatures, the ruling party wins the votes on redistricting plans that usually favor the ruling party, both on districts established for local and State elections as well as the State's Congressional districts. While minority parties sometimes succeed in suing for proper redistricting, the legal process is not the best way to draw district lines.

We need to remove State political machinations from the elections for Members of Congress.[25] The only way to do that is to transfer the responsibility for drawing districts to an independent and semi-nonpartisan body such as the Commission. The primary task for drawing district lines within a Region will presumably fall upon the two Commissioners representing each Region who will have the greatest familiarity with that Region, although the entire Commission will have the final say.

The Commission will take the most recent census, divide the population by ten, and then start building each Region with contiguous land on which approximately ten percent of the population lives. According to the 2020 census, there were 331,449,281 people living in the U.S.[26] Each Region, then, would have a little over 33 million people, and each District would have 3.3 million people.

By way of illustration, the six States comprising New England (Maine, New Hampshire, Vermont, Massachusetts, Rhode Island, and Connecticut) have almost 15 million inhabitants, roughly half a Region. Add to that Westchester County, New York, which borders Connecticut, plus the five counties comprising the boroughs of New York City, and Long Island, and we would need only another 5 million in upstate New York and/or northern New Jersey to form Region 1.

The Regions, themselves, will have little or no political significance because the only officials to be elected on a Region-wide basis would be the two Commissioners, one of whom will be nonpartisan.

The Commission will use a similar methodology to draw the District lines, with the result that people will get to vote for their own Member of Congress as now, except that each Member will represent more constituents than now, as explained with respect to the makeup of the reconstituted Congress in Article III, below.

As with the Regions, the Districts need not be drawn within the confines of a single State. Adherence to the boundaries of States for electing members of Congress no longer makes sense. People living near State borders cross the borders frequently for work, home, grocery and general shopping, and recreation. They often root for the same professional sports teams. For example, all of New England tends to root for Boston teams, except the southern half of Connecticut, which favors the nearby New York teams. Television markets, including the "local" news, encompass metropolitan areas regardless of State lines and are more regional in nature.

As a result of geographical proximity, people who live near State borders tend to have more in common with their neighbors in the State next door than with residents farther away in their same State. For instance, residents of New York City have more in common with residents in Northern New Jersey and Southern Connecticut than with people in upstate New York. People living close together have similar interests in local infrastructure, employment opportunities, and environment.

Consequently, the Commission should consider formulating Districts without strict conformity to traditional State borders. As a practical matter, if we are to downsize Congress to 100 Members each representing 3.3 million people to start with and more as the population continues to grow, the Commission will have to establish Districts that cross State borders for those States with fewer than 3.3 million residents.

Alternatively, the Commission can try to build Regions and Districts by adhering to State boundaries and grouping States, but this may be difficult to accomplish because geography and population do not always correspond.

QUALIFICATIONS OF COMMISSIONERS

2. **Only a citizen who is 35 years or older, who has been a United States citizen for more than eight years prior to election, and who is at the time of election domiciled in the Region may be elected to represent that Region on the Commission. When a vacancy occurs in the Commission before a national election, the Commission shall hold a special election by the people in the affected Region to fill the vacancy until the next national election.**

Eligibility to serve as a Commissioner is based on a hybrid of qualifications for different Constitutional offices. Since Commissioners will control the process for electing the President and Vice President, they should have to meet the same age requirement of those offices in Section 1 of Article II of the Constitution. The age threshold of 35 to serve as President and Vice President appears to be based on a presumption that a person of that age will have acquired sufficient experience and will have shown his or her character and abilities to handle the job.

The length of eight years as a U.S. citizen comes from splitting the difference between the requirement of seven years as a citizen for members of the House in Section 2 of Article I of the Constitution and nine years for Senators in Section 3 of Article I. That same compromise of eight years of citizenship is employed for Members of Congress in

Section 3 of Article III of the Restated Constitution. Sections 2 and 3 of Article I of the Constitution provide the requirement that representatives live in the geographical area of their constituency.

The Commission shall hold special elections by the people in the affected Region to fill any vacancies that occur before a national election.

NATIONAL ELECTIONS

3.	**The Commission shall hold elections for the President and Vice President on the first Saturday and Sunday following the first Monday of November in the four-year cycle in effect on the Effective Date of this Restated Constitution. The Commission shall hold the initial national election for Members of Congress and Commissioners on the first Saturday and Sunday following the first Monday of November in the year that is two years after the next election for President and Vice President following the Effective Date of this Restated Constitution. Subsequent national elections for Members of Congress and Commissioners shall be held on the first Saturday and Sunday following the first Monday of November every four years and shall include a vote on any amendments to this Restated Constitution proposed in accordance with Article VII. The Commission shall hold and monitor national elections and Presidential elections and shall work with the Department of Justice in enforcing all election laws.**

This Section sets up the system of national elections and Presidential elections organized, conducted, and monitored by the Commission. The national elections will be the means by which we select the Members of Congress and the Commissioners, themselves, on the first Saturday and Sunday following the first Monday of November every four years.

After the Effective Date of the Restated Constitution, the next Presidential election will take place in the same year as it would have under the Constitution but will be held on the first Saturday and Sunday, rather than the first Tuesday, following the first Monday of November. The initial national election will be held in the year that is two years after the next Presidential election following the Effective Date of the Restated Constitution.

One of the reasons the Restated Constitution is restructuring Congress is to eliminate the rolling election of one-third of the Senate every two years so that now the entire Congress will be up for election every four years. Congress will no longer be elected in the same year as the President and Vice President because Presidential elections tend to skew the results of Congressional elections held in the same year through the "coattail" effect. Now, the staggered elections of the President and Congress will result in mutual midterm elections that should provide a check-and-balance and a reality and accountability check on each branch.

We have been holding national elections on the first Tuesday following the first Monday of November since 1845, when Congress enacted a statute standardizing election day pursuant to Section 4 of Article I of the Constitution, known as the "Elections Clause," which empowers Congress to regulate the times, places, and manner of electing federal officials that any State has established.[27] In *The Federalist* No. 59, Alexander Hamilton stated that "[n]othing can be more evident, than that an exclusive power of regulating elections for the national government, in the hands of the state legislatures, would leave the existence of the union entirely at their mercy."

In the 1932 case of *Smiley v. Holm*, 285 U.S. 355, 366 (1932), the Supreme Court held that the Elections Clause's times, places, and manner language empowers Congress to enact "a complete code for congressional elections, not only as to times and places, but in relation to notices, registration, supervision of voting, protection of voters, prevention of fraud and corrupt practices, counting of votes, duties of inspectors and canvassers, and making and publication of election returns – in short, to enact the numerous requirements as to procedure and safeguards which experience shows are necessary in order to enforce the fundamental right involved."

The Commission will now take over from Congress the power to regulate national and Presidential elections. As we saw in 2020, we need to bolster national oversight of national elections to prevent interference from State actors, including governors, secretaries of state, and state legislators, and from the States' elected officials in Congress. Entrusting full responsibility for national elections to the independent and semi-nonpartisan Commission is the solution. That responsibility will include enforcing all election laws in tandem with the U.S. Department of Justice.

In an effort to increase voter turnout, election day will move from a single day on Tuesday to two days on Saturday **and** Sunday, which should make in-person voting easier for people who work during the week. Holding elections on two days will also help alleviate the excessively long lines in

States that seem to intentionally discourage voting by failing to staff polling places sufficiently, particularly in less affluent and heavily minority locations.

The national election will also provide the only way, pursuant to Article VII, to ratify proposed amendments to the Restated Constitution. Now, the People, rather than the State legislatures, will be able to ratify amendments directly through the popular vote.

That's how the national and Presidential elections will work in the future. How, though, do we determine when to hold the first national election? The timing is tricky because obviously the Restated Constitution has to first be ratified and then become effective before the initial national election and the Effective Date needs to occur sufficiently before that first weekend following the first Monday in November to allow time for the Commission to be appointed and set up shop, including its demarcation of the Regions and Districts. Also, there has to be enough time for candidates to campaign for Congress and the Commission.

A minimum of almost four years after ratification should be enough to satisfy all these factors. Since Section 1 requires Congress to appoint the initial Commission within 30 days after ratification, the Commission will have at least 47 months to prepare for the initial election. Since that would be the shortest lead-up to the first election, the Commission should set the boundaries for the Regions and Districts as soon as possible and, in no event, later than one year before the election so that candidates for the Commission and Congress know which Regions and Districts they can represent and know where they need to campaign. If the lead-up to the national election is more than four years, the Commission should announce the boundaries earlier to accord more time for campaigns.

The timing of the election depends on the date of ratification and, as a result, could range from four to eight years after ratification. The chart in **Appendix B** illustrates a few examples of dates of ratification and the timing of the election based on the formula that sets the initial national election for the "**Saturday and Sunday following the first Monday of November in the year that is two years after the next election for President and Vice President following the Effective Date of this Restated Constitution.**"

The earliest Presidential election dates that could be used to determine the initial national election are Saturday and Sunday, November 11 and 12, 2028, and the next ones are Saturday and Sunday, November 6 and 7, 2032.

As the chart in **Appendix B** demonstrates, there will be a four-year cycle in which the lead time fluctuates between four and eight years from ratification to the initial national election. Most of the fluctuation is gradual except for when we reach the shortest gap time of four years after ratification on November 10, 2026 and November 5, 2030 and then, three days later, leap to a gap of eight years on November 13, 2026 and November 8, 2030, respectively. Ratification on November 11, 2026 and November 6, 2030 would result in Effective Dates on election days, but since the initial national election must be held two years following the next election for President and Vice President <u>after the Effective Date</u>, the initial national election would be held eight years later.

Four years is a reasonable lead time for this transition, and eight years may be too long to wait for an initial national election, but once we hold the first election, the four-year cycle will take over and remain in place for years to come.

The first election will be like moving homes. Packing up and moving is an ordeal, but after unpacking, you're happy in your new home.

TERM LIMIT

4.   The initial Commissioners shall serve until noon on the third day of January following the initial national election by popular vote for Commissioners. At the initial national election, two Commissioners shall be elected by popular vote in each Region as representatives of that Region and shall serve for a term of four years each. One of the two Commissioners from each Region must not be affiliated with or a member of any political party. Each initial Commissioner may run for election in the initial election. Thereafter, the Commissioners shall be elected at each national election. No Commissioner may serve on the Commission for more than a total of 12 years after the initial election. The terms of each Commissioner shall end at noon on the third day of January following an election, and the terms of their successors shall then begin.

At the initial national election, the People will vote for two Commissioners in their Region. One seat in each Region can be filled only by an Independent or Unaffiliated person. Presumably, the ballots will have two categories from which voters shall select candidates—one listing Independent or Unaffiliated candidates and the other listing party-affiliated candidates. The term of the initial Commissioners appointed by the House will end at noon on January 3 following the initial national election, just like the terms of Congress end under the 20th Amendment.

Thereafter, elected Commissioners will serve four-year terms ending at noon on January 3 following each national election.

This Section could have made the initial Commissioners ineligible to run in the initial election with the thought that that might keep them from making decisions on drawing the boundaries of the Regions that would favor their own campaigns for election. Barring them from the initial election, however, might discourage some highly qualified persons from serving as initial Commissioners. In any event, there will be 19 other initial Commissioners who should prevent any hanky-panky from a Commissioner drawing self-serving lines.

In keeping with term limits imposed on the President, Congress, judges, and other officials, a maximum term is set of 12 years *after the initial national election* that Commissioners may serve. That means that the initial Commissioners, who may serve for four to eight years before the initial national election, depending on the date of ratification as explained in the prior section, may be eligible to serve for up to 20 years. Alternatively, we could make the term limit 12 years *including time served as an initial Commissioner*, but, again, we shouldn't discourage people from serving as initial Commissioners.

CENSUS

5. **The Commission shall determine the initial boundaries of the Regions based on the most recent national census. A national census shall be conducted in every year ending in a zero, and the Commission shall redraw the boundaries of the Regions and Districts within two years after and based on each new census.**

The national census was mandated by Section 2 of Article I, as modified by Section 2 of the 14th Amendment, for the purpose of determining the number of House of Representatives members each State may elect. The first census was taken in 1790, and a census has been taken every ten years since.[28] This Section does not transfer responsibility for the census from Congress and the President but rather requires the Commission to base its determinations of the Regions and Districts on the census and within two years after each census.

DECLARATION OF VICTORS

6. **The Commission shall administer and conduct all elections for the President and Vice President, for Members of Congress, and for Commissioners, shall count all ballots cast in such elections, and shall determine and declare, on or before the 15th day of December following each election, the winners of the elections for the President, Vice President, and Members of Congress based on the popular vote. The Commission shall declare as the victor the person receiving the most votes in each of these elections, regardless of whether the candidate received a majority of the votes.**

This Section puts the Commission in charge of administering and conducting all national elections and determining and declaring the winners of the elections for President, Vice President, and Congress. Congress will no longer be "the Judge of the Elections, Returns, and Qualifications of its own Members," as under Section 5 of Article I of the Constitution.

The Electoral College is abolished, as explained in connection with Section 1 of Article IV, below.

The deadline of December 15 for declaring the winners approximates the current requirement of the first Monday after the second Wednesday in December when State Electors must meet and vote. If December 15 falls on a weekend, the Commission should declare the winners by the preceding Friday.

The person receiving the most votes will be declared the winner. This standard recognizes races in which more than two candidates run or in which a substantial number of write-in votes are submitted, thereby permitting victory by a plurality rather than a majority.

ELECTION OF THE COMMISSION

7.   **To avoid any appearance of a conflict of interest, within ten days after the Commission declares the winners of the elections for Congress, the then sitting Congress shall determine and declare, as the victors of the election for the Commissioners, the two persons, subject to the conditions of Section 4 of this Article, receiving the most votes in each Region resulting from the popular vote within each Region regardless of whether they received a majority of the votes.**

This Section is pretty straightforward. Congress will declare the winners in the election of the Commissioners to avoid any conflict of interest.

APPOINTMENT OF JUDGES

8.   The Commission shall select and appoint judges from the list of eligible and highly qualified candidates prepared by the Judicial Appointment Council in accordance with Article V.

It makes no sense for politicians to appoint judges who are supposed to be impartial. The independent and semi-nonpartisan Commission, therefore, will take over appointments of judges from the President. The discussion under Article V, below, sets forth the rationale for this change and the procedure.

DETERMINATION OF COMPENSATION

9.   The Commission shall determine and fix the compensation of the President, the Vice President, Members of Congress, and the members of the Judicial Appointment Council, whose compensation shall neither be increased nor decreased during their terms, and any change in their compensation shall take effect only after their next election or appointment. The Commission shall also determine and fix the compensation of the judges of the United States, which **may be increased but** shall not be diminished during their continuance in office. [Art. II, Sect.1; Art. III, Sect. 1; 27th Amend.]

Congress has traditionally determined the compensation for all three branches. For some reason, Congress often ties judges' compensation to its own. Because Congress fears that voters will vote out anyone who awards themselves a pay raise, they are reluctant to raise their own compensation and, as a result, compensation for judges.

Consequently, judges' pay remains way below what they could earn in private practice and discourages many highly qualified attorneys from serving, particularly at the stage of their careers when they are incurring high college tuition and fees for their children.

Now that we have an independent, semi-nonpartisan body like the Commission, we can finally assign compensation decisions to an objective and non-interested entity that will determine salary and benefits. The Commission will also decide the compensation for the new Judicial Appointment Council established under Article V.

The language about freezing compensation during an official's term is borrowed from Section 1 of Article II of the Constitution regarding the President's compensation, and the language postponing any changes in compensation until the official's next term is based on the 27th Amendment, which was originally proposed in 1789 but not ratified until 203 years later in 1992.

The provision regarding judges' compensation is addressed separately because their terms will be much longer and start at different times, and, unlike the other positions, the judges' compensation should never be diminished due to the policy of encouraging them to make honest decisions without worrying that controversial decisions will cause a pay cut. Language prohibiting diminishment of their pay is borrowed from Section 1 of Article III of the Constitution, and the Commission may increase judges' pay during their terms, which are continuous.

COMPENSATION OF COMMISSIONERS

10.   The Commissioners shall receive compensation for their services, to be ascertained by Congress. Their compensation shall neither be increased nor decreased during their terms, and any change in their compensation shall take effect only after their next election or appointment.

The Commissioners' compensation will be determined by Congress and will be circumscribed by the same provisions as in Section 9 for the President, the Vice President, and Congress.

IMMUNITY

11. The Commissioners shall in all cases, except treason, felony, and breach of the peace, be privileged from arrest during their attendance at any session of the Commission and in going to and returning from the same, and for any speech or debate in the Commission, they shall not be questioned in any other place.

This Section is lifted from Section 6 of Article I of the Constitution and provides the same immunity and protection for the Commissioners in performing their functions as accorded to Congress. The purpose is to encourage the Commissioners to act in the best interests of the country and not fear any criminal repercussions or civil liability for unpopular stances they may take.

THE TWO-HATS BAN

12.   No Commissioners shall, during the time for which they were elected, be appointed to any civil office under the authority of the United States, which shall have been created, or the emoluments whereof shall have been increased, during such person's time on the Commission. Similarly, no persons holding any office under the United States shall be Commissioners during their continuance in office.

This Section is also lifted from Section 6 of Article I of the Constitution, whose purpose appears to have been to remove the possibility that the President might influence Senators and Representatives with promises of newly created positions or appointment to offices whose compensation shall have been increased. This Section applies that restriction to Commissioners, as well, and also prohibits other officers of the United States from serving as Commissioners while retaining their offices.

ARTICLE III

LEGISLATIVE BRANCH

Article III makes five fundamental changes in Congress. First, the House and the Senate are consolidated into a single chamber with "Members." Second, the current total of 100 Senators and 435 Representatives plus six non-voting members of the House (Washington, D.C., Puerto Rico, American Samoa, Guam, the Northern Mariana Islands, and the U.S. Virgin Islands) is reduced to 100 Members of Congress. Third, the duration of an elected term in Congress is changed to four years for all Members. Fourth, a Member may serve no more than 16 years in Congress. Fifth, filibusters and most supermajority votes are eliminated.

Aside from these changes, the powers of Congress in Article I of the Constitution remain in place with a little wordsmithing to combine previous division of duties between the Senate and House, such as in the case of impeachment, and to modernize the language and punctuation.

NAME OF CONGRESS
1.   **The legislative branch of the United States government shall be called, "Congress."** [Art. I, Sect. 1]

Pretty much the same gist as the original but with no mention of the superseded Senate and House of Representatives.

COMPOSITION
2.   **Congress shall be comprised of a single chamber with 100 "Members." Each District shall elect one Member of Congress by popular vote to represent**

that District for a term of four years, which shall end at noon on the third day of January **following each national election,** and the terms of their successors shall then begin. **The terms of all Senators and Representatives elected before the initial national election held pursuant to Section 3 of Article II shall end at noon on the third day of January following the initial national election, regardless of whether certain Senators may have any years remaining in their terms as of the date of the initial national election. No Member may serve in Congress for more than a total of 16 years, whether or not consecutive, after the initial national election held following the Effective Date. When a vacancy occurs in Congress, the Commission shall hold a special election to fill the vacancy.** [20th Amend.]

This Section announces four dramatic changes in the makeup of Congress.

Single-Chambered Congress

The Constitution set up Congress to have two chambers, the House of Representatives and the Senate, as a balance between the larger States' desire for voting power based on population and the smaller States' fear of getting pushed around or ignored. The resulting two chambers arose from what is referred to as "the Connecticut Compromise," in which Roger Sherman of Connecticut proposed that States elect members of the House in proportion to their population but each State would send two members to the Senate. Accordingly, every State has an equal voice in the Senate.[29]

The Connecticut Compromise may have made sense in the early years as the colonies of England matured into States striving to overcome past suspicions and rivalries among themselves in a new, independent union of sovereign States.

Does the Connecticut Compromise continue to make sense today, 235 years later? Or, is it time to streamline Congress?

Section 2 of Article I of the Constitution required Congress to apportion Representatives "among the several States which may be included within this Union." To solve the chicken-or-the-egg problem, this Section set the initial apportionment of Representatives among the 13 original States as reflected in **Appendix C**.

That same Section 2 required Congress to make an "actual Enumeration within three Years after the first Meeting of the Congress" and every ten years thereafter "in such Manner as they shall by Law direct." In 1790, Congress passed the first Census Act, and the U.S. Marshals conducted the first census, which reported a population of over 3.9 million.[30]

Congress' task, then, was to figure out how to assign the number of Representatives for each State. Section 2 of Article I directed that the "number of Representatives shall not exceed one for every thirty Thousand, but each State shall have at Least one Representative." While a State could not have more than one Representative for every 30,000 residents, a Representative could represent more than 30,000, as eventually occurred as the country grew. Also, the Constitution placed no cap on the total of Representatives.

Section 2 also described how to determine apportionment of Representatives: "by adding to the whole

Number of free Persons, including those bound to Service for a Term of Years, and excluding Indians not taxed, three fifths of all other Persons." This was called the "Three-Fifths Compromise," as explained in Section 3 of Article I of the Restated Constitution regarding citizenship, above. Not only did the Three-Fifths Compromise add seats in the House for the Southern States, but it gave them extra votes for President in the Electoral College since each State had as many Electors as its total of Representatives and Senators, pursuant to Section 1 of Article II.

As a result of the 1790 census, the House was reconfigured—after the first Presidential veto ever—to contain 105 Representatives from now 15 States with the addition of Vermont and Kentucky,[31] as shown in **Appendix D**.

As Appendices C and D illustrate, the uniform addition of two Senators to each State's Congressional delegation did not really change the total voting power of the States' delegations in any significant way. The percentage of the delegations of the five States with the largest populations diminished the most, and the percentage of the delegations of the five States with the smallest populations increased the most, but still we're talking a small range of -2.2% to 1.8% under the original apportionment in the Constitution for a swing of 4.0% and a similar range of -2.6% to 1.1% after the 1790 census for a lesser swing of only 3.7%.

Where the impact was felt the most was in the Senate, where the smallest States increased their individual voting power to 7.7% in the original apportionment (2 out of 26 Senators), which decreased to 6.7% as a result of the 1790 census (2 out of 30 Senators). As the number of States kept increasing, any advantage the smallest States perceived they held in the Senate kept decreasing, to the point where today their voting power amounts only to 2.0% (2 out of 100 Senators).

Another way to view the small States' voting power in the Senate is in absolute numbers rather than percentages. In the first Senate of 26 Senators, a small State's two Senators could reasonably be expected to exert influence beyond their State's relative size, particularly on issues where the 13 States' interests were closely divided and one or two votes could pass or defeat a motion or proposed statute. Likewise, with the Senate of 30 Senators based on the 1790 census. Nowadays, however, two Senators from a small State do not have anywhere near the same influence in a Senate of 100 Senators.

The disproportionate influence a small State can have in the Senate is more a factor of the capabilities, personality, and popularity of its Senators than of the number of persons it sends to the Senate. For example, when George Mitchell of Maine served as Senate Majority Leader from 1989 to 1995, he wielded more power on behalf of Maine than its small population warranted. Mitch McConnell of Kentucky, a mid-size State, has done likewise while serving variously as Senate Majority Leader and Minority Leader since 2007.

In the recent Senates, votes seem to go fairly uniformly along party lines rather than State interests, such as when Republican and Democratic Senators representing the same State vote differently.

One exception in these times of slim political majorities in the Senate is the way that Senator Joe Manchin of West Virginia, nominally a Democrat, has managed to secure concessions favorable to his State by twisting the arms of his fellow Democrats, who desperately needed his vote to maintain a majority. Again, this results more from the political makeup of the current Senate and his personality than from the small population of West Virginia. If, on the other hand, the Democrats had built a 55-45 majority, they would not have felt as much pressure to placate him.

Consequently, the benefit to small States of having a body like the Senate that is equally apportioned among the States rather than based on their populations has lost its value over the years due to the increase in size of the Senate and the increasing intensity of overarching party partisanship.

The notion of a two-chambered legislature was not hatched in the Constitution. The British House of Lords and House of Commons served as a model, as did the two-chambered legislatures in many of the colonies and young States. In fact, by providing in Section 3 of Article I that the Senators would be chosen by the States' legislatures rather than by popular vote as in the House of Representatives, the Constitution set up a parallel to the British system with the Senators akin to the privileged class of the House of Lords and the House of Representatives more like the People's House of Commons.

On the other hand, the Continental Congress was a single-chambered legislature to which the colonies sent delegates from 1774 to 1781 and to which the States sent delegates under the Articles of Confederation from 1781 until the two-chambered Congress under the Constitution was first convened in 1789. Also, there were single-chambered legislatures in some colonies and States in the 18th Century, and today Nebraska has only one chamber, as do the District of Columbia, Guam, and the U.S. Virgin Islands.[32] Moreover, local government, such as City Councils, Town Councils, and Boards of Selectmen, are all unicameral.[33] It seems obvious that a single chamber is more efficient and less costly than two chambers.

In a two-chamber legislature or Congress, the chambers and their work are often duplicative. Their committees have the same or similar titles, functions, and purposes, investigate the same issues, and draft bills on the same topics. Then, more time and resources are wasted on trying to reconcile bills passed by the two chambers on the same subjects, resulting in the passage of a sausage-like statute with quirky provisions or no statute at all.

The Framers of the Constitution also believed that a Congress of two chambers would prevent a despotic Congress because each chamber would provide a check on the other. While there is merit to that logic, those checks have resulted in Congressional gridlock in the 21st Century. A shift to a single chamber should enable Congress to move more swiftly in general and especially in times of crisis. Any check on despotism that may still be needed is furnished by the exhaustive round-the-clock media coverage and the rabid news junkies and policy wonks that feed on it. Plus, we will always have recourse to federal judges, who will be better qualified and less partisan under the new appointment process in Article V, below.

Some people argue that the two-chamber system is ideal because it is designed to ensure a slow, deliberative process and prevent sudden, cataclysmic changes. If that is the goal, then we should revert to a part-time Congress, which can accomplish just as little as a full-time Congress in a third or a half of a year. Forty States have part-time legislatures,[34] and, until the 1970s, Congress convened on a part-time basis.[35]

100 Members

In an effort to make Congress more efficient and effective, Congress is reduced in size from 535 Senators and Representatives, plus six nonvoting delegates, to 100 Members.

In the private sector, large Boards of Directors tend to get bogged down in discussions because everyone feels compelled to put in their own two cents. Moreover, large Boards delegate work to committees and subcommittees, many of which are never heard from again. By nature, large bodies move more slowly and often stagnate under their own weight.

In *The Federalist* No. 55, James Madison discussed the pros and cons of various sizes for Congress. Because the Constitution required that there be one Representative for at least 30,000 people, unless a State had a lower population, Madison observed that the original apportionment of 65 Representatives would continue to increase as the country grew over time. He accurately predicted the 1790 census count and the resulting growth of Congress in size. He also noted that at some point Congress could get too large.

The Reapportionment Act of 1929 finally capped the number of seats in the House at 435, where it had been stuck since 1912 due to Congress' failure to reapportion after the 1920 census. In the Congress of 1913, the first with 435 seats, there was an average of 224,000 people for each Representative. After the reapportionment resulting from the recent 2020 census, those 435 seats have been distributed throughout the country in such a way that each Representative has an average constituency of about 761,000 people, 25 times as many as originally established in the Constitution.[36]

There are proposals of enlarging the House through different methodologies that would increase the House variously to 571 seats, 692 seats, and even 1,560 seats in an effort to provide what the proponents believe would be a more representative democracy.

These proposals are going in the wrong direction. As Madison pointed out in *The Federalist* No. 55, "Sixty or seventy men may be more properly trusted with a given degree of power, than six or seven. But it does not follow, that six or seven hundred would be proportionably a better depository. . . . The truth is, that in all cases, a certain number at least seems to be necessary to secure the benefits of free consultation and discussion; and to guard against too easy a combination for improper purposes: as on the other hand, the number ought at most to be kept within a certain limit, in order to avoid the confusion and intemperance of a multitude."

Adding more Representatives would vastly increase bureaucratic red tape, staffing costs, and gridlock. Any improvement in the ratio of Representative to constituents would be nominal and inconsequential. After all, how much more access to a Representative would a single constituent have if the ratio is reduced from the current 1:761,000 to 1:578,000 (571 seats), 1:478,000 (692 seats), or 1:212,000 (1,560 seats)?

Instead, let's cap Congress at 100 Members, each of whom would represent an average of 3.3 million people, about four times as many as now. The number 100 is chosen for several reasons. First, it's a nice round number. Second, we're used to having 100 Senators. Third, it simplifies the arithmetic by electing one Member from each of ten Districts in each of the ten Regions.

By the way, under Section 1 of Article II of the Restated Constitution, the Regions will include over 4 million people living in Washington, D.C., Puerto Rico, American Samoa, Guam, the Northern Mariana Islands, and the U.S. Virgin Islands who will have voting Members of Congress for the first time. So, this proposal actually increases representation for people residing in those territories and possessions.

Reducing the size of Congress, coupled with a term limit of 16 years as discussed below, should attract Members who are committed to rolling up their sleeves and working hard to accomplish something meaningful during their tenure rather than simply focusing on how to remain in power forever. Each Member of a single-chambered Congress of only 100 Members will have better opportunities to make a difference than the many "back-benchers" of Congress as now constituted. This new Congress should perform much better than the log-jammed Congress that has evolved into "the confusion and intemperance of a multitude" predicted by Madison, spouting the unproductive, soap box oratory and name-calling we see on TV and the internet every hour of every day.

Additionally, while many Senators and Representatives work pretty hard, others do not. How many pages of the 400-page American Recovery and Reinvestment Act of 2009 or the 955-page Affordable Care Act of 2010 did they sit down and write, let alone read? The drafters of federal legislation are the many staff attorneys who toil over the structure and wording of these extensive statutes. Those staff will continue their herculean work after ratification of the Restated Constitution, and, so, the reduction in the numbers of those elected to Congress will not impede legislation. On the contrary, with fewer politicians running around

Congress focused on pursuing their own personal agendas while constantly running for re-election or higher office, we should see an increase in legislation that makes our lives better and our country a better place in which to live.

Four-Year Terms

Under Sections 2 and 3 of Article I of the Constitution, Representatives are elected every two years and Senators every six years, respectively.

A two-year term for Representatives is too short. As soon as Representatives are elected for the first time, they are told by their party leaders in Congress that their primary job is to get re-elected and they are pressured to devote much of their time immediately to fundraising for the next election two years down the road. This approach subverts the process. Voters send the Representatives to Congress to work for them, not to worry primarily about getting re-elected. Even after the first re-election campaign, Representatives are constantly running on the two-year hamster wheel cycle.

On the other hand, a six-year term for Senators is too long. They need to be more accountable to their constituents through a shorter leash for their tenure.

The simple solution is four years for all Members of Congress, which is the middle ground between two and six years. Moreover, four years is the length of the President and Vice President's term, so making all terms the same for all officials elected to national office makes sense. Plus, under Section 3 of Article II of the Restated Constitution, the elections of Congress will take place every two years after Presidential elections. Thus, the national election of Congress and the Presidential election will serve as midterm elections vis-à-vis the other and provide an opportunity for the People to make adjustments every two years.

Finally, by eliminating the Senate, we also eliminate the whacky staggered election of a third of the Senate every two years. To accomplish this, this Section truncates the remaining two years of Senators elected four years before the initial national election and the remaining four years of the Senators elected two years before the initial national election. Thus, their terms will end at noon on the third day of January following the initial national election, when the term of the final Congress under the original Constitution expires.

Allowing the Senators with two and four years remaining on their terms to complete their terms is unworkable. When the 17th Amendment changed the method of selecting Senators from the State legislatures to a popular vote, it added that "[t]his amendment shall not be so construed as to affect the election or term of any Senator chosen before it becomes valid as part of the Constitution." Allowing such Senators to complete their terms was easy to do because the structure of staggered terms remained in place. With the revamping of Congress under the Restated Constitution, however, that would not be possible because there will be no separate Senate chamber and the number of Members of Congress will be reduced. So, there is no place to put Senators with time remaining in their terms. Plus, there will be no new election in two years for those Senators with two years remaining in their terms.

Don't feel too sorry for these Senators. They can run to become a Member of the new Congress, a Commissioner, President, or Governor, join a President's administration, enter the private sector, or retire.

16-Year Term Limit

The Framers did not contemplate a class of professional politicians who made careers out of holding office for decades.

George Washington twice set an example for how to serve our country. At the behest of the Continental Congress, he left his farm at Mount Vernon to lead the Continental Army in the Revolution. At the end of the war, he resigned his commission and returned to farming. Four years later, however, he once again acceded to requests to attend and preside over the Federal Convention that drafted the Constitution and, then, to serve as the first President. After two terms, he relinquished his position of power and returned to his farm.

Washington's temporary and intermittent service to the country no doubt was influenced by the story of Cincinnatus told by the Roman historian Livy in his *History of Rome*. In the Fifth Century B.C.E., a contingent of Roman Senators visited Cincinnatus, a retired military general, while he was plowing the fields on his farm. They implored him to lead the Roman army once again against the invading Aequians and made him dictator. He lay down his plow and defeated the invaders in two weeks. Instead of remaining in power, however, he returned to his farm, having accomplished his mission.

Unfortunately, many Representatives and Senators have not followed the fine examples set by Cincinnatus and George Washington. One view is that periodic elections serve as *de facto* term limits because the People could vote politicians out if dissatisfied with their performance. The clout and domination of incumbency, however, enhances the electability of Representatives and Senators not only through name-recognition at the ballot box but also by facilitating fundraising and all the advertising money can pay for. Even one term alone improves an incumbent's advantage over any challenger significantly.

Why do incumbents want to remain in office for so long? While some may genuinely view themselves as public servants seeking to help Americans and the country, others seem more interested in enjoying the power, prestige, and trappings of their position and in trying to impose their personal values on the country. As a result, everything they do and say is intended to best position themselves for re-election. Witness the Republicans who tried to sabotage the 2020 Electoral College, refused to vote against Trump in his impeachment trial after the January 6th insurrection, even though it threatened their own lives, or refused to join the House committee investigating the insurrection, lest they anger Trump's MAGA mob and lose votes.

Senators Ted Cruz and Josh Hawley are brilliant lawyers with prestigious pedigrees, who have to know in their heart of hearts that there was no factual or legal basis for Trump's frivolous lawsuits contesting the 2020 election and that he instigated a treasonous insurrection to subvert the election and seize the Presidency illegally. The reason for their steadfast support of a tyrant can only be to ride his coattails for votes down the road by appeasing his rabid following. In other words, self-preservation as Senators and, perhaps, a shot at the Presidency were greater motivations to them than doing the right thing for our country.

Liz Cheney and Adam Kinzinger, on the other hand, were two Republican Representatives who courageously decried the Emperor's new clothes, despite realizing that faithfully fulfilling their duties and responsibilities pursuant to their oaths under Article VI to support the Constitution would bring about the end of their time in the House.

Another reason Representatives and Senators may wish to stay so long in office is based on dollars and cents. Although many of them have amassed or inherited large fortunes or could earn more money in the business world or as lawyers at mega firms, some others actually earn more money in Congress than they were making in the real world. The base salary for Congress is currently $174,000, and they receive great healthcare benefits. After five years of service, they are eligible for a pension, which could reach 80% of the average of their three highest annual salaries, depending on the length of service.[37] Plus, there are all sorts of Congressional allowances and perks. As a result, many in Congress have financial incentives to prolong their stay.

So, what is the problem with long incumbencies? The problem is that the desire to continue in power often takes priority over concerns for what is best for America. While Representatives and Senators should always take into consideration the views and needs of their constituents whom they were elected to represent, they cannot simply cater to them blindly to the detriment of the nation at large. Voting for a statute that is good for the country but may endanger re-election is a bold stand that is difficult to take.

Another problem with long incumbencies is that they tend to induce staleness. People naturally fall into the habit of acting and thinking the same way after a number of years. They don't like reinventing the wheel or looking at the same issue in different ways. While the adage, "If it ain't broke, don't fix it," usually makes sense, that attitude can also lead toward failure to recognize what is broken.

On the flip side, a benefit to long incumbencies is that one gains experience, insight, and, we hope, wisdom after a number of years, such as on a specialized committee, that will be lost if there are term limits. While the country does benefit from such experience, that is not a sufficient reason to bar term limits. Rather, that should be a factor in determining the length of term limits.

For over 160 years, there was no term limit on the Presidency. After the Republicans gained control of Congress in 1946, however, they pushed for a two-term limit so they wouldn't have to suffer another four-term Democratic President like Franklin Roosevelt again. In 1951, the ratification of the 22nd Amendment imposed a two-term limit on the Presidency, with an allowance for serving up to two years "of a term to which some other person was elected President," such as when, under the 25th Amendment, a Vice President succeeds a President who dies, resigns, becomes incapacitated, or is removed after impeachment with fewer than two years remaining in the term. A Vice President in that situation would be eligible for election to two terms after serving out the remainder of the prior President's term. That's why Lyndon Johnson could have run for re-election in 1968, since he had completed only the remaining year of Jack Kennedy's term.

A term limit of 16 years for Members of Congress would be appropriate. This is an absolute total of 16 years of service, which means it includes any time serving out the remainder of a seat that becomes vacant and it covers non-consecutive terms that may have been interrupted by an election defeat or resignation to serve in another branch or to take a break from politics. It is twice as long as the term limit of the Presidency and gives Members time enough and incentive enough to get some meaningful things done without giving them the prospect of decades in power. If they aren't capable of using four terms in Congress as a springboard to a lucrative job afterwards, well, maybe they weren't too qualified to serve in Congress in the first place.

This term limit provision alone will most likely be the primary reason why Congress will vote against proposing to the States ratification of the Restated Constitution pursuant to Article V of the Constitution. Indeed, it is inconceivable that the Judiciary Committee of either the House or the Senate would allow the Restated Constitution out of committee for a vote so long as it contains this term limit. Although some in Congress have advocated for term limits, the self-interests of the majority would presumably never approve this term limit. Consequently, as discussed in the context of Article VII, below, ratification of the Restated Constitution will have to bypass Congress and go through the State legislatures, which should not have a conflict of interest regarding the term limit.

Filling Vacancies

Section 2 of Article I of the Constitution provides that "[w]hen vacancies happen in the Representation from any State, the Executive Authority thereof shall issue Writs of Election to fill such Vacancies." That provision applies only to vacancies in the House.

For vacancies in the Senate, the 17th Amendment has an identical provision but also adds that "the legislature of any State may empower the executive thereof to make temporary appointments until the people fill the vacancies by election as the legislature may direct." In over two-thirds of the States, the Governor may appoint a person to fill the vacancy on an interim basis until a special election can be held.[38]

In keeping with the design of the Restated Constitution to place the election process for Congress in the hands of the Commission, this Section provides that "the Commission shall hold a special election to fill the vacancy."

ELIGIBILITY

3.   Only a citizen who is 25 years or older, who has been a United States citizen for more than **eight** years prior to election, and who is at the time of election **domiciled in** the **District** may be elected to represent that **District in and serve as a Member of Congress**. [Art. I, Sect. 2]

The current minimum age requirement for the House is 25 and for the Senate, 30. With the combining of the Senate and House into the new Congress, it makes senses to go with the younger threshold. First, unlike the compromise between the two-year term of Representatives and the six-year term of Senators, there is no sensible average or even intermediate age between 25 and 30. Second, if any 25-year old candidates are able to win an election that should be even more competitive in the slimmed-down Congress, more power to them. Third, as a practical matter, there aren't many Representatives under 30 in a typical Congress.

Currently, a Representative must be a citizen for at least seven years and a Senator for at least nine years, under Sections 2 and 3, respectively, of Article I. The average of eight years is the obvious compromise.

The language for the requirement of being "an Inhabitant of that State" in Sections 2 and 3 of Article I is changed to being "**domiciled in the District**." A domicile is one's legal primary home and the place of one's present intention of making a permanent home. It seems more definite than "inhabitant."

The purpose of this requirement is to ensure that Members actually live in the Districts they are elected to represent and to prevent carpetbaggers who move to a District simply because it may present the easiest place to win an election due to a vulnerable or retiring incumbent, for example. Often, such purported relocations are temporary and just for the sake of the election, consisting of nothing more than bringing a change of underwear for a stay on the couch of a friend or relative who actually does live within the boundaries of the district.

SPEAKER AND PRESIDENT OF CONGRESS

4.   Congress shall choose its Speaker and other officers. The Vice President of the United States shall be President of **Congress** but shall have no vote except to break a tie. [Art. I, Sects. 2 and 3]

The substance of this Section is lifted from Sections 2 and 3 of Article I of the Constitution with but slight modifications in wording. With the merger of the House and Senate, the position of Speaker for the day-to-day functioning of Congress remains and the ceremonial position of President, filled by the Vice President of the United States, continues simply for breaking ties.

IMPEACHMENT

5.   **Congress** shall have the sole power of impeachment, **by a majority vote, of any United States officer or official, including judges, Commissioners, members of the Judicial Appointment Council, and Members of Congress**, and to try all impeachments.

When trying an impeachment, Members shall be on oath or affirmation. When the President of the United States is tried, the Chief Justice of the Supreme Court shall preside. No person shall be convicted except upon a vote of at least two-thirds of the Members present. **A conviction of impeachment shall serve to remove such convicted persons from any current office and ban them from any future office or position in the United States government. Congress may impeach and convict any United States officers or officials subject to this Section even after they have resigned from such positions or after their terms have expired. A conviction or acquittal under this Section is not a defense to any criminal charges or civil claims based on the same facts and shall not serve as a reason for dismissal of criminal charges on the grounds of double jeopardy.** [Art. I, Sects. 2 and 3]

The process of impeachment is another aspect of our government whose imperfections have been exposed thanks to Trump.

Only three Presidents (Andrew Johnson, Bill Clinton, and Donald Trump, twice) have been impeached by the House, one was headed that way before becoming the only President to resign (Richard Nixon), and none have been convicted by the Senate. It's not easy to impeach a President and, obviously, even harder to convict one.

The process of impeachment was intended to be difficult and to serve as the last resort to oust someone who is really, really bad and really, really dangerous to the country's welfare. It was not intended as a political weapon with which to attack a President of an opposing party. Impeachment and conviction are a more difficult way to get rid of a President than, say, a vote of no confidence in parliamentary systems like Great Britain. In fact, the impeachment of Clinton was more in the nature of a vote of no confidence for something having nothing to do with the performance of his duties as President or any threat to the nation.

Under Sections 2 and 3 of Article I of the Constitution, the House has the sole power to impeach by a majority vote, and the Senate has the sole power to try all impeachments and render judgment by a supermajority vote of two-thirds. This two-step process is retained in the unified Congress and the corresponding, differing levels of votes required. While the process could have been collapsed into a single proceeding in the new Congress, this slower, more deliberative process is necessary in light of the seriousness of impeachment and how it tends to interrupt and shut down the functioning of government.

Trump's second impeachment occurred after Joe Biden was certified as the winner of the 2020 election and just one week before Trump's term was scheduled to end at noon on January 20, 2021 under the 20th Amendment. In the House impeachment and in the Senate trial, Republicans straddled the fence between party loyalty and patriotism by arguing that the imminent end of Trump's term mooted any conviction of impeachment because one of the punishments sought was removal from office. In other words, they tried to sidestep a decision on the merits by claiming any conviction would be academic and inconsequential in effect.

That argument was blatantly disingenuous because the impeachment provision of Section 3 of Article I states that "[j]udgment in Cases of Impeachment shall not extend further than to removal from Office, *and disqualification to hold and enjoy any Office of honor, Trust, or Profit under the United States."* Emphasis added. So, the second available punishment would not have been mooted by the impending end of Trump's term because it is prospective in nature.

Not only does the Constitution expressly permit the Senate to ban the impeached person from holding any federal office in the future, but the history of impeachment in English law, upon which this provision is based, supports a ban on future public service. In fact, in practice under English law, impeachment was resorted to often after office holders left office and their misdeeds were uncovered.[39]

To make the point even clearer and avoid such superficial arguments in the future, the two punishments are merged by providing that "**[a] conviction of impeachment shall serve to remove such convicted persons from any current office and ban them from any future office or position in the United States government. Congress may impeach and convict any United States officers or officials subject to this Section even after they have resigned from such positions or after their terms have expired.**" This formulation is much clearer and forceful than the one in Section 3 of Article I of the Constitution, quoted above.

This Section ends with a sentence that declares that a person convicted or acquitted of impeachment remains subject to prosecution for crimes and liable civilly for the same conduct, notwithstanding the freedom from double jeopardy guaranteed in Section 9 of Article I of the Restated Constitution. This concept appears in Section 3 of Article I of the Constitution.

Section 4 of Article II of the Constitution subjects the "President, Vice President and all civil Officers of the United States" to possible impeachment. It was decided early on that this phrase did not encompass Congress but did cover federal judges, seven of whom are the only persons to have been convicted upon a trial of impeachment.[40] The view is that although there are no provisions expressly subjecting judges to impeachment, judges are "civil officers," within the meaning of Section 4 of Article II, and "shall hold their Offices during good Behaviour," under Section 1 of Article III. This Section makes it clear that impeachment is a way to remove judges for bad behavior.

Instead of impeachment, Congress has the power to "punish its Members for disorderly Behavior, and, with the Concurrence of two thirds, expel a Member," under Section 5 of Article I, which is incorporated into Section 7 of new Article III. That provision probably makes it easier to expel than impeach a Member but doesn't provide for banning a Member from holding any future offices. There is no reason why Members of Congress are not deemed subject to impeachment. They, too, are "civil officers of the United States" and, like "all executive and judicial Officers," "shall be bound by Oath or Affirmation, to support this Constitution," under Article VI.

Consequently, we should retain the provision that makes it easier to expel a Member but add this Section that also subjects Members to impeachment and provides a ban on holding future offices. Congress can decide which avenue to pursue depending on the situation.

"Conviction of impeachment" is not considered a criminal conviction, and, therefore, the Fifth Amendment's protection against double jeopardy does not shield the person so convicted from criminal prosecution. This concept appears in Section 3 of Article I of the Constitution and is reworded for clarity.

Finally, the newly created positions of Commissioners and members of the Judicial Appointment Council are added as United States officers and officials subject to impeachment.

MAJORITY VOTE AND FILIBUSTERS

6.   Congress shall assemble at least once in every year, and such meeting shall begin at noon on the third day of January, unless it shall by law appoint a different day. A majority of the Members of Congress shall constitute a quorum to conduct business, but a smaller number may adjourn from day to day and may be authorized to compel the attendance of absent Members in such manner and under such penalties as Congress may provide. **Except as otherwise provided in this Restated Constitution, all votes shall be determined by a simple majority of those Members present. No filibusters shall be permitted.** [Art. I, Sects. 4 and 5; 20th Amend., Sect. 2]

Nothing has slowed down the Senate like filibusters and the requirement of passage of certain votes by a super-majority.

The Constitution requires supermajority votes in only half a dozen instances, namely, conviction of impeachment (Article I, Section 3), expulsion of members of Congress (Article I, Section 5), overriding a veto (Article I, Section 7), approving treaties (Article II, Section 2), proposals to amend the Constitution (Article V), and declaring the President incapacitated (25th Amendment, Section 4). All such votes require a two-thirds majority. Some of these circumstances rarely occur, such as declaring the President incapacitated, although Trump once again brought attention to that provision when his own staff questioned his sanity in the aftermath of the 2020 election and seriously considered starting the process.

Supermajority votes are antithetical to the majority rule that forms the basis for our system of representative democracy. A supermajority standard that requires passage by 60%, two-thirds, or 75% necessarily allows a minority to block a vote by the simple majority. Thus, a supermajority vote should only be required in instances where the issue is so important that we want to ensure that more than a simple majority supports the measure. In other words, that there exists a mandate for passage.

Both the Senate and the House have gone beyond the Constitution and required supermajority votes by rule in certain circumstances. In the Senate, the most egregious of these rules is the one that requires a 60% vote to end a filibuster. A filibuster is a technique by which a Senator or Senators can stifle a bill and prevent it from coming up for a vote by prolonging the debate without end. Filibusters historically were used by Southern Senators to prevent voting on civil rights laws. Because neither party has enjoyed a 60% majority in the Senate in recent years and since Senators tend to stick to the party line nowadays, this rule means that filibusters cannot effectively be stopped.

The practice of filibusters is contrary to the parliamentary system used by Congress for bringing debate to a head and voting on motions and bills. The House does not permit filibusters. Consequently, this Section bans filibusters and Congressional rules requiring supermajority votes, other than those required by the Restated Constitution, which have been carried over from the Constitution and its Amendments.

MISCELLANEOUS CHANGES

Sections 7-15 of Article III of the Restated Constitution are pretty much a verbatim incorporation of the balance of Article I (specifically, Sections 4-10), the 14th Amendment's Public Debt Clause (Section 4), and the 16th Amendment (income taxes) of the Constitution, with a number of minor stylistic changes for grammar, punctuation, spelling, and clarity that do not appear in **bold**. Other than the changes discussed above, the powers and responsibilities of Congress basically remain intact.

Section 4's Elections Clause and Section 5's clause providing that "[e]ach House shall be the Judge of the Elections, Returns, and Qualifications of its own Members" have been deleted because the Commission will now be serving those functions.

The vaguely worded first sentence of Section 9, which prohibited Congress from prohibiting the importation of slaves until 1808, has been deleted. Let's hope that provision is no longer necessary. In any event, The Trafficking Victims Protection Act of 2000 provides criminal punishment for persons running slave trade, usually for prostitution and forced labor.

Section 15 states, "Congress shall have power to enforce **and implement Articles I and II** by appropriate legislation." This provision is borrowed from the 13th, 14th, 15th, 19th, 24th, and 26th Amendments, which basically state a right or process and then empower Congress to enact enabling statutes. For example, the 13th Amendment abolishes slavery and empowers Congress to enact legislation to enforce that ban, such as criminal punishments for enslaving another human being.

Section 15 makes sure that Congress has the power not only to enact statutes enforcing but also implementing the rights, liberties, and freedoms set forth in Article I and the structure and processes of the Commission in Article II. Particularly with respect to the Commission, there are surely details and refinements that have been overlooked and that Congress will need to supply down the road. This Section also makes it clear that Congress can and should enable and implement the freedom of safety and the freedom from violence by enacting stricter gun control, especially with the repeal of the 2nd Amendment.

ARTICLE IV

EXECUTIVE BRANCH

The President of the United States is often referred to as the most powerful man in the world. On the contrary, while the United States is one of the most powerful nations in the world, if not the most powerful nation, our President is not the most powerful person in the world.

In the 19th Century, the most powerful man in the world was Queen Victoria of Great Britain. In the 20th Century, the most powerful man in the world was, at various times, Adolf Hitler, Josef Stalin, and Mao Zedong. In the 21st Century, it is Vladimir Putin or Xi Jinping.

When it comes to power, the American President cannot hold a candle to foreign monarchs and dictators who hold their countries in thrall. Our Presidents may hold more power politically than any other single person in America, but the Constitution and our traditions impose constraints on them that leaders of other countries do not labor under. Heck, even Benjamin Netanyahu of a tiny parliamentary democracy like Israel can stay and has stayed in power longer than any U.S. President, including Franklin Roosevelt.

Because America began as a rebellion against the tyranny of a monarch, Americans have been wary about granting the President too much power. Despite the amount of care and precautions that the Framers took in creating our first-of-a-kind, elected leader, this experiment has needed more tweaking over the years than any other branch of the government or article of the Constitution. In fact, Article II of the Constitution has been amended four times by the 12th, 20th, 22nd, and 25th Amendments.

Trump's abuse of the Office of the Presidency cries out for more tweaking.

ELECTION OF THE PRESIDENT AND VICE PRESIDENT

1.   The executive power shall be vested in a President of the United States of America. **The President and the Vice President shall hold office** during a term of four years **and shall be elected as a team, provided they are not domiciled in the same State, based on the national popular vote of citizens 18 years of age or older without regard to the boundaries of the States, Districts, Regions, possessions, and territories. The Commission shall declare as the victor the team receiving the most votes in the Presidential election, regardless of whether that team receives a majority of the votes. The Electoral College is hereby abolished.** [Art. II, Sect. 1; 12th Amend.]

Popular Vote Replaces Electoral College

As explained earlier in the context of merging the Senate and the House into a single-chambered Congress, it makes no sense to perpetuate the myth that giving each State two Senators somehow levels the playing field among States of different sizes. That same explanation applies equally to the manner we continue to vote for the President through an Electoral College established in Section 1 of Article II of the Constitution, which provides that "[e]ach State shall appoint . . . a Number of Electors, equal to the whole Number of Senators and Representatives to which the State may be entitled in the Congress." In simpler language, the number of votes each State has in the Electoral College is the same as the sum of its Representatives and two Senators.

Every Presidential election night, the talking heads on TV begin tallying and predicting the Electoral votes as soon as the polls begin closing at 8:00 p.m. on the East Coast. While they spend a little time analyzing the votes in small States, those votes have no material impact on the outcome.

Based on the reapportionment of Congressional seats after the 2020 census,[41] **Appendix E** compares the Electoral College voting power of the ten States with the largest populations to the Electoral College voting power of the ten States with the smallest populations.

We can draw a few important conclusions from the comparison in **Appendix E**. First, California and Texas can each outvote the ten smallest States combined, and Florida and New York fall just four and six votes shy, respectively, of doing the same. Second, the total of 254 votes controlled by the ten largest States is just 16 votes below the total number of 270 needed for a candidate to become elected President. Third, the Connecticut Compromise, which was designed to give smaller States a slightly disproportionate influence in Congress and in the Electoral College when the differences in State populations were within spitting range in 1787, no longer works 235 years later when California has 39,576,757 residents, Texas has 29,183,290, Vermont has 643,503, and Wyoming has 577,719.

Of course, these observations assume the extreme case where the ten largest States vote for one candidate and the ten smallest States vote for the other. That rarely happens, however, as when McGovern won only Massachusetts in 1972. Instead, California and New York team up to beat out Texas and Florida, Illinois cancels Ohio, and so on.

The population and political shifts of the States in the last 40 years have reworked the arithmetic of the Electoral

College to the point where only six so-called "battleground" or "swing" States are projected to control the 2024 election: Arizona (11 votes), Georgia (16 votes), Michigan (15 votes), Nevada (6 votes), Pennsylvania (19 votes), and Wisconsin (10 votes). These are purple States with significant Electoral votes where the outcome is not a foregone conclusion and where the victor in the 2020 election won by less than 5% of the vote.[42] These six States have 50 million people (16% of total U.S. population) and only 77 of the 538 Electoral votes (14%).

A feature of the Electoral College contributes to this situation where only a half dozen States will determine our next President. Under Section 1 of Article II, "[e]ach State shall appoint, in such Manner as the Legislature thereof may direct, a Number of Electors . . . ." So, each State gets to determine how to translate the popular vote into Electoral votes.

In the beginning, the States allocated their Electoral votes somewhat pro rata based on the popular vote, but today only Maine and Nebraska award Electoral votes in a manner that can give some recognition to the candidate with fewer statewide popular votes.[43] The other 48 States and Washington, D.C. award Electoral votes on a winner-take-all basis, meaning that if Candidate A loses by only 500,000 votes in California, where 17 million people voted in 2020, the votes of the 8.25 million voters who voted for Candidate A will not count because Candidate B will garner all of California's 52 Electoral votes.

So, not only does the Electoral College fail to deliver any meaningful benefit to small States now, but it also deprives the losing candidate in 48 States and D.C. of votes that could count toward an aggregate total of popular votes that may bring about a different result from counting Electoral votes.

In other words, the voices of voters who backed a losing candidate in 48 States and D.C. are never heard.

A candidate who lost the popular vote has nevertheless become President five times.[44] In 1824, Andrew Jackson won a plurality of the popular and Electoral votes in a race among four candidates, but the 12th Amendment requires winning the majority of Electoral votes. It fell to the House to decide, and it picked John Quincy Adams. In 1876, Samuel Tilden won 250,000 more popular votes than Rutherford B. Hayes and was one shy of a majority of Electoral votes. There was a dispute, however, over 20 Electoral votes, which the House awarded to Hayes, putting him over the top. In 1888, Grover Cleveland won the popular vote by 90,000, but Benjamin Harrison won the Electoral vote by 233 to 168.

After 112 years of Presidents winning both the popular votes and Electoral votes, Al Gore won 500,000 more popular votes in 2000, but George W. Bush won the Electoral vote by 271 to 266 (one D.C. Elector abstained), thanks to a margin of only 537 votes declaring Bush the winner in Florida after the Supreme Court stopped further recounting. In 2016, Hillary Clinton won 2.8 million more popular votes than Trump, who won the Electoral vote 304-227 due in large part to margins of victory of less than 1% in Wisconsin, Pennsylvania, and Michigan.

While the popular vote and the Electoral vote have been out of synch only five times in 59 elections, do we really want Presidential races decided by a method that could nullify and, essentially, disenfranchise 2.8 million voters as in 2016?

To alleviate the contrivances, quirks, and idiosyncrasies of the Electoral College that the Framers most likely could not foresee, this Section of the Restated Constitution elects the President and Vice President by a pure popular vote and abolishes the Electoral College. Whoever wins the most votes as counted on every ballot cast will be the winner, regardless of State, Region, District, county, city, or town boundaries. Election by popular vote will not deprive the smaller States of any boost they may have thought they enjoyed from the Electoral College in the 18th Century.

Also, the requirement of winning a majority of the votes cast, as in the Electoral College, has been eliminated. Whoever garners the most popular votes, even if that is less than a majority of votes cast, wins.

The President and Vice President are the only officials for whom the entire country votes. Each vote should count.

Team Vote

The original process of electing the President and Vice President in Section 1 of Article II contemplated that the person receiving the most votes would become the President and the runner-up would become the Vice President. That worked fine when George Washington was elected President and John Adams, Vice President. It didn't work so well when John Adams beat out his enemy, Thomas Jefferson, or when Jefferson beat his adversary, Aaron Burr. Consequently, in 1804, the 12th Amendment changed the methodology by requiring the Electors to vote for President and Vice President on separate ballots.

At this point, we should simply recognize that Presidential candidates now have running mates and that they are running as a team. So, let's just vote for the team.

A certain quirk from the early days of the Constitution persists today. In the original Section 1 of Article II of the Constitution, the Electors voted for two persons for President but they could not vote for two persons from their own State.

The thought was that the largest States could control the Presidency and, effectively, the country if they could always cast their votes for two persons from their own States. When the method of choosing the President was changed by the 12th Amendment and separate ballots were cast for President and Vice President, the bar on voting for two persons from the Electors' State was retained and an Elector could not vote for a President and a Vice President both of whom were from that Elector's State. Strictly speaking, though, that bar did not prevent an Elector from Virginia from voting for two New Yorkers for President and Vice President.

Nevertheless, it makes sense to prohibit the election of a President and Vice President from the same State to bring some geographical diversity to the Executive Branch, even if they are next-door neighbors like Bill Clinton (Arkansas) and Al Gore (Tennessee).

As in elections for Congress and the Commission, the team with the most votes will win, even if the team gains only a plurality and not a majority of the votes cast, as when more than two teams run.

ELIGIBILITY

2.   Only a natural born citizen who is 35 years or older and has resided within the United States for at least 14 years before the national election shall be eligible to serve as President or Vice President. **No person may hold the office of President or Vice President while incarcerated.** [Art. II, Sect. 1; 12th Amend.]

This Section simplifies and condenses language from Section 1 of Article II and from the 12th Amendment.

There's no reason to change the basic requirements of eligibility to serve as President. A foreigner who becomes a citizen through naturalization is eligible to serve in Congress, on the Commission, or in the courts and can hold other offices in the U.S. government but cannot become President. The Presidency is a unique position, and it should be reserved for natural born citizens because many Americans would not trust or accept a naturalized citizen as their leader, even though England has coronated monarchs who were foreigners, such as William III and George I. At this point, there is no cogent reason to change this requirement.

The prospect of Donald Trump running for President while convicted of 34 counts of falsifying business records related to hush money paid to Stormy Daniels and while under several state and federal indictments prompts the additional requirement that **"[n]o person may hold the office of President or Vice President while incarcerated."** It would be farcical to have a President running the country while in prison, like a Mafia Don directing the mob from behind bars. We do not need a repeat of James Curley who was convicted and imprisoned while serving as Mayor of Boston in the late 1940s.[45] For a similar reason, Section 15 of this Article prohibits a President from pardoning or granting a reprieve to himself or herself.

The last sentence of the 12th Amendment states, "But no person constitutionally ineligible to the office of President shall be eligible to that of Vice-President of the United States." This requirement is maintained by making the Vice President subject to the same eligibility requirements as the President. Needless to say, it makes no sense to elect someone as Vice President if he or she would not be eligible to serve as President when the President dies, resigns, becomes incapacitated, or is convicted after impeachment.

EMOLUMENTS CLAUSE

3.   The President **and the Vice President** shall, at stated times, receive compensation for their services, which **shall be determined by the Commission and** shall neither be increased nor diminished during the period for which they shall have been elected. They shall not receive within that period any other compensation or emolument from the United States or any State. **They shall not accept, without the consent of the Congress, any present, emolument, office, or title of any kind whatever from any king, prince, or foreign state.** [Art. I, Sect. 9; Art. II, Sect. 1]

The first two sentences come from Section 1 of Article II of the Constitution regarding the President's compensation. The Vice President is added to the provision, and the Commission is assigned the task of determining their compensation, as provided in Section 9 of Article II of the Restated Constitution.

The second sentence continues the provision from Section 1 of Article II of the Constitution, which prohibits the President from receiving any other compensation or emolument from the federal government or from any State. An "emolument" is basically a fancy synonym for "compensation for work."

While we're on the topic of emoluments, it can't hurt to remind the President and Vice President in this Section of the "Emoluments Clause" in Section 9 of Article I of the Constitution, which is incorporated as Section 13(g) of Article III in the Restated Constitution. The original Emoluments Clause applies to any "Person holding any Office of Profit or Trust under [the United States]," which includes the President and Vice President. It appears, however, in Article I, which pertains primarily to Congress.

Thus, it is important to repeat it here in Article IV to remind the President and Vice President that they, too, are bound by the Emoluments Clause.

The Emoluments Clause was intended to prevent any officer of the United States from accepting bribes from foreign governments. Apparently, Trump didn't recognize that the Emoluments Clause applied to him and prohibited him from accepting gifts from foreign states without the consent of Congress. He seems to have believed he could keep and not report over 100 gifts valued at almost $300,000 that foreign governments gave him and his family,[46] in violation of the Foreign Gifts and Decorations Act, 5 U.S.C. § 7342, which delineates the protocol for accepting and dealing with such gifts. That Act recognizes that diplomacy may require acceptance of such gifts to avoid offending a foreign government, but, aside from gifts of less than minimal value (defined as $415 or less during Trump's term in office), the gifts have to be reported and become the property of the U.S. government, unless the recipient purchases them from the government.

Trump accepted gifts from, among others, Chinese President Xi Jinping, Crown Prince Mohammad bin Salman of Saudi Arabia, and Indian Prime Minister Narendra Modi. Clearly, gifts from these rulers and their countries are suspect. To avoid any semblance of undue influence, Trump should have reported the gifts under the Foreign Gifts and Decorations Act and let the State Department handle their disposition.

OATH OF OFFICE

4.   Before entering on the execution of office, the President shall take the following Oath or Affirmation:

"I do solemnly swear (or affirm) that I will faithfully execute the Office of President of the United States and will, to the best of my ability, preserve, protect, defend, **and abide by** the **Restated** Constitution of the United States." [Art. II, Sect. 1]

This is a really simple but important addition to the formal oath of office taken by the President at the inauguration. In light of Trump's attempt on January 6, 2021 to disrupt Congress' functions in certifying the winner of the Electoral College pursuant to the 12th Amendment, the oath needs to be augmented to ensure that the President must swear also to abide by the Restated Constitution. It is not enough for the President to swear just to "preserve, protect, and defend" the Restated Constitution. The President has to affirmatively recognize the duty to follow and not undermine the terms of the Restated Constitution.

The phrase "abide by" is added to similar oaths for all U.S. officers in Article VIII.

MISCELLANEOUS CHANGES

Sections 5-14, 16, and 17 of this Article IV incorporate fairly closely the powers, duties, and conditions granted to or imposed on the President in Article II of the Constitution and the 20th, 22nd, and 25th Amendments. These various provisions are rearranged into a more comprehensive and comprehensible sequence.

These Sections address: (a) dates for the start and finish of the President's term of office (Section 5); (b) death or disqualification of the President-Elect or Vice President-Elect before the term begins (Section 6); (c) Congressional choice of a successor of a President or Vice President when the choice falls to Congress (Section 7); (d) the limit of Presidential terms (Section 8); succession of the Vice President upon the President's removal, death, or resignation (Section 9); (f) filling a vacancy in the office of Vice President (Section 10); (g) the inability or incapacity of the President to discharge his or her duties (Sections 11-13); (h) service as Commander in Chief of the armed forces (Section 14); and (i) making treaties and nominating ambassadors and officers (Section 16).

One significant departure from these Article II Sections and the Presidential Amendments is the removal from Section 16 of the President's power to appoint federal judges subject to the "Advice and Consent of the Senate." That power to appoint federal judges will now fall under Section 8 of new Article II to the Commission, which will choose judges from lists prepared by the Judicial Appointment Council under Section 4 of new Article V.

Another change in Section 16 limits the duration of recess appointments by the President to when Congress reconvenes from the recess rather than to the next session of Congress, which currently could be up to two years later.

PARDONS

15.   The President shall have power to grant reprieves and pardons for offenses against the United States, except in cases of impeachment. **The President may not, however, grant himself, herself, or a co-conspirator a reprieve or pardon.** [Art. II, Sect. 2]

When Trump was being tried for impeachment the second time in connection with the January 6th Insurrection, the question arose whether he could pardon himself and others who were close to him. The simple and straightforward language in Section 2 of Article II of the President's "Power to grant Reprieves and Pardons for Offenses against the United States" seems pretty absolute. This makes sense because the Executive Branch is entrusted with enforcing laws, and, therefore, the President, as head of the Executive Branch, should be allowed to exercise clemency, as historically done by monarchs.

The only exception was "in Cases of Impeachment," which also makes sense because Congress is in charge of impeachments of all officers of the United States and, under the separation of powers of the different branches of government, should not be overruled by a Presidential pardon.

While the Presidential right to pardon seems absolute, except in cases of impeachment, some Constitutional scholars opined that if Trump pardoned himself, such a pardon would be void based on history and other provisions in the Constitution that imply the President must act in good faith and not contrary to his duty to support the Constitution. These arguments seem a bit attenuated and shaky.

Consequently, this Section expressly states that "[t]he **President may not, however, grant himself, herself, or a co-conspirator a reprieve or pardon.**" Presidents should not feel free to break the law because they can simply pardon themselves before their term ends. This provision should warn them that they are not above the law and they cannot escape criminal liability through the contrivance of granting themselves a pardon prospectively at any time while in office.

Let's first address prospective pardons because no President has ever been indicted while in office, and it is doubtful that the President's own Justice Department would indict him, even though the Justice Department is supposed to be somewhat autonomous and independent from the President. Furthermore, there is nothing in the Constitution or in the Supreme Court's decisions interpreting the Constitution that directly addresses whether a sitting President can be indicted for federal crimes committed while in office.

In 1867, the Supreme Court held in *Mississippi v. Johnson*, 71 U.S. (4 Wall.) 475 (1867), that the doctrine of separation of powers prevented the federal courts from hearing the State of Mississippi's claim for an injunction prohibiting President Andrew Johnson from enforcing the Reconstruction Laws. It is puzzling that Mississippi would sue him personally because he wasn't doing a good job of Reconstruction anyway and his failure to treat the South more harshly led to his impeachment trial.

Fast forward a hundred years to 1974 when the Supreme Court held in *United States v. Nixon*, 418 U.S. 683 (1974), that President Richard Nixon was subject to a subpoena from the special prosecutor to produce the Watergate tapes.

Neither of these cases addressed whether a President could be indicted while in office or whether a President must first be convicted upon impeachment before being indicted, as Nixon's lawyers argued as tangential support for their claim that he wasn't subject to a subpoena. In the latter case, of course, the President would be removed from office after such a conviction.

Trump once again presents another possibility that wasn't addressed in the Constitution. With indictments coming down after he has been out of office and during his campaign for a second term, there is a scary likelihood that he would pardon himself if he were to win a second term. In fact, many people believe that his primary motivation in seeking office again is to pardon himself. This Section's exception to the historical pardon power is intended to eliminate any doubt about whether such a pardon would be valid.

While we're at it, we may as well add a ban against the President pardoning a co-conspirator to prevent pardons like the ones Trump granted his cronies, Paul Manafort, who was convicted of tax and bank fraud, witness tampering, obstruction of justice, and conspiracy to defraud the United States related to his ties to Russia; Roger Stone, who was convicted of witness tampering and lying in special counsel Robert Mueller's investigation of Trump's 2016 campaign; and Steve Bannon, who was charged with fraud and money laundering in procuring funds to support Trump's efforts to build a wall along the border with Mexico. Pardons of co-conspirators can stymie at the outset investigations that may lead to evidence that would be damaging or embarrassing to a President.

IMPEACHMENT

18.   **In accordance with Section 5 of Article III,** the President, Vice President, and all civil officers of the United States shall be removed from office on impeachment for and conviction of treason, bribery, **sedition, fomenting rebellion or insurrection, advocating the overthrow of the United States government by force,** or other **felonies. A conviction of impeachment shall serve to remove such convicted persons from any current office and ban them from any future office or position in the United States government. Congress may impeach and convict any United States officers or**

officials subject to this Section even after they have resigned from such positions or after their terms have expired. A conviction or acquittal under this Section is not a defense to any criminal charges or civil claims based on the same facts and shall not serve as a reason for dismissal of criminal charges on the grounds of double jeopardy. [Art. II, Sect. 4]

Section 4 of Article II of the Constitution concerning the Executive Branch does not reference the related provisions regarding impeachment in Sections 2 and 3 of Article I concerning Congress' role. Here, the provision regarding impeachment in this Section 18 of Article IV (the Presidency) is expressly tied to the impeachment provision in Section 5 of Article III (Congress) of the Restated Constitution. Thus, the discussion regarding Section 5 of Article III, above, applies equally to this Section.

The difference between Section 5 of Article III and this Section 18 of Article IV lies in the list of offenses that will serve to subject the President and other officers and officials to impeachment. The original list was "Treason, Bribery, or other high Crimes and Misdemeanors." Added to this list are the crimes of "**sedition, fomenting rebellion or insurrection, advocating the overthrow of the United States government by force,**" and "**felonies**" replaces "high Crimes and misdemeanors."

Once again, Trump prompted these additions to the list. During his second impeachment trial, some of his supporters argued that he was not being charged with "Treason, Bribery, or other high Crimes and Misdemeanors." While it seemed that inciting a mob to disrupt Congress from proceeding with certifying the results of the Presidential election was treasonous because it sought the overthrow of the government by interfering with action by Congress in performing its Constitutional duties, Section 3 of Article III of the Constitution provides, "Treason against the United States, shall consist only in levying War against them, or, in adhering to their Enemies, giving them Aid and Comfort." Thus, treason is not simply seeking the overthrow of the government but must involve war or conspiring with foreigners. The insurrection, however, didn't rise to the level of war, and most, if not all, of the insurgents were Americans.

This Section, therefore, adds sedition, fomenting rebellion or insurrection, and advocating the overthrow of the United States government by force, which should subject to impeachment any similar exhortations and machinations by a President to undermine the results of a Presidential election in the future.

Sedition is a felony prohibited by 18 U.S.C. § 2384, which provides that "[i]f two or more persons in any State or Territory, or in any place subject to the jurisdiction of the United States, conspire to overthrow, put down, or to destroy by force the Government of the United States, or to levy war against them, or to oppose by force the authority thereof, or by force to prevent, hinder, or delay the execution of any law of the United States, or by force to seize, take, or possess any property of the United States contrary to the authority thereof, they shall each be fined under this title or imprisoned not more than twenty years, or both."

Rebellion or insurrection are felonies prohibited by 18 U.S.C. § 2383, which provides that "[w]hoever incites, sets on foot, assists, or engages in any rebellion or insurrection against the authority of the United States or the laws thereof, or gives aid or comfort thereto, shall be fined under this title or imprisoned not more than ten years, or both; and shall be incapable of holding any office under the United States." The additional punishment of banning anyone convicted of rebellion or insurrection from holding any federal office matches a similar punishment for conviction of impeachment, thereby making it all the more sensible to add these crimes to the list for which a President and other officers and officials may be impeached.

During Trump's second impeachment, the talking heads on TV debated the meaning of "high crimes and misdemeanors" for which a President may be impeached. The phrase comes down to us from medieval English law. Since misdemeanors are petty crimes that are punishable by imprisonment for less than one year, it seems overkill to subject the President to impeachment for committing a misdemeanor and could too easily lead to politically motivated impeachments. True, all impeachments to date have been politically motivated, perhaps with the exception of the investigation of Richard Nixon in which Republicans in Congress participated, but it seems the possibility of an impeachment based on commission of a misdemeanor would be more egregiously politically motivated.

"High crimes" is too vague a term and invites more legal argument and debate as to its meaning. Usually, "high crimes" are considered felonies. Consequently, the entire phrase of "high Crimes and Misdemeanors" has been replaced with "felonies," which is defined under 18 U.S.C. § 3559 as crimes punishable by more than one year in prison.

Trump's lawyers have argued that his acquittal in his second impeachment arising out the Insurrection should preclude a later criminal prosecution for the same conduct. The new language makes it clear that neither a conviction nor an acquittal precludes a later criminal prosecution or a civil suit based on the same conduct.

PROSECUTION AND SUIT

19. **Presidents are absolutely immune from civil suit for any act they committed while in office. They are not, however, immune whatsoever from criminal prosecution for any act they committed while in office. Nevertheless, no such criminal prosecution may be initiated until a President has left office as President, at which time any applicable statute of limitations shall begin to run.**

An immunity is an exemption from the law, meaning that "the law does not apply to the immunized person . . . ." *Trump v. United States*, 603 U.S. ___, 144 S. Ct. 2312, 2372 (July 1, 2024) (Jackson, J., dissenting).

For example, government officials such as police officers are often granted qualified immunity from civil lawsuits, which means that to sue an officer, a plaintiff has the burden of proving that the officer has exceeded certain standards.

In *Nixon v. Fitzgerald*, 457 U.S. 731 (1982), a former Air Force employee sued former President Nixon after he left office for damages, alleging that Nixon approved a reorganization of the Air Force that caused the employee to be wrongfully terminated from his job. The United States Supreme Court held that Presidents were absolutely immune from civil suits based on their actions taken within the outer perimeter of their official responsibilities. The Court reasoned that Presidents should not be distracted in their decision-making process by concern over whether someone may later sue them civilly.

After all, anyone can easily start a lawsuit, even without a lawyer, and countless frivolous suits are filed every year. In any event, plaintiffs who cannot sue an absolutely immune President will still have a remedy available because they can always sue the Government.

Accordingly, this Section preserves a President's absolute immunity from civil suits, thereby making it simple for a President or former President to have such a suit expeditiously dismissed at the outset.

On the other hand, the novel issue presented in the federal prosecution of former President Trump is whether a former President enjoys any immunity from criminal prosecution for official acts while in office. In *Trump v. United States*, 603 U.S. ___, 144 S. Ct. 2312 (July 1, 2024), Trump moved to dismiss the federal indictment against him for asserting false claims of election fraud to persuade State officials to change electoral votes, organizing fake electors, attempting to use the Justice Department to conduct sham election fraud investigations, attempting to persuade Vice President Pence to use his ceremonial duty to change the certification of the electoral vote, and exploiting the rioting at the Capitol on January 6, 2021 to convince Members of Congress to delay the certification.

The Supreme Court's conservative bloc created a three-part test for Presidential immunity from criminal prosecution.

First, Presidents are absolutely immune in exercising core constitutional powers. Previous Supreme Court decisions found absolute immunity for granting pardons, removing officers in the Executive Branch, and recognizing foreign nations, areas that are within a President's conclusive and preclusive core Constitutional authority.

Second, Presidents are entitled to presumptive immunity for acts they committed within the outer perimeter of their official responsibilities. In other words, for acts performed beyond the Presidential powers expressly provided in the Constitution or Acts of Congress but still within the scope of official Presidential acts, Presidents are immune from criminal prosecution "unless the Government can show that applying a criminal prohibition to that act would pose no 'dangers of intrusion on the authority and functions of the Executive Branch.'" 144 S. Ct. at 2331-32 (citation omitted). The Court reasoned that "[s]uch an immunity is required to safeguard the independence and effective functioning of the Executive Branch, and to enable the President to carry out his constitutional duties *without undue caution.*" *Id.* at 2331 (emphasis added).

Third, Presidents have no immunity from criminal prosecution for unofficial acts beyond the scope of their responsibilities.

This three-part is unnecessary, a threat to democracy, and judicial activism at its worst.

To begin with, there is no immunity granted to Presidents anywhere in the Constitution. The absence of an express grant of immunity in the Constitution should have been enough for the conservative bloc to reject Trump's immunity claims summarily. After all, only two years earlier in *Dobbs*, this same bloc overturned *Roe v. Wade* by reasoning that there was no mention of abortion or privacy in the Constitution and that *Roe* exhibited judicial legislation. Failing to adhere to that same reasoning in *Trump* shows how outcome-oriented and intellectually dishonest this bloc of justices is.

Furthermore, the bloc exaggerates the need to create immunities to ward off the threat of future criminal prosecutions of former Presidents. This prosecution of Trump is the first one of a former President, making it the only one out of 44 former Presidents in over 235 years. Also, the protections of a grand jury and other procedures in a prosecution make it more unlikely that a prosecution will be brought against a former President than a civil law suit.

The bloc argues that "[a]lthough the President might be exposed to fewer criminal prosecutions than the range of civil damages suits that might be brought by various plaintiffs, the threat of trial, judgment, and imprisonment is a far greater deterrent. Potential criminal liability, and the peculiar public opprobrium that attaches to criminal proceedings, are plainly more likely to distort Presidential decision-making than the potential payment of civil damages." *Id.* at 2331.

The logical conclusion to that pronouncement should have been that the prospect of criminal prosecution with no immunity is an indispensable deterrent to protect the People and the United States from a President who, as the most powerful person in America, has the potential to inflict the most harm if given a get-out-of-jail-free card. Why should the President be free to make decisions and commit acts without worrying about whether they are legal or not when everyone else is constricted by and subject to the laws? As a practical matter, Presidents have routinely consulted with the Office of Legal Counsel of the Justice Department and the White House Counsel for legal advice about the legality of contemplated actions.

The bloc's conclusion that immunity is necessary "to enable the President to carry out his constitutional duties *without undue caution," id.* (emphasis added), flies in the face of the criminal justice concept of deterrence, as explained in the discussion of Section 11 of Article I, above, and the American principle that no one is above the law. It resuscitates the notion that the King is above the law, which the Founders clearly rejected.

The only provision in the Constitution similar to immunity appears in Section 6 of Article I, which protects Senators and Representatives from arrest going to, attending, and returning from sessions of their respective Houses, except in cases of "Treason, Felony and Breach of the Peace," and provides they "shall not be questioned in any other Place" "for any Speech or Debate in either House."

Nothing remotely similar appears in Article II regarding the President. To the contrary, Section 3 of Article I of the Constitution provides that a President convicted of impeachment "shall nevertheless be liable and subject to Indictment, Trial, Judgment, and Punishment according to Law." Various statements of the Framers also indicate that they envisioned the President would be subject to prosecution. *Id.* at 2358-59 (Sottomayor, J., dissenting).

President Ford did not believe former President Nixon was immune from criminal prosecution when he pardoned him for his coverup of the Watergate break-in. Certainly, no pardon would have been necessary if former Presidents were deemed immune from prosecutions.

Trump, himself, acknowledged his exposure to criminal prosecution when his lawyers argued in his second impeachment trial before the Senate that he could be tried in a court of law like any other citizen. *Id.* at 2360 (Sottomayor, J., dissenting). When he was later prosecuted, he changed his tune and claimed immunity. Like a true con man, he played both the Senate and the Supreme Court.

Consequently, the conservative bloc has violated its own espoused principles of judicial restraint by legislating from the bench, by reading into the Constitution provisions that do not appear expressly or even by implication and that lack historical support, and by usurping powers of Congress. Despite condemning the *Roe* Court for developing a trimester test, the *Trump* Court has created its own three-part immunity test.

It appears that the bloc was more intent on working backwards to justify a result that threw a lifeline to Trump, who nominated three of the six, than of working forwards from legal principles towards a conclusion. Their path to the result lacked legal, Constitutional, and historical foundations.

The Court sent the case back to the district court to determine the presumptive immunity of certain charges in the indictment. The problem with this approach is that it allows courts to play word games.

The Court, itself, demonstrated how judges can manipulate seemingly straightforward fact situations to find immunity. Ask high schoolers studying the Constitution in an American civics or history course to describe the President's role in certifying the results of a Presidential election, and most of them would recognize that as a trick question because he has no such role.

Chief Justice Roberts, however, went around and around on this point. He acknowledged that it is the Vice President, not the President, who presides over the certification of the election and that that role emanates from his position as the President of the Senate under Article I and not from his position within the Executive Branch. Nevertheless, the Chief Justice opined that it could be argued that since the Vice President advises and assists the President within the Executive Branch, Trump might have immunity from a charge that he improperly tried to coerce Pence into changing the election results through the certification process. *Id.* at 2335-37.

Presidents do not need immunity to protect themselves from prosecution. Even if former Presidents lack immunity from prosecution, they can still assert defenses to criminal charges by justifying their actions. They will also have at their disposal the whole arsenal of rights, defenses, and tactics available to any other criminal defendant.

Consequently, this Section makes it clear that Presidents enjoy no immunity from criminal prosecution for any act committed while in office. If an act falls with a President's core constitutional duties, it is doubtful the Justice Department would indict the former President and, if it did prosecute, the former President could assert a defense based on the core duties.

The last sentence of this Section postpones initiation of any prosecution of a President until he or she leaves office. The Justice Department '"has long recognized' that 'the separation of powers precludes the criminal prosecution of a sitting President.'" *Id.* at 2332 n.2 (citation omitted). Prosecution by the Justice Department of a President to whom it reports within the Executive Branch poses a problem. For a renegade sitting President, impeachment should be the primary protection. Let's hope that Congress and the courts will be able to restrain a criminal President and limit the harm sufficiently while he or she remains in office.

So, Article IV ends with a bang, a warning to all Presidents, after enumerating their mighty powers, that they nevertheless must answer to Congress and, ultimately, to the People and can be removed from office, banned from future offices for conduct detrimental to the country, and prosecuted for crimes after they leave office.

ARTICLE V

JUDICIAL BRANCH

How would you like a job that pays between $223,000 and $286,000 a year with benefits, where there are no defined prerequisites for employment and where you can slow down after age 65 or retire entirely and still get paid your full salary for doing nothing? Oh, and, no matter how many mistakes you make, no matter how much your superiors disagree with your opinions and criticize your work product, no matter how low the public rates you, and no matter how much you slack off, you can't get fired or have your pay cut. Welcome to the federal judiciary established under Article III of the Constitution.

While most federal judges are very capable and hardworking and the federal judiciary on the whole is better in many respects than state judicial systems, the federal judicial system really needs to be revamped. Article V proposes establishing eligibility for becoming a judge, setting a term limit on service, altering the process for appointing judges, and subjecting the Supreme Court to a Code of Conduct.

ESTABLISHMENT OF THE JUDICIARY

1.   The judicial power of the United States shall be vested in one Supreme Court **comprised of a Chief**

Justice and eight Associate Justices and in such inferior courts as the Congress may from time to time ordain and establish, **including trial courts, special subject matter courts, and intermediate courts of appeal**. [Art. III, Sect. 1]

Section 1 of Article III of the Constitution established a Supreme Court but left it to Congress to set up lower courts, as did Section 8 of Article I, also. This Section specifies some of the "inferior courts" that Congress has ordained and established, such as the district courts at the trial level, special subject matter courts like bankruptcy courts, tax courts, and courts for asserting claims against the United States, and circuit courts of appeals.

Article III also did not specify the number of justices on the Supreme Court. Rather, the Judiciary Act of 1789, the very first bill introduced in the very first Congress, set the initial number of Supreme Court justices at six, which had more to do with assigning two justices to each circuit than with a concern over the possibility of ties with an even number of justices. The number changed several times until it stuck on nine in 1869.[47]

Since then, Presidents have threatened to push Congress to increase the number of justices so they could appoint more justices more favorable to their liking to outnumber and outvote justices who rejected their policies. For example, Franklin Roosevelt threatened to "pack the Court" to counter the Court's rulings holding that Congress lacked the power under the Commerce Clause in Section 8 of Article I to enact legislation creating New Deal programs and agencies. After his threat, the Court started interpreting the Commerce Clause more broadly and upholding the programs and agencies, prompting the saying, "A switch in time saves nine." Satisfied, FDR stopped floating the idea of increasing the seats on the Supreme Court.

With Trump's appointment of three justices, the first and third of which should have been Obama's and Biden's appointments, respectively, talk of packing the Court arose again.

This Section fixes the number of justices at nine to recognize the accepted number for over 150 years and to quell future Court-packing talk for political maneuvering. The number can still be changed via amendment of this Section, but at least such an amendment will have to be passed by the People under Article VII rather than changed by statute whenever a peeved President and an accommodating Congress disagree with the Court's decisions. Furthermore, with the new appointment process for judges by the Commission under Section 8 of Article II from lists compiled by the Judicial Appointment Council under Section 4 of this Article V, the impact of politics on selection of judges should be extinguished or significantly diminished.

ELIGIBILITY

2. **Only a citizen who is 45 years or older, has resided within the United States for at least 14 years before appointment, and is an attorney in good standing admitted to any State bar or the bar of a possession or territory shall be eligible to serve as a judge in the courts of the United States.**

As discussed earlier, the Constitution contains eligibility requirements for the House of Representatives, the Senate, the President, and the Vice President. There are no eligibility requirements, however, to become a federal judge. More specifically, there are no citizenship, age, or residency requirements, as there are for the Legislative and Executive Branches.

If such requirements are deemed necessary for candidates for the other two branches, candidates for the judiciary should meet similar requirements. Consequently, to be eligible for appointment as a federal judge, this Section mandates that a person must be a citizen, at least 45 years old, a resident of the U.S. for at least 14 years before appointment, and, because of the special skills required to serve as a judge, a lawyer admitted to the bar of any State, possession, or territory.

Citizenship

It seems obvious that a judge must be a citizen. Federal district court judges wield enormous power over the lives and fortunes of the parties that appear before them. Since most cases never go beyond the district court level, either because they settle or the loser can't afford to throw good money after bad with an appeal, district court judges often have the final say. Even when a jury renders a verdict, the district court judge influences that verdict through evidentiary rulings before and during the trial and can also throw out the jury verdict.

Appellate court judges make rulings often on general principles that affect great numbers of people. Supreme Court rulings announce, extend, create, and, more recently, take away rights affecting just about everyone. Judges at all levels can strike down statutes enacted by Congress and overrule Presidential actions by declaring them unconstitutional.

It is not clear why the President, the Vice President, and Members of Congress must be citizens. Some historians believe the citizenship requirement arose from a fear that a foreigner would have allegiance to another country or make decisions favorable to that country, especially at the time in 1787 when Great Britain, France, and Spain still controlled lands in North America close to the U.S. borders.[48]

Because of the profound effect judges have on our lives, Americans should be assured that such power is entrusted to a fellow citizen. If the citizenship requirement is good enough for the Executive and Legislative Branches, it's good enough for the Judicial Branch. In other words, you have to be a member of the club to run the club.

Residency

Federal judges should be subject to the residency requirement of 14 years for Presidents found in Section 1 of Article II of the Constitution, which is maintained in Section 2 of Article IV of the Restated Constitution. Again, it's not clear whether there is any magic to that number of years, but since the power of federal judges is more similar to that of the President than of Congress, the residency requirement should be the same.

After all, like the President, a district court judge acts on his or her own, appellate court judges act primarily through panels of three, and the Supreme Court acts through a panel of nine or fewer when there is a vacancy or when justices recuse themselves from cases. A member of Congress, on the other hand, acts only as part of a body with many others, namely, 100 in the Senate and 435 in the House. So, for whatever reasons Presidents must have been a resident for 14 years prior to serving, the same reasons should apply to judges.

Age and Training

As to an age requirement, the specialized duties a judge performs clearly call for greater skill, training, and experience than for the offices of President or Congress. The President and Members of Congress are politicians, who, like ordinary citizens at a town hall meeting, need no particular background to stand up and voice their opinions. Take a look at some of the nut jobs that have been elected to Congress and the White House.

A dozen Presidents lacked a college degree, including Abraham Lincoln, and, most recently, Harry Truman.[49] Presidents have come from all walks of life: surveyor (Washington), tailor (Andrew Johnson), school teacher (Garfield, Arthur, Lyndon Johnson), university professor and president (Wilson), newspaper editor (Harding), engineer (Hoover), haberdasher (Truman), journalist/author (Kennedy), football coach (Ford), peanut farmer (Carter), B-movie actor (Reagan), oil executive (George H.W. Bush), Major League Baseball team owner (George W. Bush), and real estate developer and TV personality (Trump). The rest were primarily lawyers and/or military officers.[50]

The range of jobs held by Representatives and Senators before they were elected is even more expansive. Many have been lawyers, which makes sense because lawyers are naturally attracted to a position that includes drafting laws and advocating on behalf of constituents.

Nevertheless, there is no reason to suggest that we add a law degree as a requirement for Congress or the Presidency. Since these are elected positions, we should continue the long tradition going back to the Greeks and Romans of being governed by fellow citizens from all occupations because of the different perspectives they add to the process of governing.

Determining that 45 is an appropriate age requirement for judges takes into account the requirement of training and experience in the law. Since law school is a three-year graduate program after college, the youngest law school graduates are usually around 25. Most lawyers, then, will have practiced law for about 20 years by age 45. If this Section were to match the age requirements for the President (35), the Senate (30), or the House (25), on the other hand, the most experience a judge would have had by the time of appointment would be ten years, five years, and none, respectively.

What is the magic to 20 years of legal experience? Twenty years of legal experience provides time for a lawyer to encounter numerous different situations and to learn more about the law, whether as a lawyer in private practice, a prosecutor, a public defender, other government attorney, a corporate in-house counsel, a law professor, or other type of position requiring legal training. Moreover, 20 years provides more time for a lawyer to grow as a person and gain insights, compassion, and wisdom that should enhance a judge's interaction with juries, counsel, and the parties, especially criminal defendants.

Case in point: Trump appointed Aileen Cannon to the U.S. District Court for the Southern District of Florida when she was 39 and had only 13 years of experience as an attorney. She was reversed and rebuked several times by the Eleventh Circuit Court of Appeals during the prosecution of Trump charging him for improperly retaining, handling, and storing classified documents after his Presidency. She eventually dismissed the indictment, agreeing with Trump's argument that the special prosecutor was not legally appointed, despite Supreme Court and Circuit Court precedent to the contrary.

In the old days, lawyers became judges near the end of their careers, partly due to their desire to cap their careers with an honored position but also partly due to the recognition that gray hair (or no hair) was a sign of elder leadership that so many cultures revered.

Because of the life tenure federal judges have enjoyed, which is addressed in the next Section, Presidents started to recognize that if they appoint young judges, they will add to their Presidential legacy, particular on the Supreme Court, that will last for another 30 or 40 years. Consequently, the tendency has been to appoint judges in their forties and early fifties to the federal courts.

Another problem with appointing young judges is that the pay they receive as judges does not keep up with the pay they could receive in private practice. As a result, when they hit their mid-forties to mid-fifties, a fair number have been resigning to return to private practice to be able to afford to send their kids to college.

In *The Federalist* No. 64, John Jay makes the following arguments for the age requirements for the President and the Senate, but his rationale is equally applicable to an age requirement for judges:

> As the select assemblies for choosing the president [the Electoral College], as well as the state legislatures who appoint the senators, will, in general, be composed of the most enlightened and respectable citizens, there is reason to presume, that their attention and their votes will be directed to those men only who have become the

most distinguished by their abilities and virtue, and in whom the people perceive just grounds for confidence. The constitution manifests very particular attention to this object. By excluding men under thirty-five from the first office [the Presidency], and those under thirty from the second [the Senate], it confines the elections to **men of whom the people have had time to form a judgment, and with respect to whom they will not be liable to be deceived by those brilliant appearances of genius and patriotism, which, like transient meteors, sometimes mislead as well as dazzle**.

Emphasis added.

Jay's point is that while certain young people may rise rapidly, they could be just a flash-in-the-pan and that the passage of time helps determine their lasting power. Waiting until they are older also gives us a chance to see if they screw up along the way. This point applies particularly to judges because, since they currently enjoy life tenure and do not stand for re-election, there is no way to get them out of office when they fail to perform, short of impeachment.

As to legal training, Article III of the Constitution is bizarrely silent regarding whether judges have to be lawyers. That's just plain nuts. Court cases involve multiple, complex legal issues with all sides spinning arguments in ways most favorable to their clients. Specialized language and terms of art, often in Latin or medieval French, are flung around by the lawyers. The judge has to analyze the arguments, understand the statutes and precedential decisions,

211

and apply the law to the facts. To one lacking legal training, sitting as a judge would be like walking into the Operating Room at a hospital and being handed the scalpel without going through medical school and surgical residencies. Who would like to be a patient or litigant under these circumstances?

Perhaps, a reason why the Constitution doesn't require legal training for judges is that, in 1787, the process for becoming a lawyer was murky. The usual route was to "read law" as an apprentice or clerk to a practicing lawyer or judge for a varying number of years and then apply to a court for admission to the bar.[51] The first law school, the Litchfield Law School in Litchfield, Connecticut, was not founded until 1774.[52] Thus, most of the lawyers who were Framers of the Constitution had not attended or graduated from law school.

Nowadays, while six States still retain some version of "reading law," the primary path to becoming a lawyer is to graduate from law school and pass a bar exam. Regardless of the method for admission to the bar, we should require that a federal judge be an "**attorney in good standing admitted to any State bar or the bar of a possession or territory**." To be "in good standing" means attorneys have not been disbarred or suspended or have any other pending grievance or limitation on their ability to practice law.

The bar admission and age-45 requirements will cause very little change, as a practical matter. It is doubtful there are currently any sitting federal judges appointed under Article III of the Constitution who were not attorneys in good standing admitted to a bar at the time of their appointments. Furthermore, most sitting judges were probably around 40 to 45 or older at the time of their appointments. Nevertheless, it's important to add the bar admission requirement as a fundamental and crucial prerequisite to serving as a judge. The age requirement will tie into the term limit that is discussed in the next Section.

TERM LIMIT

3. **No judge shall serve in any courts of the United States for more than 25 years in the aggregate or beyond the age of 75 years, whichever occurs sooner. The positions of Senior Judge and Senior Justice are hereby abolished. Notwithstanding the foregoing, for the purpose of calculating the remaining terms of judges serving as of and prior to the Effective Date, only half of the previous service time shall count toward the 25-year limit and no age limit shall be imposed.** The judges of the courts of the United States shall hold their offices during good behavior **within their terms as defined in this Section,** and shall, at stated times, receive for their services, a compensation, which **may be increased but** shall not be diminished during their continuance in office **and which the Commission shall determine and fix**. [Art. III, Sect. 1]

Impartiality and Independence

It is fundamental to the proper administration of justice and the judicial system that judges remain unbiased and non-partisan and make objective decisions and rulings. We want judges to wear blindfolds like the allegorical statues of Lady Justice holding her scales so that they cannot see and, as a result, are not swayed by considerations and factors beyond the law and the facts before them. Consequently, the Framers wanted to make sure that no sword of Damocles threatening dismissal would be constantly dangling over the judges' heads, dissuading them from making tough decisions that might anger and provoke recriminations from the President, Congress, or the People.

How best to accomplish the goal of reassuring judges that they will not be fired for making unpopular decisions that the law, nevertheless, mandates? One way, which the Framers chose, is to appoint judges rather than elect them.

There are several problems with electing judges, although some States do so. First, candidates for a judgeship must campaign for office and, inevitably, will make promises and express views about how they will perform as judges to garner votes. Second, elected judges will eventually have to run for re-election, at which time their record will be up for review. During their term, therefore, they may make decisions in cases with an eye toward the impact on the next election. Imposing a sentence that is too harsh or too lenient in a notorious case will certainly be raised by the judge's opponents in an upcoming election. Third, judges running for election and re-election will need to raise funds for the campaign. Their primary targets for raising funds will necessarily be other lawyers, who will want to curry favor with the judges before whom they will be appearing. This is obviously unseemly and tantamount to bribery.

Lifetime Tenure

Another way to ensure judicial independence is to provide judges with tenure, which is protection from dismissal or the cutting of compensation based on the quality and effect of judges' decisions and rulings. The Framers provided judges with such tenure in Article III of the Constitution.

People are more familiar with tenure in the context of faculty tenure. Colleges and universities began granting tenure to faculty after the issuance of the 1940 Statement of Principles on Academic Freedom and Tenure drafted by the American Association of University Professors and the Association of American Colleges and Universities. The purpose of faculty tenure is to encourage and protect the exploration and expression of novel and, often, controversial ideas in academia without fear of reprisal. A tenured professor can be discharged only for misconduct or for financial reasons, such as elimination of the professor's field from the curriculum.[53] During the 1950s and 1960s, faculty tenure became widespread across the country, but now there has been a reduction in tenure-track positions due to financial constraints.

Currently, federal judges enjoy lifetime tenure. While the concept of judicial tenure seems the best way to ensure judicial independence and the fair administration of justice, its term must be limited by objective milestones that have nothing to do with the decisions and rulings judges render.

Where in the Constitution does it say that judges shall enjoy lifetime tenure? There is no language in Article III that specifically and clearly makes that statement. Rather, Section 1 of Article III states, "The Judges, both of the supreme and inferior Courts, shall hold their Offices during good Behaviour, and shall, at stated Times, receive for their Services, a Compensation, which shall not be diminished during their Continuance in Office."

The simple and plain meaning of the clause, "The Judges . . . shall hold their Offices during good Behaviour," is that they cannot be dismissed so long as they perform their functions and do not do bad things, like take bribes, embezzle from court funds, or, perhaps, commit crimes un-related to judicial matters. We can infer from the phrase that so long as judges exhibit good behavior, they cannot be dismissed. Alternatively, the phrase "shall hold their Offices" suggests that Congress can define "Offices" to cover a limited term of years or to require judges to step down after a certain age.

The only explanations that holding "Offices during good Behaviour" equates to lifetime tenure appear in several passages in Alexander Hamilton's essay in *The Federalist* No. 78. Hamilton noted that holding office "during good be-haviour" was the standard in "the most approved of the state constitutions." He argued that while the judiciary is the weakest of the three branches because it "has no influence over either the sword or the purse," as do the Executive Branch and the Legislative Branch, respectively, the judiciary has the power and responsibility to declare acts of the legislature void if contrary to the Constitution and to interpret the Constitution and statutes. In order to do so, the judiciary must be able to act without fear of reprisal from the other branches. So far, all these points make sense.

He then concluded, however, that the only way to ensure judicial independence is through permanent appointments:

> . . . that as from the natural feebleness of the judiciary, it is in continual jeopardy of being overpowered, awed or influenced by its coordi-nate branches; and **that as nothing can contribute so much to its firmness and independence, as permanency in office, this quality may therefore be justly regarded as an indispensable ingredient in its constitution**; and in a great

measure as the citadel of the public justice and the public security.

. . .

If then the courts of justice are to be considered as the bulwarks of a limited constitution against legislative encroachments, **this consideration will afford a strong argument for the permanent tenure of judicial offices, since nothing will contribute so much as this to that independent spirit in the judges**, which must be essential to the faithful performance of so arduous a duty.

. . .

That inflexible and uniform adherence to the rights of the constitution, and of individuals, which we perceive to be indispensable in the courts of justice, can certainly not be expected from judges who hold their offices by a temporary commission. Periodical appointments, however regulated, or by whomsoever made, would, in some way or other, be fatal to their necessary independence. If the power of making them was committed either to the executive or legislature, there would be danger of an improper complaisance to the branch which possessed it; if to both, there would be an unwillingness to hazard the displeasure of either; if to the people, or to persons chosen by them for the special purpose, there would be too great a disposition to consult popularity, to justify a reliance that nothing would be consulted but the constitution and the laws.

Emphasis added.

While temporary and periodic appointments run the same risk as elections and re-elections of instilling inherent bias and skewing decisions and rulings with an eye toward reappointment hearings, it doesn't follow that permanent appointments of lifetime tenure are the only bulwark against undue influence from the President, Congress, or the People.

Cap Based on Years of Service and Age

This Section, therefore, proposes a lengthy but non-permanent appointment term of a maximum of 25 years of service or reaching the age of 75, whichever comes first. These are objective, factual thresholds that should have absolutely no adverse or undue influence or bearing on a judge's decisions and rulings.

If, in fact, some State constitutions at the time Hamilton was writing bestowed tenure upon their judges "during good Behaviour," more than half of the States now have mandatory retirement of State court judges at ages ranging from 70 to 75, depending on the State.[54] Apparently, those States do not believe the mandatory retirement age supplies incentives or disincentives that influence judges' decisions in any respect.

The upper age limit of 75 is chosen for a couple of reasons. First, considering the minimum age of 45 for eligibility to serve in Section 2 of this Article V and coupling that with the term limit of 25 years, an appointment at age 50 would allow a judge to serve the full term of 25 years by age 75. Second, judges, like all of us, start slowing down in their mid-sixties and really crawling by their mid-seventies. It is not fair, therefore, to the parties and their lawyers to be assigned to Senior Judges over 75 who tend to take longer to issue decisions and who appear to have lost something off their fast ball on the bench during oral arguments and trials. Of course, there are exceptions, but they are few and far between.

A term limit of 25 years is in keeping with the beliefs expressed as to the term limits of 16 years for Congress and 12 years for the Commission, namely, that government employment should be considered service and not a career and that longevity tends to produce staleness. Recognizing how the judiciary differs from politicians, though, judges should enjoy longer terms.

Also, we don't need judges to serve the maximum of 25 years. The Commission can appoint judges older than 50 who will necessarily serve less than 25 years. After all, judges appointed in their sixties bring a lot more experience and wisdom to the job.

The cap of 25 years covers the aggregate of service without regard to position within the judiciary. Justice Sonia Sotomayor has served in the federal judiciary for over 30 years, starting when President George H.W. Bush appointed her to be a district court judge in the Southern District of New York in 1992. President Clinton appointed her to the Second Circuit in 1998, and then President Obama elevated her to the Supreme Court in 2009 where she continues to this day. Under the new scheme, she would have completed her service in 2017 because the 25-year clock does not start up fresh again with each new appointment.

Before people start feeling sorry for judges who will no longer enjoy lifetime tenure, the Commission can feel free to continue the generous pension of judges' full annual compensation upon retirement. Additionally, many state court judges in States with mandatory retirement ages join law firms and parlay their judicial experience and reputations into arbitration and mediation practices, as well as presiding over mock trials and appellate arguments to help lawyers prepare for their court appearances. They also teach at colleges and law schools. So, a retired federal judge can continue with a legal career and make more in retirement than by remaining on the bench.

Accordingly, there will be no need to preserve the status of Senior Judge or Senior Justice. Those positions are now available to judges who are 65 years or older and whose years of service plus age equal 80 or more. So, the earliest a judge may take senior status is upon serving 15 years and hitting 65 years of age. Senior Judges carry reduced caseloads but still have staff and receive full compensation. Instead of part-time Senior Judges, let's just give them a gold watch and replace them once they have served 25 years or are 75 years old. Senior Justices are rare because Supreme Court Justices tend to hang around until they die in office, like Justices Antonin Scalia and Ruth Bader Ginsburg, although retired Justices David Souter and Stephen Breyer continued to sit on the First Circuit Court of Appeals in Boston after stepping down from the Supreme Court.

Transition

This Section provides a transition method for the various situations of judges in office at the time when the Restated Constitution takes effect. For such judges, we will count only half of their previous service time toward the 25-year term limit and no age limit will apply to them. So, if on the Effective Date, a 65-year old judge will have already served 25 years, he or she can continue for another twelve and a half years to age 77 and a half for a total of 37 and a half years on the bench. It is hard to see how they can complain about that, unless they don't want to spend more time with their spouses and families.

The only time the Constitution has been amended to impose a term limit was when the 22nd Amendment, ratified in 1951, capped the Presidency at two elected terms of four years plus less than two years of someone else's term, for an absolute max of ten years. Section 1 of that Amendment made it inapplicable to whoever was President at the time when it was proposed by Congress, meaning Harry Truman. It was also expressly inapplicable to whoever would be President when the Amendment would become ratified, but only to the extent of allowing that President to complete the present term. Thus, Truman, who had served more than two years of FDR's fourth term and who had later been elected on his own in 1948, would remain eligible to serve with no term limit, but if his successor were in office when the Amendment was ratified, which didn't happen, the successor could finish the term but would otherwise be constrained by the cap.

The 22nd Amendment's process for transition could have been followed for transition from lifetime tenure for judges to the new 25 Years/Age 75 model. Exempting all sitting judges, however, would perpetuate the current system for decades. For example, judges recently appointed in their early forties could choose to remain on the bench for 40 or so more years into their eighties. The compromise of counting only half of prior service time with no age limit is a fairer approach to sitting judges while expediting implementation of the new caps. So, a 54-year old judge who has served four years can serve another 23 years until 77 years old for a total of 27 years. Not a bad run.

Removal from Office

Finally, this Section retains the concepts and language of Section 1 of Article III of the Constitution by providing that "[t]he judges of the courts of the United States shall hold their offices during good behavior **within their terms as defined in this Section,** and shall, at stated times, receive for their services, a compensation, which **may be increased but** shall not be diminished during their continuance in office **and which the Commission shall determine and fix.**"

Accordingly, as before, the judges cannot be removed from the bench for issuing unpopular decisions. The only way to remove them during their term would be via impeachment by Congress for bad behavior pursuant to Section 5 of Article III of the Restated Constitution.

Since the creation of the judiciary in 1789, 15 federal judges have been impeached. Of those, eight were convicted by the Senate, four were acquitted, and three resigned. The charges of misconduct for the eight that were convicted and removed from the judiciary included mental instability, intoxication on the bench, refusing to hold court and, instead, waging war against the United States during the Civil War, improper business relationships with litigants before the court, favoritism in appointing receivers, maintaining a private law practice while sitting on the bench, conviction of income tax evasion, perjury, conspiring to solicit a bribe, and accepting bribes.[55] Certainly, not good behavior.

One of the four judges who were acquitted was Justice Samuel Chase, the only Supreme Court Justice to be impeached. At his trail in 1805, he argued that the impeachment clause, which appears in Section 4 of Article II, subjects "the President, Vice President and all civil Officers of the

222

United States," presumably including federal judges, to impeachment only for "Treason, Bribery, or other high Crimes and Misdemeanors." Since he was not charged with any of these crimes but rather for his non-criminal conduct in several trials, including a refusal to dismiss purportedly biased grand jurors and his exclusion of testimony, he claimed that he could not be impeached. He also argued that the impeachment was politically motivated by his enemies, the Democratic-Republicans in Congress.[56]

Chase's acquittal came to stand for the proposition that judges cannot be impeached and convicted solely for their judicial conduct. Nevertheless, his argument that grounds for impeaching a judge are confined to those listed in Section 4 of Article II is not accurate because the "good Behaviour" clause in Section 1 of Article III adds another standard for impeachment of judges.

Likewise, judges' compensation cannot be reduced during their terms. Reduction of pay in the business world usually reflects an adverse performance evaluation. In the context of the judiciary, the ability to reduce a judge's compensation would invite retaliation for issuing unpopular decisions and, thus, present judges with the dilemma of rendering decisions that might cut their livelihood.

In keeping with the goal of removing politics from judicial appointments, discussed in the next Section, the Commission assumes the power of Congress under Section 8 of Article I of the Constitution to determine judges' compensation.

In sum, this Section provides reasonable caps on judges' tenures based on their length of service and age, objective standards that do not exert any influence over their decisions and rulings. The caps give them a pretty lengthy gig in an honored position in the community. Well qualified and deserving lawyers will continue seeking judgeships, despite the caps.

APPOINTMENT PROCESS

4.   Upon ratification of this Restated Constitution, a Judicial Appointment Council (the "Council") of 20 persons shall be established for the purpose of compiling and updating lists of recommended candidates deemed eligible and highly qualified to serve as judges in the courts of the United States. The Council shall be comprised of five judges of the courts of the United States appointed by the Judicial Conference of the United States (notwithstanding any provision in this Restated Constitution to the contrary), five non-governmental attorneys appointed by Congress, five persons who are not attorneys appointed by Congress, and five persons appointed by the President, and they shall serve for a term of five years and may be reappointed by the same or a different appointing authority for a second term of five years but shall serve no more than ten years. If a vacancy occurs on the Council, the entity that appointed the vacated seat shall appoint another person to fill that vacancy and such person shall be eligible for reappointment but in no event may serve more than 12 years. The Commission shall select and appoint judges to fill vacancies and new positions in the courts of the United States only from the lists compiled by the Council. The Commission shall determine and fix the compensation of the Council members, which shall neither be increased nor diminished during their continuance in office.

Politicization of Judgeships

Section 2 of Article II of the Constitution empowered the President to nominate, "and by and with the Advice and Consent of the Senate," appoint federal judges and other officials. The judicial appointments, however, are the only ones outside of the Executive Branch. This is one of only a few instances in the Constitution where the President or Congress gets to fill a position in another branch.

The other instances appear in the 12th and 20th Amendments where Congress picks the President under unusual circumstances. In the 25th Amendment, Congress may confirm the President's choice of a new Vice President if a vacancy occurs and may confirm the inability of a President to discharge the powers and duties of office, in which case the Vice President shall serve as Acting President. Under the 25th Amendment, however, Congress merely confirms and doesn't select the Vice President or President.

The President chooses all officers within the Executive Branch, subject to confirmation by the Senate depending on how high the positions are.

The House chooses its "Speaker and other Officers" under Section 2 of Article I of the Constitution, and the Senate chooses its "Officers, and also a President pro tempore, in the Absence of the Vice President," under Section 3 of Article I of the Constitution. The House and Senate make their selections unilaterally without input or approval from any other branch.

So, why should the President select all the judges upon confirmation by the Senate as a matter of course? Clearly, the confirmation by the Senate provides a check on the President's ability to dish out patronage positions to unworthy persons and cronies. But giving the President the right to make the selection in the first place and granting the Senate a veto simply invites political maneuvering and manipulation. Plus, if the Senate is controlled by the President's party, it usually rubber-stamps the confirmation.

As a matter of practice starting early on, Presidents have granted Senators the opportunity for input in the selection of judges being considered to sit in federal courts in their State, particularly if the Senator belongs to the same party as the President. This Senatorial courtesy, as it is called, has evolved to the point where Senators of the same party as the President propose to the President a candidate or several candidates for a judgeship in their home State. This process is seen as an opportunity for the Senators to play the patronage game themselves, although some dread it because for every person they delight, they disappoint and anger hundreds of others they bypass. Senatorial courtesy has been cleverly referred to as appointment of judges by Senators by and with the advice and consent of the President.

Before the 21st Century, the President's choices for Supreme Court justices, if qualified, were given great deference even by Senators of the opposing party. For example, Ruth Bader Ginsberg, who was clearly very liberal and a groundbreaker in the field of sex discrimination, was confirmed in 1993 by a Senate vote of 96 to 3.[57] Those days are gone, however, with the Democrats voting against all three of Trump's appointees to the Supreme Court. Then, Republicans united against President Biden's nomination of Ketanji Brown Jackson, whose credentials and experience pretty much mirrored Ginsberg's, and she was confirmed by a slim margin of 53 to 47, with only three of 50 Republicans voting for her.[58] Obviously, appointment and confirmation of judges has become way more political than before.

In the 21st Century, it seems that new vacancies in the judiciary have cropped up to such an extent due to deaths, retirements, assumption of senior status, and creation of additional seats that each new President has had the opportunity to refashion the complexion and legal philosophy of the judicial system as a whole.

Since 1953, the American Bar Association's Standing Committee on the Federal Judiciary has evaluated each person nominated by the President to serve on the federal bench through peer reviews conducted by interviews of colleagues, opposing counsel, judges, and others. The Committee strives to evaluate only a nominee's professional qualifications, such as integrity, professional competence, and judicial temperament and not political or legal philosophies. The Committee submits to the President and the Senate its evaluation of Well Qualified, Qualified, or Not Qualified.[59]

From its inception in 1953, the Committee has submitted to the President its evaluations of potential candidates being considered by the President before his nomination, with the exceptions that George W. Bush and Donald Trump declined to seek pre-nomination input from the Committee.

Appointment of judges by the President, a politician, subject to confirmation by Senators, more politicians, is fraught with the risk of cronyism and patronage and encourages the appointment of judges based on their biases and political bent rather than on their legal abilities, fairness, objectivity, temperament, and open minds. In fact, when the media reports on pending cases and decisions at any level of the federal judiciary, they now tend to point out which President appointed the judges, implying that the judges' rulings should be read within a political context. Rejecting pre-nomination, nonpartisan input from the ABA highlights the politicization of judicial appointments.

We can't blame only Presidents for playing politics with judicial appointments. Republican Senate Majority Leader Mitch McConnell has twice influenced the makeup of the Supreme Court. First, he sat on Obama's nomination of Merrick Garland when Justice Antonin Scalia died in February 2016, nine months before the next Presidential election. McConnell declared that no hearings would be held on the nomination because it was too close to the election and that the choice of a new Justice should be made by the new President.[60] That was a clear dereliction of the Senate's obligation under Section 2 of Article II of the Constitution to confirm or reject the President's nomination for a Supreme Court Justice. McConnell's stalling forced the Supreme Court to operate with a vacant seat for over a year until it was filled by Trump's first appointee, Neil Gorsuch.[61]

Second, McConnell showed how unprincipled he is by rushing through the confirmation of Amy Coney Barrett in the last days of Trump's term when Ruth Bader Ginsburg died less than two months before the Presidential election. Ginsburg died on September 18, 2020, and Barrett was confirmed a month later, only a week before the election. When questioned about the contrast between freezing the Garland nomination and rushing through the Barrett nomination, McConnell acknowledged that that's politics.[62]

New Method for Appointing Judges

In light of all the games that Presidents and the Senate play, this Section proposes a new system for appointment of judges based, in part, on processes followed in some States. This Section creates a 20-person Judicial Appointment Council (the "Council") whose mission will be to prepare lists of potential judges that they rate as eligible and highly qualified to serve as federal judges.

To avoid political favors, only persons rated "highly qualified" can be placed on the list. Consequently, we should have no more judges lacking the necessary abilities who are nominated simply because of whom they know or as a favor to someone. It will be up to the Council to figure out how to continually prepare and update these lists. They could solicit recommendations from the public, State Bar Associations, State and nationally elected officials, and even judges. They could post a fillable application form on the Council's website for anyone who wants to apply for a judgeship. They could ask the ABA Standing Committee to evaluate candidates. In any event, we will end up only with "highly qualified" judges and not merely "qualified" or "not qualified" judges.

When vacancies occur or new seats are created, the Commission will then ask the Council for lists of appropriate candidates, and the semi-nonpartisan Commission will then select judges only from the Council's lists.

This is similar to the process in some States where a judicial review committee prepares a list of qualified candidates from which the governor may appoint judges upon the legislature's confirmation.

While trying to de-politicize the selection process in favor of a merit system, it is important to construct the Council in such a way that permits some aspects of politics to participate in an effort to ensure that the Council itself does not become an elitist club. The following formula will determine the composition of the Council: "**The Council shall be comprised of five judges of the courts of the United States appointed by the Judicial Conference of the United States (notwithstanding any provision in this Restated Constitution to the contrary), five** non-governmental attorneys appointed by Congress, five persons who are not attorneys appointed by Congress, and five persons appointed by the President."

Thus, at least half of the Council will have legal training, five will have no legal training, and five may have legal training or not and may be governmental lawyers, depending on whom the President appoints. This way, all three branches will have input into the makeup of the Council, but the final selections will be made by the semi-nonpartisan Commission.

The Judicial Conference of the United States was created by Congress in 1922 and is comprised of the Chief Justice of the Supreme Court, the Chief Judge of each of the 12 judicial circuits, the Chief Judge of the Court of International Trade, and a district judge from each regional judicial circuit. The Judicial Conference proposes to Congress matters involving the administration of justice for Congress to promulgate statutes affecting the Judicial Branch.[63]

The appointment of judges to the Council is qualified by stating, "**notwithstanding any provision in this Restated Constitution to the contrary,**" to avoid any confusion with the principles prohibiting Commissioners (Section 12 of Article II), Members of Congress (Section 10 of Article III), and the President and Vice President (Section 3 of Article IV) from serving in two offices at the same time. Serving on the Council can be seen as part of the judges' judicial functions as if they were sitting on a federal judicial committee like the Judicial Conference, itself, and the various Advisory Committees on Appellate, Bankruptcy, Civil, Criminal, and Evidence Rules. If the extra compensation for serving on the Council is a problem, the sitting judges who are appointed to the Council can serve without extra pay, which may alleviate any concerns about holding two positions simultaneously. If that is not acceptable, then the Judicial Conference can appoint retired federal judges to the Council, instead.

Council members will serve five-year terms and can be reappointed once by the same appointing body. They can also be appointed after an initial five-year term to a seat allocated to a different appointing body if they meet the qualifications for that seat, provided that they do not exceed the term limit. Vacancies will be filled by the body that originally appointed the vacant seat. As in the 22nd Amendment, no one who has served more than two years by filling a vacant seat can be reappointed for more than one full term. In other words, no one can serve for more than a total of 12 years.

Finally, as with Congress and the President, the Commission shall determine the Council members' compensation, **"which shall neither be increased nor diminished during their continuance in office."**

CODE OF CONDUCT

5. **A Code of Conduct for United States Judges shall be issued by the Judicial Conference of the United States and shall apply to all United States judges and magistrate judges, including the Justices of the Supreme Court.**

In 1973, the Judicial Conference issued a Code of Conduct for United States Judges that sets forth rules for federal judges to follow on such ethical subjects as the avoidance of the appearance of impropriety, impartiality, conflicts of interest, recusal, outside activities like speaking engagements and publication of articles and books, and re-fraining from political activity.[64]

For some reason, the Code of Conduct does not apply to Supreme Court Justices. As a result, we have seen instances where Justice Ginsburg made with impunity arguably polit-ical statements critical of Trump during the 2016 campaign that may have violated the Code.[65] Similarly, Justice Clarence Thomas did not recuse himself from a decision that arguably involved or affected his wife.[66]

Furthermore, Justice Thomas has gotten into hot water for failing to disclose free air flights and vacations paid for by a Texas billionaire, as well as the billionaire's purchase of Thomas' mother's house, partly owned by Thomas, and the billionaire's payment of tuition at a private school for Thomas's great-nephew, for whom Thomas served as guardian.[67] Justice Alito similarly failed to report a free luxury fishing trip to Alaska provided by a billionaire with cases before the Supreme Court.[68] These transactions arguably should have been disclosed in accordance with the Ethics in Government Act of 1978, a post-Watergate law that mandates reporting of financial transactions by employees of the federal government.

Lawyers are bound by the model Rules of Professional Conduct or some variation in every State, state court judges are bound by codes of conduct, and all federal judges except Supreme Court Justices are bound the Code of Conduct. The problem is that, aside from impeachment, there are hardly any checks and balances monitoring and controlling the Supreme Court. As the Roman satirist Juvenal asked, *"Quis custodiet custodes ipsos?"* Who will guard the guards them-selves?

In light of these other ethical issues, the Chairman of the Senate Judiciary Committee, Senator Dick Durban, requested that Chief Justice Roberts testify before the Committee about ethics reform in the Supreme Court, but the Chief Justice respectfully declined, which was a polite way of snubbing the Committee.[69] Presumably, Roberts declined to testify on the grounds of separate of powers, meaning he did not feel obligated to subject himself and the Court to the jurisdiction of Congress, even for information purposes.

Roberts' shunning of the Judiciary Committee was questionable. First, Congress has the right to call in anyone in the United States to gather information under its investigatory powers.

Second, despite the doctrine of separation of powers, Congress still regulates the judiciary to a certain degree beyond simply confirming Presidential appointments to the bench. Section 8 of Article I empowers Congress "[t]o make all Laws which shall be necessary and proper for carrying into Execution the foregoing Powers, and all other Powers vested by this Constitution in the Government of the United States, or in any Department or Officer thereof." Thus, as discussed in the next Section, Congress determines the dollar amount in controversy for the courts' jurisdiction in diversity of citizenship cases in 28 United States Code § 1332. Also, under Section 2 of Article III, "the supreme Court shall have appellate Jurisdiction . . . under such Regulations as the Congress shall make." Finally, while the Judicial Conference proposes rules such as the Federal Rules of Civil Procedure and Federal Rules of Evidence and amendments to those rules, their implementation is subject to Congress' approval or rejection.

In November 2023, the Supreme Court unexpectedly issued its own "Code of Conduct for Justices of the Supreme Court of the United States."[70] While this new, special Supreme Court Code of Conduct tracks many provisions of the Code of Conduct for United States Judges, it contains a number of tweaks of those provisions. Most importantly, the Supreme Court Code merely states that Justices "should" disqualify themselves in certain circumstances while the Judge's Code states they "shall" disqualify themselves in those same circumstances. The use of such precatory and suggestive rather than mandatory language shows that the Justices are still not willing to answer to a higher power. They apparently feel that no one has the right to demand they recuse themselves from a case. Additionally, the new Supreme Court Code does not address the lack of an enforcement process to rein in a runaway Justice.

If Congress were to enact a statute imposing a Code of Conduct on the Supreme Court, the Supreme Court might ignore that statute and, if a case were brought to enforce the statute, the Supreme Court might deem it unconstitutional. To avoid a Constitutional crisis, therefore, let's do the sensible thing and bind Supreme Court Justices to the Code of Conduct for United States Judges via the Restated Constitution, since they have refused to do so themselves.

SUBJECT MATTER JURISDICTION

6.   The judicial power shall extend (a) to all cases, in law and equity, arising under this **Restated** Constitution, the laws of the United States, and treaties made, or which shall be made, under their authority; (b) to all cases affecting ambassadors, other public ministers, and consuls; (c) to all cases of admiralty and

maritime jurisdiction; (d) to controversies to which the United States shall be a party; (e) to controversies between two or more States, (f) to controversies between citizens of different States, and (g) to controversies between citizens of the same State claiming lands under grants of different States. [Art. III, Sect. 2]

Subject Matter Jurisdiction

The general concept behind the creation of federal courts was (a) to provide a forum for resolution of cases involving federal issues and (b) to provide a neutral forum for certain cases between States or based on State laws but involving a party from a different State who might suffer from being "home-towned" in a State court. The types of claims and issues that a federal court is empowered to hear and rule on is referred to as its subject matter jurisdiction.

Federal Question Jurisdiction

All cases relating to the Restated Constitution, federal statutes and agency regulations, treaties with foreign countries, foreign emissaries, and the United States government involve federal issues.

Sections 8 and 10 of Article I and Sections 2 and 3 of Article II of the Constitution (Sections 12 and 14 of Article III and Sections 14, 16, and 17 of Article IV of the Restated Constitution, respectively) make it clear that Congress and the President, and not the individual States, have complete authority to act on behalf of the United States with respect to interstate and foreign commerce, war with foreign countries, and admiralty, piracy, and maritime matters.

Consequently, these are federal matters that should be adjudicated in federal and not State courts. Subject matter jurisdiction for federal issues is today referred to as federal question jurisdiction and is succinctly defined in 28 United States Code § 1331: "The district courts shall have original jurisdiction of all civil actions arising under the Constitution, laws, or treaties of the United States."

Diversity Jurisdiction

As explained in the 1806 Supreme Court case of *Strawberry v. Curtiss*, 7 U.S. (3 Cranch) 267 (1806), Section 2 of Article III of the Constitution endows the federal courts with jurisdiction over cases in which no plaintiff is a citizen of the same State as any defendant even if no federal question is at issue, such as a breach of contract dispute in which a State's law on contracts applies or a car accident case where a State's negligence law would control. This is referred to as "diversity of citizenship jurisdiction" or "diversity jurisdiction," for short. In 28 United States Code § 1332, Congress added a minimum dollar amount at stake, which was $3,000 from 1911 to 1958, when it was raised to $10,000, then to $50,000 in 1988, and finally to $75,000 in 1996.[71]

This type of jurisdiction arose most likely from a perception that a State court would show bias in favor of a citizen of the same State in a lawsuit against a citizen of a different State. This seems to be a simple inference to draw that warrants the provision of a neutral forum, such as the federal courts, for such cases.

The assumption that the federal district court presents a neutral forum, however, is questionable. After all, federal district court judges live in the communities in which they preside, and the federal jury pools come from the same communities as the State jury pools. Thus, any prejudices against out-of-staters that a State court judge and jury might harbor will most likely be shared by a federal judge and jury in the same State. Perhaps, the protection against home-towning comes more at the next level when an appeal is taken to the Circuit Court of Appeals, which often sits in another State or, even if it does not, will have a three-judge panel consisting of at least one or more judges from another State. Of course, if the case moves on to a second appeal to the Supreme Court, chances are that very few, if any, of the nine justices will be citizens of the same States as the parties appearing before them.

Retroactive Effect

This Section follows Section 2 of Article III of the Constitution, as amended by the 11th Amendment. The sole word that is added makes it clear that the federal court's subject matter jurisdiction will extend to cases arising under this "**Restated**" Constitution and will no longer extend to cases under the original Constitution. This retroactive effect makes sense because once the Restated Constitution becomes effective, we can't have courts applying two constitutions depending upon when the conduct occurred. One word, big change.

For example, if a case challenging a State law banning or restricting abortion is pending before the Effective Date, the new provision granting the right of abortion in Section 2 of Article I of the Restated Constitution will control and not the Supreme Court decision under the original Constitution in *Dobbs*. Likewise, a case challenging a State or federal gun control law on the grounds of the 2nd Amendment will be decided under the Restated Constitution, which no longer contains the 2nd Amendment. After all, a court should not be deciding whether a gun control law might have violated a 2nd Amendment right if such a right no longer exists.

The common rule of thumb is that a new law, usually a statute, supersedes a conflicting prior law regarding the same topic, even if the conduct at issue occurred before the new law became effective. This does not violate the prohibitions against ex post facto laws in Sections 9 and 10 of the Constitution because the Supreme Court decided in the 1798 case of *Calder v. Bull*, 3 U.S. (3 Dall.) 386 (1798), that the ex post facto bans pertained to criminal laws, not civil laws.

The changes in the Restated Constitution do not create criminalization of any conduct, let alone retroactively. To the extent the freedom of safety and freedom from danger in Section 6 of Article I of the Restated Constitution prohibit **"the right to carry any firearm in any area reasonably declared by the Government to be gun-free and off-limits to firearms,"** they do so after the Effective Date. That Section also restricts any **"right to use, carry, or possess any weapon of war, including assault weapons and high-capacity magazines or ammunition"** but does so one year after the Effective Date, just like the 18th Amendment did with respect to Prohibition. Neither of these provisions makes carrying or using weapons a criminal violation, although such follow-up enabling legislation from Congress and the States is envisioned.

In the past, amendments to the Constitution did not grandfather conduct that had previously been legal. The 13th Amendment abolishing slavery had no exception keeping then current slaves in bondage. The 18th Amendment did not grandfather saloons and permit them to continue selling alcohol.

MISCELLANEOUS

The 11th Amendment and Sections 2 and 3 of Article III of the Constitution are incorporated as the remaining four Sections of Article V.

The original language in Section 2 of Article III of the Constitution invested the federal courts with subject matter jurisdiction to hear cases "between a State and Citizens of another State" and "between a State, or the Citizens thereof;-- and foreign States, Citizens or Subjects." The 11th Amendment overrode and essentially repealed this language in response to the 1793 case of *Chisolm v. Georgia*, 2 U.S. (2 Dall.) 419 (1793), in which a South Carolina citizen sued Georgia in federal court. Georgia viewed this suit as an affront to its sovereignty and refused to appear, but the Supreme Court ruled in favor of Chisolm because Section 2 of Article III expressly conferred on the federal courts jurisdiction in such cases. States joined forces quickly to ratify the 11th Amendment, which now requires citizens of one State or a foreign country to sue a different State in the latter's own courts and not in federal court.

The 11th Amendment is repeated verbatim in Section 7 of Article V of the Restated Constitution: "The judicial power of the United States shall not be construed to extend to any suit, in law or equity, commenced or prosecuted against one of the States by citizens of another State or by citizens or subjects of any foreign state." [11th Amend.]

STATES RIGHTS

ARTICLE VI

THE STATES

S ections 1-6 of Article VI are lifted verbatim from the entire Article IV of the Constitution regarding interaction between and among States. Minor changes have been made in capitalization and punctuation, and different concepts have been broken into separate sections, but the changes are not meant to alter the meaning of the original. Two provisions are added from the 2nd and 10th Amendments regarding States that logically belong with the other Sections in this Article.

FULL FAITH AND CREDIT

1.   Full faith and credit shall be given in each State to the public acts, records, and judicial proceedings of every other State. Congress may by general laws prescribe the manner in which such acts, records, and proceedings shall be proved and the effect thereof. [Art. IV, Sect. 1]

"Full faith and credit" means judgments in one State shall be enforced in another State. For example, if a court in New York enters a money judgment against a defendant who owns property in Ohio, the plaintiff can register the New York judgment in Ohio and then follow Ohio law on how to execute on the property in Ohio to satisfy the New York judgment. The defendant cannot interfere with that execution by claiming that the New York judgment is not enforceable, unless the New York court lacked personal jurisdiction over the defendant or there was some other fundamental defect.

The Framers provided for full faith and credit to facilitate a system of federalism where the States would cooperate with one another and honor one another's judgments rather than act as separate sovereign domains.

TREATMENT OF CITIZENS FROM DIFFERENT STATES

2.   The citizens of each State shall be entitled to all privileges, **rights, liberties, freedoms,** and immunities of citizens in the several States. [Art. IV, Sect. 2]

This provision also facilitates federalism by ensuring citizens of one State that they will be treated just like the citizens of another State by that other State. This protection encouraged early Americans to travel to and do business with citizens of other States without fear of reprisal or mistreatment. In essence, this was a limited version of an equal protection clause that protected all citizens from discrimination based on residence.

Since Black slaves were not citizens, however, it was necessary to add the equal protection clause in the 14th Amendment, which established that they were citizens and that their native State could not discriminate against them.

The litany of "**rights, liberties, freedoms**" used in Sections 3 and 16 of Article I, the new Bill of Rights of the Restated Constitution, is inserted.

EXTRADITION/RENDITION

3.   Persons charged in any State with treason, felony, or other crime, who shall flee from justice and be found in another State, shall on demand of the executive authority of the State from which they fled, be delivered up to be removed to the State having jurisdiction of the crime. [Art. IV, Sect. 2]

This Section empowered States to request extradition, which is sometimes referred to as "rendition" depending on the situation, of criminal fugitives. Again, establishing a standing procedure for extradition helped reinforce the concept of a single nation by treating States not as separate sovereigns but rather as branches of one tree. Thus, a fugitive could not escape a State's criminal justice system by slipping over the border to a neighboring State.

ADDITION AND FORMATION OF NEW STATES

4.   New States may be admitted by Congress into this Union, but no new State shall be formed or erected within the jurisdiction of any other State; nor any State be formed by the junction of two or more States or parts of States, without the consent of the legislatures of the States concerned as well as of Congress. [Art. IV, Sect. 3]

Congress may admit new States, as it has done 37 times since the original 13 States. Five States have been formed from other States. Vermont was formed from New York, Kentucky from Virginia, Tennessee from North Carolina, Maine from Massachusetts as part of the Missouri Compromise to maintain the balance between free and slave States, and West Virginia broke off from Virginia during the Civil War to remain in the Union.[72]

For years, there has been talk of whether to make Puerto Rico a State or grant it independence. There has also been talk of making Washington, D.C. a State.

It appears that we will not be adding any new States anytime soon. We have been stuck at 50 States for over 60 years, the longest stretch of time without the admission of a new State. The number 50 is a round number, and the 50 stars on the flag are depicted in an iconic, symmetrical design. Most likely, Betsy Ross will not be given a new commission anytime soon.

Nevertheless, this process for adding new States is retained, just in case.

TERRITORIES

5.   Congress shall have power to dispose of and make all needful rules and regulations respecting the territory or other property belonging to the United States, and nothing in this Restated Constitution shall be so construed as to prejudice any claims of the United States or of any particular State. [Art. IV, Sect. 3]

This Section addressed the territories to the west of the original East Coast States. For example, as part of its royal charter, Connecticut had been granted ownership of all land between certain latitudes extending all the way to the Pacific Ocean. It eventually ceded most of that territory to the United States but kept a portion consisting of 3.5 million acres in what is now northeastern Ohio that was referred to as the Western Reserve. In 1795, it sold those acres to developers who named settlements after towns in Connecticut, such as Canton, Norwich, Saybrook, New London, Litchfield, Mansfield, and Plymouth. This Section protected Connecticut's rights to the

Western Reserve but probably has no purpose today, as no States own territories anymore.[73]

This Section also empowered Congress to control and govern territories that came into the possession of the United States, like the land obtained in the Louisiana Purchase. Because the U.S. still owns territories (Washington, D.C., Puerto Rico, American Samoa, Guam, the Northern Mariana Islands, and the U.S. Virgin Islands), this Section continues to have vitality with respect to the federal government.

REPUBLICAN FORM OF GOVERNMENT

6.   The United States shall guarantee to every State in this Union a republican form of government and shall protect each of them against invasion and, on application of the State legislature or of the State executive (when the legislature cannot be convened), against domestic violence. [Art. IV, Sect. 4]

This Section established the obligation of the national government to defend each State against invasion by a foreign nation or even another State. In the early days of the American experiment, it was not assured that all the States would play nice with one another, and, in fact, over 7,000 died and over 33,000 were wounded at the Battle of Gettysburg four score and seven years after the signing of the Declaration of Independence.[74]

The guarantee of a republican form of government empowered the national government to intercede if a State tried to replace its representative democracy with, say, a monarchy.

Finally, the provision that Governors primarily invoke is the one that permits them to request the President to send the

National Guard of the United States to quell domestic violence in their State. In Washington, D.C., the equivalent of the "State executive" within the meaning of this Section is the President. During the January 6, 2021 attack on Congress, which was the epitome of "domestic violence," Trump refused to call up the National Guard, and Vice President Pence eventually felt compelled to do so.[75]

STATE NATIONAL GUARDS

7. **Each State shall maintain a National Guard unit.** [2nd Amend.]

As discussed regarding the freedom of safety and freedom from violence in Section 6 of Article I, the focus of the Second Amendment was on permitting the States to maintain militias. This is the only aspect of the Second Amendment that remains in the Restated Constitution.

State militias evolved into State National Guards in each State, Washington, D.C., and the territories in a series of steps starting in 1903 and culminating in the National Guard Mobilization Act of 1933, which required all National Guard soldiers to be enlisted or commissioned in both a State National Guard unit and the National Guard of the United States.

The National Guard not only helps protect property and lives during riots but also assists in rescue missions and other live-saving measures when natural disasters strike. It is worth keeping.

RESERVATION OF POWERS

8. The powers not delegated to the United States by **this Restated** Constitution, nor prohibited by it to the

States, are reserved to the States, respectively, or to the People. [10th Amend.]

In this Section, the entire 10th Amendment is maintained in full, inserting only **"this Restated"** before the word "Constitution" to refer to what will become the operative document.

This Section makes it clear that the States or the People remain the reservoir of all powers, except for those powers granted to the United States elsewhere in the Restated Constitution and except for those powers that the Restated Constitution prohibits States from exercising, such as in this Article and in Section 14 of Article III of the Restated Constitution (Section 10 of Article I of the Constitution), which primarily prohibits States from meddling in matters that the national government controls.

This is the provision on which the argument for States rights rests, an argument that has been going on since the Federal Convention of 1787 at which the Constitution was drafted. The delegates to the Convention espoused divergent ideologies that either favored a strong national government or a weak national government with more power exercised by the individual States. These ideologies developed into political parties, with John Adams and Alexander Hamilton leading the pro-national government Federalists and Thomas Jeffersons leading the anti-Federalists or States-rights Democratic Republicans.[76]

In the last generation or so, Republicans have appeared to advocate for weakening the national government in favor of States rights. Before *Roe v. Wade* was overturned, they argued that abortion was a local interest that should be regulated by each State. Now, in light of the backlash from

Dobbs even in Red States, however, they keep talking about enacting a national law banning abortion. Similarly, during the chaotic counting of the Electoral votes in Congress on January 6, 2021, Republican Senators and Representatives challenged the Electoral votes certified by States that they did not even represent. So much for respecting States rights.

In the overview of the restructuring of the national government discussed above, the purpose behind maintaining both a national government and a system of 50 different sub-sovereignties with different laws, structures, and customs was questioned. The Restated Constitution, however, is proposing enough dramatic changes without opening up that can of worms.

Also, it may be idealistic to imagine that an America with no diverse State laws would have only reasonable and fair national laws, rules, and regulations. What if, on the other hand, the uniform national laws were more like the State laws that many find to be offensive and unjust? Be careful what you wish for.

Representative Marjorie Taylor Greene has called for shrinkage of the national government and "a national divorce" so that Red States and Blue States with irreconcilable differences can go their separate ways.[77] Needless to say, she was just spouting off and has no real plan that could possibly be implemented.

Nevertheless, as we witness more and more absolutely crazy things happening in other States like Arizona (time-consuming and costly recount of the 2020 election into the following year), Texas (a civil bounty statute permitting private suits against abortion providers), and Florida (anti-LGBTQ+ laws), it is frightening that certain States are dragging America down. Would the Blue States and Red

States be better off without the other? We are rapidly devolving into a country like 1950s America where segregation by law made living in Mississippi a lot different from living in New York.

Did you ever wonder why Abraham Lincoln fought to keep the Southern States from seceding? If they wanted to leave, why didn't he let them go? There's no express provision in the Constitution requiring a State to remain in the Union or prohibiting it from seceding. In fact, the 10th Amendment, as incorporated into this Section, seems to imply that States have retained the right to secede.

In *Texas v. White*, 74 U.S. 700 (1869), however, the Supreme Court held in 1869 that Texas' secession was null and void because when it became a State, it entered into a perpetual and final Union with the other States that could not be dissolved. Nowhere in the Supreme Court's homage to patriotism, though, is there any analysis of the Constitution that supports that conclusion.

So, while there is nothing in the Constitution prohibiting secession, no one has seriously joined Marjorie Taylor Greene in calling for a national divorce. Despite our different beliefs and values, we are stronger and better off as a nation if we stick together and work through our problems and disagreements in a civil and respectful way, as hard as that has become to do. If the States are truly married for eternity as the Supreme Court declared in 1869, what we really need, rather than a national divorce, is a family and marriage counselor.

ORGANIC AND STRUCTURAL COMPONENTS

T he last three Articles address how the Restated Constitution works. Article VII expands on how to amend the Restated Constitution. Article VIII affirms the primacy of the Restated Constitution as the supreme law of the land and requires national and State officers to take an oath to support and abide by the Restated Constitution. Article IX defines ratification and the Effective Date of the Restated Constitution.

ARTICLE VII

AMENDMENT

No document is perfect. No drafters can foresee every possible application, ramification, or inconsistency of their language. No drafters can predict and provide for all future needs.

Consequently, it is necessary to establish methods for amending the Restated Constitution. There is a natural tension between the goals of a constitution with definitive and permanent terms and rules that continuously guide the Government and everyday life, on the one hand, and of a constitution that is easily amendable and, as a result, easily adaptable as the world changes, on the other hand. We should strive for a constitution that is not so easy to amend that it changes every year but not so hard to amend that changes become rare.

Clearly, we don't want to keep messing with the Restated Constitution by way of amendments unless they are truly material and necessary. This Article, then, provides ways to amend the Restated Constitution that discourage tinkering but do not erect insurmountable obstacles.

LIVING DOCUMENT

1.   **This Restated Constitution is intended to be a living document to be adapted to future times.**

A battle has been waging in the Supreme Court between the adherents of "original intent" and the advocates for a living Constitution.

The Originalists maintain that interpretation of the Constitution and its amendments must be confined to the original intent of the section of the Constitution or the amendment at issue as evidenced in contemporaneous documentation at the time of ratification. Justice Scalia was one of the most ardent Originalists.[78]

Supporters of a living Constitution believe that the words of the Constitution should be read to apply to modern life and technology through analogy or expanded readings without the need for formal amendments to update the language. Thus, the 4th Amendment, which requires warrants for searches of homes and papers, has been applied to searches of automobiles and wiretaps of telephones, neither of which existed in 1791. This approach is also called "judicial pragmatism."[79]

The problem with Originalism is that it treats the Constitution as if it were written in stone, and we are then stuck in 18th Century agrarian America with only 13 States along the Atlantic seaboard. We saw that approach in Justice Alito's reasoning in *Dobbs*, which reviewed and relied on the history of the criminalization of abortion from colonial days. As pointed out in the discussion of Section 2 of Article I of the Restated Constitution, one problem with that historical approach is that the laws in 18th and 19th Century America were written almost exclusively by white men because women and Black slaves had no right to vote and did not serve as legislators.

The risk in a living Constitution, on the other hand, is that 21st Century readings may expand too far beyond the original language and meaning. In such an instance, the courts may be informally amending the Constitution through the guise of updating and adapting it to modern situations.

All things considered, the better approach is the living Constitution viewpoint, which is spelled out in this Section. Like the bylaws in a corporation, the Constitution should be specific enough to give definitive answers but also broad enough to permit application to unforeseen circumstances without the need to go through the amendment process. By stating that "**[t]his Restated Constitution is intended to be a living document to be adapted to future times**," this Section is directing courts to treat the Restated Constitution as flexible and applicable to modern times and the future.

By the same token, courts are not prohibited from researching and analyzing the original intent of a passage in the Constitution as an aid in interpretation. After all, in construing a State statute or Act of Congress, courts often seek guidance from the legislative history of the promulgation of the law, although finding definitive meaning in the sausage-making process can be challenging and uncertain.

This directive appears in Article VII regarding amendment because treating the Restated Constitution as a living document should significantly moderate the need to amend it.

PROPOSALS FOR AMENDMENT

2.　　**A proposal for amendment to this Restated Constitution may be made by:**
   a. a two-thirds vote of Congress;
   b. a convention for proposing amendments called for by the legislatures of two-thirds of the several States; **or**
   c. **a resolution or referendum by popular vote of two-thirds of the several States.** [Art. V]

The procedure for amending the Constitution is set forth in a single, lengthy and confusing sentence that comprises the whole of Article V. For the sake of clarity, the two main components, namely, proposing amendments and ratifying proposed amendments, are set forth in two separate Sections of Article VII of the Restated Constitution.

The two original ways of proposing amendments are maintained. First, Congress can propose an amendment by a two-thirds vote. Second, the legislatures of two-thirds of the States can call for a national convention, like the Federal Convention of 1787, that will propose amendments. This second method is slightly modified by allowing the States to call for the national convention directly and not requiring them to apply to Congress for the formal call for the convention, as Article V currently requires.

To date, Congress has proposed 33 amendments, 27 of which have been ratified by the States. No amendments have been proposed by way of a convention applied for by the States. No amendment has been proposed by Congress since the Equal Rights Amendment in 1972, which grants equal rights to women but has not been ratified. The 27th Amendment, which prohibits the enactment of any law giving Congress a raise taking effect during that term, was ratified by the States in 1992 but had been proposed by Congress 203 years earlier in 1789.[80] Thus, Congress has proposed no amendments in over 50 years.

To these two methods, a third amendment route is added that bypasses Congress and State legislatures completely. Now, proposals to amend the Restated Constitution can also be made by the People directly through "**a resolution or referendum by popular vote of two-thirds of the several States.**"

Many States place proposed State constitutional amendments on their election ballots. In fact, two months after *Dobbs* overruled *Roe v. Wade* on June 23, 2022, Kansas voters rejected a proposed amendment to the Kansas constitution that would have banned abortions, and Kentucky voters did the same in the general election several months later in November. Also in the November 2022 election, Michigan and Vermont voters approved amendments to their State constitutions guaranteeing the right to abortion.[81] While the ways that States propose amendments to their constitutions vary, it only makes sense that if the People may vote on proposed amendments, then they should be permitted to propose amendments by a popular vote.

In the original procedure, the Framers were fearful of letting the People amend the Constitution and, therefore, required proposals to be made by Congress or a convention of State delegates and required ratification by State legislatures or State conventions. Here, in keeping with the theme of giving the People a more direct say in their government, as in the direct election of the President and Vice President, this Section enables them to make proposals by a popular vote of two-thirds of the States. Each State can determine how to place proposals for amendments on their State ballots and when.

Two-thirds is the supermajority required in Article V of the Constitution for proposing amendments, and there appears no reason to change that. A supermajority should be required for momentous steps like proposing amendments to the Constitution. A two-thirds vote will minimize a flood of proposals without making it too onerous for proposals to make it to the next step of approval.

APPROVAL OF PROPOSED AMENDMENTS

3. **After a proposal for an amendment has satisfied any of these requirements, the proposed amendment shall be submitted for a popular vote in the next national election conducted by the Commission. If three-fourths or more of the States vote in favor of the amendment, it shall become part of this Restated Constitution. A vote in favor of the amendment by more than half of the votes cast in a State shall be deemed by the Commission to be a vote by that State in favor of the amendment.**

The next step in the amendment process is fairly straightforward. Once an amendment has been proposed under Section 2, the Commission will place it on the ballot in the next national election. The Commission will determine whether the amendment passes by a majority vote in each State. If three-fourths of the States approve the amendment, as currently required by Article V of the Constitution, it becomes part of the Restated Constitution.

ARTICLE VIII

SUPREME LAW OF THE LAND

In this Article, two clauses of Article VI of the Constitution are joined with a related clause regarding oaths of office from Section 3 of the 14th Amendment.

The first clause of Article VI affirming the validity of debt incurred before the adoption of the Constitution has been deleted. The statute of limitations for collecting on such debts ran over 200 years ago.

SUPREMACY CLAUSE

1.   This **Restated** Constitution, the laws of the United States made pursuant thereto, and all treaties made under the authority of the United States shall be the supreme law of the land, and the judges in every State shall be bound thereby, anything in the constitution or laws of any State to the contrary notwithstanding. [Art. VI]

This Section replicates the second clause of Article VI, with several stylistic changes in diction, capitalization, and punctuation. This Supremacy Clause means that if a State constitution or law clashes with the Restated Constitution, Act of Congress, or a treaty, the federal law wins, even in State court. This provision prevents States from essentially vetoing federal law by passing and enforcing State laws to the contrary. We can't have States undermining the national system. To the extent they disagree with federal law, they have their representatives in Congress and the President who can work to change that law.

OATH OF OFFICE

2.   The Members of Congress, **the Commissioners, the members of the Council**, the members of the several State legislatures, and all executive and judicial officers, both of the United States and of the several States, shall be bound by oath or affirmation to support **and abide by** this Restated Constitution, but no religious test shall ever be required as a qualification to any office or public trust under the United States. [Art. VI]

An oath or affirmation is a formal promise made orally and aloud. Oaths are made in the Old Testament, even by God. Romans took oaths, and the practice has continued since.

The purpose of requiring an oath or affirmation in the Restated Constitution for all public officers, both national and State, is to reinforce the solemnity of the obligations they are undertaking to support and abide by the Restated Constitution. The newly created Commissioners and Council members are added to the oath requirement. More importantly, the phrase **"and abide by"** is added to make sure that officers taking the oath understand that supporting the Restated Constitution includes abiding by its terms.

The instigation of the January 6th Insurrection and the actions of a number of Senators and Representatives who tried to assist Trump in a coup attempt by making baseless challenges to the election results demonstrated failures to abide by the Constitution. Consequently, this Section spells out their obligation to abide by the Restated Constitution in the hope of curbing such betrayals of their oaths of office in the future.

DISQUALIFICATION FROM OFFICE

3.   No person shall be a Member of Congress, **President, Vice President, Commissioner, judge, or member of the Council** or hold any office, civil or military, under the United States or under any State, who, **as determined by the Commission in the case of offices of the United States, has** engaged in **treason, sedition,** insurrection, rebellion, **advocating the overthrow of the United States government by force, or similar conduct** against the **United States** or given aid or comfort to the enemies thereof. **Nevertheless,** Congress may by a vote of two-thirds remove such disability. [14th Amend., Sect. 3]

This provision was added as part of the 14th Amendment in 1868 to ban from federal and State public and military offices any person who previously took an oath to support the Constitution but then violated the oath by taking part in the South's rebellion against the Union in the Civil War. Fool me once, shame on you—fool me twice, shame on me.

In light of the January 6th Insurrection, this Section expands the offenses that would preclude continued or future public service by a person who participates in or aids others in such conduct, namely, "**treason, sedition, . . . advocating the overthrow of the United States government by force.**" These offenses are borrowed from Section 18 of Article IV regarding bases for impeachment of the President, Vice President, and civil officers of the United States. The phrase "**or similar conduct**" is added to extend the ban to conduct that may not fit neatly under any of these terms but nevertheless has the same effect and causes the same type of harm to our nation.

The more difficult issue to be addressed is how to implement this ban.

In 2023, the Colorado Supreme Court affirmed a state trial judge's finding after a bench trial that Trump had instigated the January 6, 2021 insurrection. While the trial judge was not sure whether Section 3 of the 14th Amendment applied to the office of the President, the Colorado Supreme Court held that it did apply to Presidents and, therefore, banned Trump from appearing on Colorado primary ballots because he was not eligible to serve as President. To avoid future spurious arguments like the one made by Trump that this provision does not apply to Presidents, this new Section expressly names Presidents.

Another issue raised by the chaos Trump has created is who determines whether persons should be disqualified under this Section from holding public office due to their disloyal conduct. Section 3 of the 14th Amendment simply disqualifies from office former office holders who "shall have engaged in Insurrection or rebellion against the same, or given aid or comfort to the enemies thereof" but does not indicate who is empowered to decide whether an individual has so engaged in insurrection or rebellion.

Whom did the drafters of the 14th Amendment intend to make that determination in the case of a Presidential candidate? Was it the Electors of the Electoral College who formally elect the President under the 12th Amendment? Was it the House of Representatives, which chooses the President if no one receives the votes of a majority of Electors under the 12th Amendment? The 12th Amendment, however, has no provision for the Electors or the House to determine the eligibility of the candidates for President equivalent to the power granted in Section 5 of Article I to each House of

Congress to "be the Judge of the Elections, Returns and Qualifications of its own Members . . . ."

Was it the States, which appoint their Electors under Section 1 of Article II? Under Maine state law, its Secretary of State, Shenna Bellows, was empowered to determine the eligibility of Presidential candidates for its ballots, and she banned Trump from the 2024 ballot.[82]

Was it the federal courts, whose "judicial Power shall extend to all Cases, in Law and Equity, arising under this Constitution," as provided in Section 2 of Article III?

Or, was it the State courts, since the States appoint the Electors who elect the President and, therefore, their courts should make the determination?

Regardless of whether it should be a federal or state court, should a judge make the decision in a civil trial, as in the Colorado case, since there would be no right to a jury trial under the 7th Amendment because no money damages would be involved in a suit seeking a declaratory judgment or an injunction? Or, should a person be banned from holding office only after a conviction in a criminal prosecution for the felonies of insurrection or rebellion under 18 U.S.C. § 2383, as discussed in the context of impeachment in Section 18 of Article IV, above?

In *Trump v. Anderson*, 601 U.S. 100 (2024), the Supreme Court unanimously held that no State is empowered to hold an oath-taking insurrectionist unqualified to hold a federal office under Section 3 of the 14th Amendment. Five justices went further and held that Section 5 of the 14th Amendment requires Congressional legislation to establish procedures for disqualifying an oath-taking insurrectionist, even though Section 3 appears to be self-executing, as pointed out in the concurring opinion of three justices.

The Constitution says very little about the qualifications for being President. Section 1 of Article II provides that the President must be a natural born citizen of the United States, over 35 years of age, and a resident of the United States for at least 14 years. The last sentence of the 12th Amendment states that "no person constitutionally ineligible to the office of President shall be eligible to that of Vice-President of the United States." Those were the only provisions in the Constitution that mentioned eligibility for President before ratification of the 14th Amendment in 1868.

Then, in 1933, Section 3 of the 20th Amendment provided that "if the President elect shall have failed to qualify," the "Vice President elect shall act as President until a President shall have qualified." That Section then empowered Congress to enact legislation for how to proceed if both the President-elect and the Vice President-elect fail to qualify.

Was the 20th Amendment envisioning a situation where the President-elect was almost but not quite 35 years old or just shy of 14 years a resident when elected, in which case the Vice President-elect would serve as President until the President-elect's birthday or completion of 14 years of residency in, say, the coming February? In a similar situation, Joe Biden was 29 years old when elected Senator from Delaware but turned the prerequisite age of 30 a few weeks later and before being sworn in as a Senator.

The other two provisions regarding eligibility for serving as President are being a natural born citizen, which cannot be cured, and not being an insurrectionist, which can only be cured by a two-thirds vote of both houses of Congress under the 14th Amendment.

Under the present Constitution, it is conceivable that Trump could be elected President in 2024 but later determined to fail to qualify under the 14th Amendment and, as a result, his Vice President-elect would act as President. While the Presidential Succession Act of 1947 sets up the line of succession when a President or President-elect dies, it is not clear what happens if the President-elect fails to qualify. Again, neither the 20th Amendment nor the Presidential Succession Act of 1947 indicates who determines the qualifications of the President-elect.

In 1968, Eldridge Cleaver, a founder of the Black Panthers, tried to run for President as a candidate of the Peace and Freedom Party, even though he would not be 35 until a year and a half after the January 20, 1969 inauguration. The Hawaii Supreme Court ruled he missed deadlines. *Jones v. Gill*, 50 Haw. 618 (1968). The New York Court of Appeals (its highest court) affirmed the trial judge's ruling that the New York Secretary of State properly refused to add to the ballot the candidates for Presidential Electors proposed by the Peace and Freedom Party because they had not listed the persons whom they were endorsing for President and Vice President, most likely because Cleaver was not yet 35. *Garst v. Lomenzo*, 22 N.Y.2d 956 (1968), *aff'g, In re Garst*, 57 Misc. 2d 1040 (N.Y. Sup. Ct., Albany Co. 1968).

As in the Hawaii case, the New York courts did not decide the issues of whether Cleaver was age-eligible to run for President or who was empowered to decide his eligibility. These cases were decided on the party's failure to comply with filing deadlines or technicalities. That is all the past case law concerning qualifications for serving as President.

One final qualification for the Presidency was added in 1951 by the 22nd Amendment, which provides that "[n]o person shall be elected to the office of the President more than twice." That amendment fails to indicate who or what body shall determine what to do if a President seeks to run for a third term.

The Supreme Court's recent decision in *Trump v. Anderson* is neither satisfactory nor sufficient. It leaves disqualification under Section 3 exclusively in the hands of Congress. As a result, any determination under Section 3 will necessarily be political in nature and will turn on the makeup of Congress at the particular time. What we need, however, is a mechanism for objectively assessing whether a person had committed or participated in insurrection.

Consequently, this Section of the Restated Constitution designates the Commission, as the body running the national elections, to make the determination of whether any person is ineligible or unqualified to serve as a federal officer under this Section. This designation is similar to the current power of the Senate and the House of Representatives to determine the qualifications of their members under Section 5 of Article I, which empowered the House to expel George Santos in 2023 without any criminal conviction for fraud or violation of election laws.

In *Trump v. Anderson*, the Supreme Court permitted a State to disqualify an oath-taking insurrectionist from State offices, and that empowerment is tacitly continued here. After all, States should be allowed to determine the qualifications of their own officers, and the Commission should not interfere.

Another issue is whether this Section should apply, as the 14th Amendment does, only to persons who have held state or federal office before and had taken an oath "to support the Constitution of the United States." In other words, should this Section serve to ban from office also the insurrectionists who stormed the Capitol on January 6, 2021 but had never taken such an oath? One could argue that their crimes were worse than Trump's instigation.

Perhaps, the 14th Amendment was intended to punish only those who violated the oath because Congress viewed them as more disloyal than the lowly farm boy forced into the Confederate Army. Today, however, there appears to be no cogent reason to shield first-time office seekers who were insurrectionists from the ban on serving as a public officer. Thus, this Section's ban applies to any insurrectionist or rebel regardless of prior public office.

Finally, the last sentence of Section 3 of the 14th Amendment, "Congress may by a vote of two-thirds remove such disability," is added reluctantly. Even insurrectionists should be entitled to an appeal, especially if they have been wrongly accused or there are mitigating circumstances. Plus, this right of appeal would provide a check on the Commission.

ARTICLE IX

RATIFICATION AND EFFECTIVE DATE

This Article addresses ratification of the Restated Constitution and when it becomes effective.

RATIFICATION AND EFFECTIVE DATE

1.   **This Restated Constitution shall be deemed ratified** when approved by the legislatures or conventions of **three-fourths of the** States **and shall take effect two years after its ratification (the "Effective Date"). Upon the Effective Date, this Restated Constitution shall be binding on all States, possessions, and territories, including those States that have not approved it, and shall supersede and replace the original Constitution and its amendments in their entirety.** [Art. V; Art. VII]

The approval of the Restated Constitution by 38 of the 50 States constitutes a supermajority of 76% of the States, thereby satisfying the requirement of a three-fourths vote in Article V for amendment of the Constitution. Because we are still operating under the Constitution, Congress will determine whether votes on the proposed Restated Constitution will be conducted by State legislatures or State conventions.

Like the creation or amendment of corporate documents, it is helpful to state in the document itself the date when it becomes effective. Sometimes, parties make the document effective as of a date in the past so that actions taken before the document could be formally signed would be deemed to have been performed pursuant to the document. Sometimes, they sign the document and designate a future date for it to become effective.

The Constitution was ratified when New Hampshire became the ninth State to approve it on June 21, 1788. Because a lot had to been done before the new government could be created, the Congress of the Confederation, which was the national government that loosely connected the sovereign States before the Constitution took effect, directed that elections be held and that the new government would commence over eight months later on March 4, 1789.[83]

Today, we have the luxury of taking two years after ratification to make the Restated Constitution effective. First, we have an ongoing, established form of government and not the same urgency for creating a new one that faced the Framers. Second, there a lot of moving parts with the reconfiguration of Congress and the creation of the Commission and the Council. Third, the Commission needs to draw the boundaries for the Regions and Districts, and candidates need lead-time to run for Congress and the Commission.

In addition to signifying the date when the Restated Constitution will replace the Constitution, the Effective Date will trigger the following provisions:

a. **All persons domiciled or residing in the United States or its possessions or territories on the Effective Date of this Restated Constitution who entered or have remained in the United States illegally shall be deemed citizens of the United States.** Article I, Section 3

b. **In furtherance of such rights** [that is, freedom of safety and freedom from violence], **after the**

Effective Date of this Restated Constitution, no civilian shall have the right to carry any firearm in any area reasonably declared by the Government to be gun-free and off-limits to firearms. Article I, Section 6

c. Moreover, commencing one year after the Effective Date of this Restated Constitution, no civilian shall have the right to use, carry, or possess any weapon of war, including assault weapons and high-capacity magazines or ammunition. Article I, Section 6

d. The Commission shall hold the initial national election for Members of Congress and Commissioners on the first Saturday and Sunday following the first Monday of November in the year that is two years after the next election for President and Vice President following the Effective Date of this Restated Constitution. Article II, Section 3

e. No Member may serve in Congress for more than a total of 16 years, whether or not consecutive, after the initial national election held following the Effective Date. Article III, Section 2

f. Notwithstanding the foregoing, for the purpose of calculating the remaining terms of judges serving as of and prior to the Effective Date, only half of the previous service time shall count toward the 25-year limit and no age limit shall be imposed. Article V, Section 3

The Restated Constitution, once ratified, will bind even States that did not approve it. Amendment of the Constitution does not require unanimity to be binding on all. As stated in the discussion on secession in Article VI, the

States have been wedded for eternity and must honor all ratified amendments.

This Section provides that the Restated Constitution is the only document serving as America's constitution because it replaces the original Constitution and its amendments altogether. This concept first appears in the Preamble and Recitals before Article I. It is repeated here to avoid any argument that the Preamble and Recitals simply explain background and are not an operative part of the Restated Constitution.

PART THREE

RATIFICATION OF THE RESTATED CONSTITUION

T he first purpose of the Constitution, as stated in its preamble, was "to form a more perfect Union." English
grammatical rules have evolved since the 18th Century, and
we are now taught that the adjective "perfect" is a super-
lative. Consequently, today's grammar police would issue a
ticket for the use of the comparative "more" to modify
"perfect." For, if something is considered perfect, it cannot
be made more perfect. In fact, the word "perfect" derives
from the Latin meaning "thoroughly done."

On the other hand, perhaps, the Framers knew perfectly
well that nothing created by humans can truly be perfect.
Maybe, they meant to imply that as great as the government
they were conceiving and constructing was, there would always be room for improvement. Surely, by adding rules for
amendment in Article V, they knew that their finished
product was not finished. In other words, the Constitution
was more perfect than the Articles of Confederation it was
replacing, and amendments to the Constitution would make
the Union more perfect in the future.

This overhaul and rewriting of the Constitution has not
been intended to be simply an intellectual exercise. It was
undertaken in an attempt to cure the defects and deficiencies
apparent in a Constitution that fails to fit the needs of

today's America, whether the shortcomings arise from the original language and structure, from the Supreme Court's interpretations and reversals over the years, or simply from a changed country and world. The discussions above criticize the Supreme Court a lot, but, to be fair, there's only so much even the best mechanics can do with an old, broken-down car whose obsolete parts are no longer available.

So, how do we implement this self-improvement guide for America? How do we go beyond discussing and debating these ideas as playful, hypothetical filler on political news shows and actually ratify the Restated Constitution?

THE CONSTITUTIONAL AMENDMENT ROUTES

The only way to substitute the Restated Constitution for the Constitution is by wholesale amendment of the Constitution. The discussion of the amendment process in Section 2 of Article VII points out that there are two ways to propose amendments under Article V of the Constitution: (1) by a two-thirds vote in both the Senate and the House or (2) through a constitutional convention called for by Congress when two-thirds of the States apply to Congress for such a convention.

The first path would be an exercise in futility. While Congress has not proposed to the States a new amendment since the Equal Rights Amendment in 1972, each year Senators and Representatives introduce bills to amend the Constitution that die quiet deaths. In fact, most of them never make it out of committee.

The more arduous obstacle to overcome, however, will be the Congressional members' self-interest in preserving their stranglehold over their offices so they can continue to enjoy power and prestige for years to come. They are not going to like the consolidation of the two houses of Congress, the reduction from 535 members combined in the Senate and the House to 100 Members in the new Congress, and the 16-year limit imposed on their terms in Section 2 of Article III. Forget about this proposed Restated Constitution getting out of committee, it is virtually inconceivable that any Representative or Senator, even one who has decided not to run for re-election, would have the courage or nerve to even introduce it. The Restated Constitution would not die a quiet death in Congress. Rather, it would be dead on arrival, the ultimate nonstarter.

Aside from Senators and Representatives, the only other group that might possibly oppose the Restated Constitution out of self-interest would be federal judges, who might not like the 25-year term limit in Section 3 of Article V, although current judges are exempted from the requirement of retirement at age 75. Since sitting judges are not involved in the amendment process, we need not worry too much about their opposition. Once the Restated Constitution is ratified, they will simply have to follow it.

There isn't any change in the Restated Constitution that would cause an upstanding President to oppose it. Because so many amendments have already refined the rules regarding the Presidency, Article IV of the Restated Constitution primarily gathers them all together in a coherent sequence. The handful of changes that are made should not be objectionable: election by popular vote (Section 1); adding "abide by" the Constitution to the Presidential oath (Section 4); prohibiting self-pardons and pardons of co-conspirators (Section 15); and more specific grounds for impeachment (Section 18). A law-abiding President should also not object to the overriding of the Supreme Court's recent creation of criminal immunity (Section 19).

So, since the path through Congress is a dead end, that leaves us with the alternative path of lobbying State legislatures to apply to Congress to call for a national constitutional convention at which the Restated Constitution can be debated, revised, and proposed by a two-thirds vote. Lobbying State legislatures removes the self-interest obstacle that Congress presents. After all, State legislators will not be greatly affected by the Restated Constitution. They will not have to run for office in a larger District for fewer seats for a capped term.

Article V of the Constitution clearly provides that "on the Application of the Legislatures of two thirds of the several States," Congress "shall call a Convention for proposing Amendments . . . ." This language, as Hamilton explained in the final essay, *The Federalist* No. 85, is mandatory and gives Congress no discretion but to call a convention once two-thirds of the States (that is, 34 States) have applied for one.

If 34 States apply for a convention and if the convention proposes the Restated Constitution to the States, then the Restated Constitution will replace the Constitution if three-fourths of the States (that is, 38 States) ratify it, either through their legislatures or State conventions as directed by Congress. If 34 State legislatures like the Restated Constitution enough to apply for a convention, then presumably their delegates will vote in favor of it at the convention, and we will need to convince only four more States to vote for it at the convention to propose it to the States for ratification. So, the first step will be to convince 34 State legislatures to call for a convention.

While the convention path is the only practical one for proposing the Restated Constitution, such a convention has never been called and neither the Constitution nor the essays in *The Federalist* explain how such a convention shall be assembled or function after Congress calls for one.[84]

Perhaps, such a convention would follow the Federal Convention of 1787 as its model, to the extent we can reconstruct what occurred, and then modernize it by, for example, following the parliamentary procedure laid out in *Robert's Rules of Order*, which was first published almost a century later in 1876. There will probably have to be a pre-convention meeting to determine such matters as how many delegates each State can send, whether each State gets a single vote or multiple votes based on population, and whether the convention shall propose amendments to the States by a simple majority vote or a supermajority vote.

One other quirk of the amendment process in Article V is that regardless of whether the proposed amendment comes from Congress or a convention, Congress may determine whether the mode of ratification is through action by State legislatures or State conventions. Again, Article V provides no information or details about State conventions.

Despite this provision, Congress has expressly directed the mode of ratification in only four amendments: the 18th Amendment instituting Prohibition (legislatures), 20th Amendment regarding Presidential and Congressional terms and Presidential succession (legislatures), 21st Amendment repealing Prohibition (conventions), and 22nd Amendment limiting the President's term (legislatures). The 21st Amendment was the only one ratified by conventions, as discussed below.

THE GRASSROOTS ROUTES

The Restated Constitution contains many provisions, changes, and innovations that should appeal to many various special interest groups.

The expanded personal rights, liberties, and freedoms in Article I, the new Bill of Rights, should appeal to libertarians and everyone who believes the Government should stay out of their bedrooms and lives and leave them alone. The right to privacy in Section 1 of Article I should appeal to the LGBTQ+ sector for its freedom of gender identity and right to gay marriage, to sexually active adults for its right to contraceptives, and to the religious right for its freedom of worship and religion. The right to abortion in Section 2 should appeal to women, medical providers, and Planned Parenthood. The citizenship provisions and amnesty for illegal aliens in Section 3 should appeal to immigrants. The voting rights in Section 4 and the Commission's control over national elections in Article II should appeal to minorities, especially Blacks, whose franchise continues to be blocked by gerrymandering and rules tending to discourage voter registration and voting. The fortified freedom of speech in Section 5 should appeal to librarians and publishers battling censorship, while the provision carving out hate crimes should appeal to groups like the Anti-Defamation League.

The freedom of safety and freedom from violence in Section 6 should appeal to survivors and families of victims of mass shootings, students of all ages, parents and relatives of students, and basically every sane person in the country. The heightened ban on excessive bail in Section 8, the repeal of capital punishment in Section 11, and the payment of minimum wage in prison in Section 14 should appeal to the poor and Blacks, both of whom suffer disproportionately in the criminal justice system. The right to basic human necessities in Section 15 should appeal to everyone because our society will become stronger and our economy will become more robust if everyone enjoys decent healthcare, housing, food, clothing, and education.

The restructure and streamlining of the national government in Articles II, III, and V should appeal to fiscal conservatives and progressive liberals, alike. The greater accountability for Presidents should appeal to everyone who cherishes our democratic republic.

While the ideologies of some of these groups overlap, some of them do not see eye to eye on multiple issues. Nevertheless, there is something in the Restated Constitution for them all, and, therefore, they should pull together for its ratification.

While most of the amendments to the Constitution arose from Congressional initiatives, the 18th Amendment (Prohibition), the 19th Amendment (women's suffrage), and the 21st Amendment (repeal of Prohibition) resulted from efforts of special interest groups.

The temperance movement advocating abstinence from alcohol consumption began in America in the mid-19th Century. It gained traction among rural, agrarian communities, Protestants (mainly, Baptists and Methodists), and nativists who were hostile to immigrants and Catholics. The movement spread through groups such as the Woman's Christian Temperance Union, the Sons of Temperance, the Prohibition party, and, most effectively, the Anti-Saloon League of America. Starting at the ground level, these organizations had succeeded in passing "dry" laws at local and State levels through intensive lobbying and litigation to the point where 33 of the 48 States had already prohibited alcohol at the time that the organizations managed to persuade Congress to propose the 18th Amendment at the end of 1917. This proposal resulted in part from the addition of 13 Western States that were admitted after the Civil War as primarily dry states.

A women's suffrage amendment was first introduced in Congress in 1869 but not proposed by Congress until 1919. In contrast to the Prohibition amendment, at the time Congress proposed the 19th Amendment, women could vote in all elections in only a third of States and could vote in Presidential elections in over half of the States. The women's suffrage movement began with the Seneca Falls Convention for Women's Rights in upstate New York in 1848. Groups like the National Woman Suffrage Association and the American Woman Suffrage Association employed protest marches, petitions, marketing, litigation, and legislation to make inroads and succeeded primarily in the West.

The repeal of Prohibition through the 21st Amendment was spearheaded by a different type of special interest group and achieved its goal much more quickly. The Voluntary Committee of Lawyers was formed in 1927 by a dozen Ivy League-educated, prominent conservative lawyers of the New York City Bar who viewed the 18th Amendment as an improper intrusion upon the powers reserved to the States and the People under the 10th Amendment. The Voluntary Committee of Lawyers and other organizations advocating for repeal, like the Association Against the Prohibition Amendment, the Women's Organization for National Prohibition Reform, the Republican Citizens' Committee Against National Prohibition, the American Bar Association, and the American

Legion, viewed Prohibition as a failed policy that resulted in crime, gangs, loss of profits to legitimate companies and organizations, loss of tax revenue, and flouting of the law by otherwise law-abiding citizens, among other things.

The Voluntary Committee of Lawyers organized sophisticated legal teams in States throughout the country. They successfully pressured both the Republican and Democratic parties to call for a Congressional proposal for repeal on their national platforms for the Presidential election of 1932. As a result, in less than six years, the Voluntary Committee of Lawyers managed to get Congress to propose the 21st Amendment on February 20, 1933, and it was ratified by State conventions on December 5, 1933, one of the shortest spans from submission of proposal to ratification in the history of Constitutional amendments.

A significant reason why the 21st Amendment was ratified so quickly after its submission to the States is that Congress stipulated in the proposed amendment itself that it must be ratified "by conventions in the several States." This was no happenstance. The Voluntary Committee of Lawyers pushed for ratification by State conventions rather than by State legislatures, believing not only that conventions were more democratic but also that the amendment stood a better chance of ratification through conventions than legislatures. The distrust of State legislatures that brought about the switch from selection of Senators by State legislatures to popular elections in the 17th Amendment in 1913 persisted at the time. Consequently, the Voluntary Committee of Lawyers sponsored a model ratifying convention law that was followed by many States just for addressing the 21st Amendment.

Currently, it appears that three States (Florida, New Mexico, and Vermont) have standing laws governing a State convention in the event Congress submits a proposed amendment and directs ratification through State conventions.[85] In the event that occurs, the other 47 States will have to decide such issues as how many delegates should attend the convention, how they should be elected or appointed, whether they should be elected or appointed at large or by district, and whether they should deliberate about the proposed amendment or simply vote in accordance with the wishes as expressed by the voters electing them, as in the Electoral College. Perhaps, we can revive and update the Voluntary Committee of Lawyers' model ratifying convention law to guide these States.

ACTION PLAN

Obviously, the only viable first step to ratification of the Restated Constitution would be to persuade the legislatures of 34 States to apply to Congress to call for a national convention for proposing the Restated Constitution. As in the discussion above concerning the makeup of State conventions for ratification, we would need to address the basic composition, structure, and operation of a national convention. Should each State have the same number of delegates or should the number be in proportion to their populations? Should each State have only a single vote or multiple votes proportionate to their populations? Should the convention vote solely yea or nay on the Restated Constitution as drafted, or should it deliberate over all provisions and, if appropriate, revise it? If the convention approves the Restated Constitution, whether as drafted or revised, should it direct Congress to direct the States to vote for ratification in their legislatures or in State ratifying conventions?

So, how do we get 34 State legislatures to apply to Congress to call for a national convention, a process that has never been utilized? We can learn from the Prohibition, women's suffrage, and repeal movements how to effect Constitutional change through lobbying, testifying, demonstrating, campaigning, and, if appropriate, litigating. If those movements could raise the necessary funding to pursue their missions through small donations from many people in the days before GoFundMe, we surely can with the resources we have to reach millions of people.

We should also call on progressive billionaires who are trying to make the country and the world a better place in which to live. Clearly, working for change within the political system by donating to the campaigns of seemingly worthy politicians and funding issue-oriented litigation is not working. Congress isn't doing anything significant on protecting us from mass shootings, and the Supreme Court is taking away rights like the right to abortion and protecting Presidents from criminal prosecution. The best way for billionaires to improve the system, then, is to financially support the restructuring of the system through the Restated Constitution.

We need to create an organization to spearhead the ratification of the Restated Constitution. Let's call it the "Reframers Alliance for a More Perfect Union Pact." That's "RAMP UP," for short.

Dire times call for bold action. Let's install Constitution 2.0. We can do this, America.

★ APPENDIX A

UNITED STATES CONSTITUTION, AS CURRENTLY AMENDED

W e the People of the United States, in Order to form a more perfect Union, establish Justice, insure domestic Tranquility, provide for the common defence, promote the general Welfare, and secure the Blessings of Liberty to ourselves and our Posterity, do ordain and establish this Constitution for the United States of America.

ARTICLE I

Section 1.

All legislative Powers herein granted shall be vested in a Congress of the United States, which shall consist of a Senate and House of Representatives.

Section 2.

The House of Representatives shall be composed of Members chosen every second Year by the People of the several States, and the Electors in each State shall have the Qualifications requisite for Electors of the most numerous Branch of the State Legislature.

No Person shall be a Representative who shall not have attained to the Age of twenty five Years, and been seven Years a Citizen of the United States, and who shall not, when elected, be an Inhabitant of that State in which he shall be chosen.

Representatives and direct Taxes shall be apportioned among the several States which may be included within this Union, according to their respective Numbers, which shall be determined by adding to the whole Number of free Persons, including those bound to Service for a Term of Years, and excluding Indians not taxed, three fifths of all other Persons.[1] The actual Enumeration shall be made within three Years after the first Meeting of the Congress of the United States, and within every subsequent Term of ten Years, in such Manner as they shall by Law direct. The Number of Representatives shall not exceed one for every thirty Thousand, but each State shall have at Least one Representative; and until such enumeration shall be made, the State of New Hampshire shall be entitled to chuse three, Massachusetts eight, Rhode-Island and Providence Plantations one, Connecticut five, New-York six, New Jersey four, Pennsylvania eight, Delaware one, Maryland six, Virginia ten, North Carolina five, South Carolina five, and Georgia three.

When vacancies happen in the Representation from any State, the Executive Authority thereof shall issue Writs of Election to fill such Vacancies.

The House of Representatives shall chuse their Speaker and other Officers; and shall have the sole Power of Impeachment.

---

[1] Language in Italics was modified and superseded by later amendments. This particular language was changed by Section 2 of the 14th Amendment.

Section 3.

The Senate of the United States shall be composed of two Senators from each State, _chosen by the Legislature thereof,_[2] for six Years; and each Senator shall have one Vote.

Immediately after they shall be assembled in Consequence of the first Election, they shall be divided as equally as may be into three Classes. The Seats of the Senators of the first Class shall be vacated at the Expiration of the second Year, of the second Class at the Expiration of the fourth Year, and of the third Class at the Expiration of the sixth Year, so that one third may be chosen every second Year; _and if Vacancies happen by Resignation, or otherwise, during the Recess of the Legislature of any State, the Executive thereof may make temporary Appointments until the next Meeting of the Legislature, which shall then fill such Vacancies._[3]

No Person shall be a Senator who shall not have attained to the Age of thirty Years, and been nine Years a Citizen of the United States, and who shall not, when elected, be an Inhabitant of that State for which he shall be chosen.

The Vice President of the United States shall be President of the Senate, but shall have no Vote, unless they be equally divided.

The Senate shall chuse their other Officers, and also a President pro tempore, in the Absence of the Vice President, or when he shall exercise the Office of President of the United States.

The Senate shall have the sole Power to try all Impeachments. When sitting for that Purpose, they shall be on Oath or Affirmation. When the President of the United States is tried, the Chief Justice shall preside: And no Person

---

[2] Changed by the 17th Amendment.
[3] Changed by the 17th Amendment.

shall be convicted without the Concurrence of two thirds of the Members present.

Judgment in Cases of Impeachment shall not extend further than to removal from Office, and disqualification to hold and enjoy any Office of honor, Trust or Profit under the United States: but the Party convicted shall nevertheless be liable and subject to Indictment, Trial, Judgment and Punishment, according to Law.

Section 4.

The Times, Places and Manner of holding Elections for Senators and Representatives, shall be prescribed in each State by the Legislature thereof; but the Congress may at any time by Law make or alter such Regulations, except as to the Places of chusing Senators.

The Congress shall assemble at least once in every Year, and such Meeting shall be on *the first Monday in December,*[4] unless they shall by Law appoint a different Day.

Section 5.

Each House shall be the Judge of the Elections, Returns and Qualifications of its own Members, and a Majority of each shall constitute a Quorum to do Business; but a smaller Number may adjourn from day to day, and may be authorized to compel the Attendance of absent Members, in such Manner, and under such Penalties as each House may provide.

Each House may determine the Rules of its Proceedings, punish its Members for disorderly Behaviour, and, with the Concurrence of two thirds, expel a Member.

---

[4] Changed by the Section 2 of the 20th Amendment.

Each House shall keep a Journal of its Proceedings, and from time to time publish the same, excepting such Parts as may in their Judgment require Secrecy; and the Yeas and Nays of the Members of either House on any question shall, at the Desire of one fifth of those Present, be entered on the Journal.

Neither House, during the Session of Congress, shall, without the Consent of the other, adjourn for more than three days, nor to any other Place than that in which the two Houses shall be sitting.

Section 6.

The Senators and Representatives shall receive a Compensation for their Services, to be ascertained by Law, and paid out of the Treasury of the United States. They shall in all Cases, except Treason, Felony and Breach of the Peace, be privileged from Arrest during their Attendance at the Session of their respective Houses, and in going to and returning from the same; and for any Speech or Debate in either House, they shall not be questioned in any other Place.

No Senator or Representative shall, during the Time for which he was elected, be appointed to any civil Office under the Authority of the United States, which shall have been created, or the Emoluments whereof shall have been encreased during such time; and no Person holding any Office under the United States, shall be a Member of either House during his Continuance in Office.

Section 7.

All Bills for raising Revenue shall originate in the House of Representatives; but the Senate may propose or concur with Amendments as on other Bills.

Every Bill which shall have passed the House of Representatives and the Senate, shall, before it become a Law, be presented to the President of the United States; If he approve he shall sign it, but if not he shall return it, with his Objections to that House in which it shall have originated, who shall enter the Objections at large on their Journal, and proceed to reconsider it. If after such Reconsideration two thirds of that House shall agree to pass the Bill, it shall be sent, together with the Objections, to the other House, by which it shall likewise be reconsidered, and if approved by two thirds of that House, it shall become a Law. But in all such Cases the Votes of both Houses shall be determined by yeas and Nays, and the Names of the Persons voting for and against the Bill shall be entered on the Journal of each House respectively. If any Bill shall not be returned by the President within ten Days (Sundays excepted) after it shall have been presented to him, the Same shall be a Law, in like Manner as if he had signed it, unless the Congress by their Adjournment prevent its Return, in which Case it shall not be a Law.

Every Order, Resolution, or Vote to which the Concurrence of the Senate and House of Representatives may be necessary (except on a question of Adjournment) shall be presented to the President of the United States; and before the Same shall take Effect, shall be approved by him, or being disapproved by him, shall be repassed by two thirds of the Senate and House of Representatives, according to the Rules and Limitations prescribed in the Case of a Bill.

Section 8.

The Congress shall have Power To lay and collect Taxes, Duties, Imposts and Excises, to pay the Debts and provide for the common Defence and general Welfare of the United States; but all Duties, Imposts and Excises shall be uniform throughout the United States;

To borrow Money on the credit of the United States;

To regulate Commerce with foreign Nations, and among the several States, and with the Indian Tribes;

To establish an uniform Rule of Naturalization, and uniform Laws on the subject of Bankruptcies throughout the United States;

To coin Money, regulate the Value thereof, and of foreign Coin, and fix the Standard of Weights and Measures;

To provide for the Punishment of counterfeiting the Securities and current Coin of the United States;

To establish Post Offices and post Roads;

To promote the Progress of Science and useful Arts, by securing for limited Times to Authors and Inventors the exclusive Right to their respective Writings and Discoveries;

To constitute Tribunals inferior to the supreme Court;

To define and punish Piracies and Felonies committed on the high Seas, and Offences against the Law of Nations;

To declare War, grant Letters of Marque and Reprisal, and make Rules concerning Captures on Land and Water;

To raise and support Armies, but no Appropriation of Money to that Use shall be for a longer Term than two Years;

To provide and maintain a Navy;

To make Rules for the Government and Regulation of the land and naval Forces;

To provide for calling forth the Militia to execute the Laws of the Union, suppress Insurrections and repel Invasions;

To provide for organizing, arming, and disciplining, the Militia, and for governing such Part of them as may be employed in the Service of the United States, reserving to the States respectively, the Appointment of the Officers, and the Authority of training the Militia according to the discipline prescribed by Congress;

To exercise exclusive Legislation in all Cases whatsoever, over such District (not exceeding ten Miles square) as may, by Cession of particular States, and the Acceptance of Congress, become the Seat of the Government of the United States, and to exercise like Authority over all Places purchased by the Consent of the Legislature of the State in which the Same shall be, for the Erection of Forts, Magazines, Arsenals, dock-Yards, and other needful Buildings;—And

To make all Laws which shall be necessary and proper for carrying into Execution the foregoing Powers, and all other Powers vested by this Constitution in the Government of the United States, or in any Department or Officer thereof.

Section 9.

The Migration or Importation of such Persons as any of the States now existing shall think proper to admit, shall not be prohibited by the Congress prior to the Year one thousand eight hundred and eight, but a Tax or duty may be imposed on such Importation, not exceeding ten dollars for each Person.

The Privilege of the Writ of Habeas Corpus shall not be suspended, unless when in Cases of Rebellion or Invasion the public Safety may require it.

No Bill of Attainder or ex post facto Law shall be passed.

No Capitation, or other direct, Tax shall be laid, *unless in Proportion to the Census or enumeration herein before directed to be taken.*[5]

---

[5] Changed by the 16th Amendment.

No Tax or Duty shall be laid on Articles exported from any State.

No Preference shall be given by any Regulation of Commerce or Revenue to the Ports of one State over those of another: nor shall Vessels bound to, or from, one State, be obliged to enter, clear, or pay Duties in another.

No Money shall be drawn from the Treasury, but in Consequence of Appropriations made by Law; and a regular Statement and Account of the Receipts and Expenditures of all public Money shall be published from time to time.

No Title of Nobility shall be granted by the United States: And no Person holding any Office of Profit or Trust under them, shall, without the Consent of the Congress, accept of any present, Emolument, Office, or Title, of any kind whatever, from any King, Prince, or foreign State.

Section 10.

No State shall enter into any Treaty, Alliance, or Confederation; grant Letters of Marque and Reprisal; coin Money; emit Bills of Credit; make any Thing but gold and silver Coin a Tender in Payment of Debts; pass any Bill of Attainder, ex post facto Law, or Law impairing the Obligation of Contracts, or grant any Title of Nobility.

No State shall, without the Consent of the Congress, lay any Imposts or Duties on Imports or Exports, except what may be absolutely necessary for executing its inspection Laws: and the net Produce of all Duties and Imposts, laid by any State on Imports or Exports, shall be for the Use of the Treasury of the United States; and all such Laws shall be subject to the Revision and Controul of the Congress.

No State shall, without the Consent of Congress, lay any Duty of Tonnage, keep Troops, or Ships of War in time of

Peace, enter into any Agreement or Compact with another State, or with a foreign Power, or engage in War, unless actually invaded, or in such imminent Danger as will not admit of delay.

ARTICLE II

Section 1.

The executive Power shall be vested in a President of the United States of America. He shall hold his Office during the Term of four Years, and, together with the Vice President, chosen for the same Term, be elected, as follows

Each State shall appoint, in such Manner as the Legislature thereof may direct, a Number of Electors, equal to the whole Number of Senators and Representatives to which the State may be entitled in the Congress: but no Senator or Representative, or Person holding an Office of Trust or Profit under the United States, shall be appointed an Elector.

The Electors shall meet in their respective States, and vote by Ballot for two Persons, of whom one at least shall not be an Inhabitant of the same State with themselves. And they shall make a List of all the Persons voted for, and of the Number of Votes for each; which List they shall sign and certify, and transmit sealed to the Seat of the Government of the United States, directed to the President of the Senate. The President of the Senate shall, in the Presence of the Senate and House of Representatives, open all the Certificates, and the Votes shall then be counted. The Person having the greatest Number of Votes shall be the President, if such Number be a Majority of the whole Number of Electors appointed; and if there be more than one who have such Majority, and have an equal Number of Votes, then the House of Representatives shall immediately chuse by Ballot one of them for President; and if no Person have a Majority, then from the five highest on the List the said House shall in like Manner chuse the President. But in chusing the President, the Votes shall be taken by States, the Representation from each State having one Vote; A quorum for this Purpose shall consist of a Member or Members from two thirds of the States, and a Majority of all the States shall be necessary to a Choice. In every Case, after the Choice of the President, the Person having the greatest Number of Votes of the Electors shall be the Vice President. But if there should remain two or more who have equal Votes, the Senate shall chuse from them by Ballot the Vice President.[6]

The Congress may determine the Time of chusing the Electors, and the Day on which they shall give their Votes; which Day shall be the same throughout the United States.

No Person except a natural born Citizen, or a Citizen of the United States, at the time of the Adoption of this Constitution, shall be eligible to the Office of President; neither shall any Person be eligible to that Office who shall not have attained to the Age of thirty five Years, and been fourteen Years a Resident within the United States.

In Case of the Removal of the President from Office, or of his Death, Resignation, or Inability to discharge the Powers and Duties of the said Office, the Same shall devolve on the Vice President, and the Congress may by Law provide for the Case of Removal, Death, Resignation or Inability, both of the President and Vice President, declaring what Officer shall then act as President, and such Officer shall act accordingly, until the Disability be removed, or a President shall be elected.[7]

---

[6] Changed by the 12th Amendment.

[7] Changed by the 25th Amendment.

The President shall, at stated Times, receive for his Services, a Compensation, which shall neither be encreased nor diminished during the Period for which he shall have been elected, and he shall not receive within that Period any other Emolument from the United States, or any of them.

Before he enter on the Execution of his Office, he shall take the following Oath or Affirmation:—"I do solemnly swear (or affirm) that I will faithfully execute the Office of President of the United States, and will to the best of my Ability, preserve, protect and defend the Constitution of the United States."

Section 2.

The President shall be Commander in Chief of the Army and Navy of the United States, and of the Militia of the several States, when called into the actual Service of the United States; he may require the Opinion, in writing, of the principal Officer in each of the executive Departments, upon any Subject relating to the Duties of their respective Offices, and he shall have Power to grant Reprieves and Pardons for Offences against the United States, except in Cases of Impeachment.

He shall have Power, by and with the Advice and Consent of the Senate, to make Treaties, provided two thirds of the Senators present concur; and he shall nominate, and by and with the Advice and Consent of the Senate, shall appoint Ambassadors, other public Ministers and Consuls, Judges of the supreme Court, and all other Officers of the United States, whose Appointments are not herein otherwise provided for, and which shall be established by Law: but the Congress may by Law vest the Appointment of such inferior Officers, as they think proper, in the President alone, in the Courts of Law, or in the Heads of Departments.

The President shall have Power to fill up all Vacancies that may happen during the Recess of the Senate, by granting Commissions which shall expire at the End of their next Session.

Section 3.

He shall from time to time give to the Congress Information of the State of the Union, and recommend to their Consideration such Measures as he shall judge necessary and expedient; he may, on extraordinary Occasions, convene both Houses, or either of them, and in Case of Disagreement between them, with Respect to the Time of Adjournment, he may adjourn them to such Time as he shall think proper; he shall receive Ambassadors and other public Ministers; he shall take Care that the Laws be faithfully executed, and shall Commission all the Officers of the United States.

Section 4.

The President, Vice President and all civil Officers of the United States, shall be removed from Office on Impeachment for, and Conviction of, Treason, Bribery, or other high Crimes and Misdemeanors.

ARTICLE III

Section 1.

The judicial Power of the United States, shall be vested in one supreme Court, and in such inferior Courts as the Congress may from time to time ordain and establish. The Judges, both of the supreme and inferior Courts, shall hold their Offices during good Behaviour, and shall, at stated Times, receive for their Services, a Compensation, which shall not be diminished during their Continuance in Office.

Section 2.

The judicial Power shall extend to all Cases, in Law and Equity, arising under this Constitution, the Laws of the United States, and Treaties made, or which shall be made, under their Authority;—to all Cases affecting Ambassadors, other public Ministers and Consuls;—to all Cases of admiralty and maritime Jurisdiction;—to Controversies to which the United States shall be a Party;—to Controversies between two or more States;— *between a State and Citizens of another State*,[8]—between Citizens of different States,— between Citizens of the same State claiming Lands under Grants of different States, and between a State, or the Citizens thereof, and foreign States, Citizens or Subjects.

In all Cases affecting Ambassadors, other public Ministers and Consuls, and those in which a State shall be Party, the supreme Court shall have original Jurisdiction. In all the other Cases before mentioned, the supreme Court shall have appellate Jurisdiction, both as to Law and Fact, with such Exceptions, and under such Regulations as the Congress shall make.

The Trial of all Crimes, except in Cases of Impeachment, shall be by Jury; and such Trial shall be held in the State where the said Crimes shall have been committed; but when not committed within any State, the Trial shall be at such Place or Places as the Congress may by Law have directed.

---

[8] Changed by the 11th Amendment.

Section 3.

Treason against the United States, shall consist only in levying War against them, or in adhering to their Enemies, giving them Aid and Comfort. No Person shall be convicted of Treason unless on the Testimony of two Witnesses to the same overt Act, or on Confession in open Court.

The Congress shall have Power to declare the Punishment of Treason, but no Attainder of Treason shall work Corruption of Blood, or Forfeiture except during the Life of the Person attainted.

ARTICLE IV

Section 1.

Full Faith and Credit shall be given in each State to the public Acts, Records, and judicial Proceedings of every other State. And the Congress may by general Laws prescribe the Manner in which such Acts, Records and Proceedings shall be proved, and the Effect thereof.

Section 2.

The Citizens of each State shall be entitled to all Privileges and Immunities of Citizens in the several States.

A Person charged in any State with Treason, Felony, or other Crime, who shall flee from Justice, and be found in another State, shall on Demand of the executive Authority of the State from which he fled, be delivered up, to be removed to the State having Jurisdiction of the Crime.

No Person held to Service or Labour in one State, under the Laws thereof, escaping into another, shall, in Consequence of any Law or Regulation therein, be discharged from such Service or

Labour, but shall be delivered up on Claim of the Party to whom such Service or Labour may be due.[9]

Section 3.

New States may be admitted by the Congress into this Union; but no new State shall be formed or erected within the Jurisdiction of any other State; nor any State be formed by the Junction of two or more States, or Parts of States, without the Consent of the Legislatures of the States concerned as well as of the Congress.

The Congress shall have Power to dispose of and make all needful Rules and Regulations respecting the Territory or other Property belonging to the United States; and nothing in this Constitution shall be so construed as to Prejudice any Claims of the United States, or of any particular State.

Section 4.

The United States shall guarantee to every State in this Union a Republican Form of Government, and shall protect each of them against Invasion; and on Application of the Legislature, or of the Executive (when the Legislature cannot be convened) against domestic Violence.

ARTICLE V

The Congress, whenever two thirds of both Houses shall deem it necessary, shall propose Amendments to this Constitution, or, on the Application of the Legislatures of two thirds of the several States, shall call a Convention for proposing Amendments, which, in either Case, shall be valid to all Intents and Purposes, as Part of this Constitution,

[9] Changed by the 13th Amendment.

when ratified by the Legislatures of three fourths of the several States, or by Conventions in three fourths thereof, as the one or the other Mode of Ratification may be proposed by the Congress; Provided that no Amendment which may be made prior to the Year One thousand eight hundred and eight shall in any Manner affect the first and fourth Clauses in the Ninth Section of the first Article; and that no State, without its Consent, shall be deprived of its equal Suffrage in the Senate.

ARTICLE VI

All Debts contracted and Engagements entered into, before the Adoption of this Constitution, shall be as valid against the United States under this Constitution, as under the Confederation.

This Constitution, and the Laws of the United States which shall be made in Pursuance thereof; and all Treaties made, or which shall be made, under the Authority of the United States, shall be the supreme Law of the Land; and the Judges in every State shall be bound thereby, any Thing in the Constitution or Laws of any State to the Contrary notwithstanding.

The Senators and Representatives before mentioned, and the Members of the several State Legislatures, and all executive and judicial Officers, both of the United States and of the several States, shall be bound by Oath or Affirmation, to support this Constitution; but no religious Test shall ever be required as a Qualification to any Office or public Trust under the United States.

ARTICLE VII

The Ratification of the Conventions of nine States, shall be sufficient for the Establishment of this Constitution between the States so ratifying the Same.

Adopted by the Federal Convention on September 17, 1787 and ratified by the requisite ninth State, New Hampshire, on June 21, 1788.

AMENDMENT I

Congress shall make no law respecting an establishment of religion, or prohibiting the free exercise thereof; or abridging the freedom of speech, or of the press; or the right of the people peaceably to assemble, and to petition the Government for a redress of grievances.

AMENDMENT II

A well regulated Militia, being necessary to the security of a free State, the right of the people to keep and bear Arms, shall not be infringed.

AMENDMENT III

No Soldier shall, in time of peace be quartered in any house, without the consent of the Owner, nor in time of war, but in a manner to be prescribed by law.

AMENDMENT IV

The right of the people to be secure in their persons, houses, papers, and effects, against unreasonable searches and seizures, shall not be violated, and no Warrants shall issue, but upon probable cause, supported by Oath or affirmation, and particularly describing the place to be searched, and the persons or things to be seized.

AMENDMENT V

No person shall be held to answer for a capital, or otherwise infamous crime, unless on a presentment or indictment of a Grand Jury, except in cases arising in the land or naval forces, or in the Militia, when in actual service in time of War or public danger; nor shall any person be subject for the same offence to be twice put in jeopardy of life or limb; nor shall be compelled in any criminal case to be a witness against himself, nor be deprived of life, liberty, or property, without due process of law; nor shall private property be taken for public use, without just compensation.

AMENDMENT VI

In all criminal prosecutions, the accused shall enjoy the right to a speedy and public trial, by an impartial jury of the State and district wherein the crime shall have been committed, which district shall have been previously ascertained by law, and to be informed of the nature and cause of the accusation; to be confronted with the witnesses against him; to have compulsory process for obtaining witnesses in his favor, and to have the Assistance of Counsel for his defence.

AMENDMENT VII

In Suits at common law, where the value in controversy shall exceed twenty dollars, the right of trial by jury shall be preserved, and no fact tried by a jury, shall be otherwise re-examined in any Court of the United States, than according to the rules of the common law.

AMENDMENT VIII

Excessive bail shall not be required, nor excessive fines imposed, nor cruel and unusual punishments inflicted.

AMENDMENT IX

The enumeration in the Constitution, of certain rights, shall not be construed to deny or disparage others retained by the people.

AMENDMENT X

The powers not delegated to the United States by the Constitution, nor prohibited by it to the States, are reserved to the States respectively, or to the people.

The first ten Amendments, known as the Bill of Rights, were ratified on December 15, 1791.

AMENDMENT XI

Passed by Congress March 4, 1794. Ratified February 7, 1795.

(**Note:** Article III, section 2, of the Constitution was modified by the 11th amendment.)

The Judicial power of the United States shall not be construed to extend to any suit in law or equity, commenced or prosecuted against one of the United States by Citizens of another State, or by Citizens or Subjects of any Foreign State.

AMENDMENT XII

Passed by Congress December 9, 1803. Ratified June 15, 1804.

(**Note:** A portion of Article II, section 1 of the Constitution was superseded by the 12th amendment.)

The Electors shall meet in their respective states and vote by ballot for President and Vice-President, one of whom, at least, shall not be an inhabitant of the same state with themselves; they shall name in their ballots the person voted for as President, and in distinct ballots the person voted for as Vice-President, and they shall make distinct lists of all persons voted for as President, and of all persons voted for as Vice-President, and of the number of votes for each, which lists they shall sign and certify, and transmit sealed to the seat of the government of the United States, directed to the President of the Senate; -- the President of the Senate shall, in the presence of the Senate and House of Representatives, open all the certificates and the votes shall then be counted; -- The person having the greatest number of votes for President, shall be the President, if such number be a majority of the whole number of Electors appointed;

and if no person have such majority, then from the persons having the highest numbers not exceeding three on the list of those voted for as President, the House of Representatives shall choose immediately, by ballot, the President. But in choosing the President, the votes shall be taken by states, the representation from each state having one vote; a quorum for this purpose shall consist of a member or members from two-thirds of the states, and a majority of all the states shall be necessary to a choice. *And if the House of Representatives shall not choose a President whenever the right of choice shall devolve upon them, before the fourth day of March next following, then the Vice-President shall act as President, as in case of the death or other constitutional disability of the President.*[10] The person having the greatest number of votes as Vice-President, shall be the Vice-President, if such number be a majority of the whole number of Electors appointed, and if no person have a majority, then from the two highest numbers on the list, the Senate shall choose the Vice-President; a quorum for the purpose shall consist of two-thirds of the whole number of Senators, and a majority of the whole number shall be necessary to a choice. But no person constitutionally ineligible to the office of President shall be eligible to that of Vice-President of the United States.

AMENDMENT XIII

Passed by Congress January 31, 1865. Ratified December 6, 1865.

(**Note:** A portion of Article IV, section 2, of the Constitution was superseded by the 13th amendment.)

---

[10] Changed by Section 3 of the 20th Amendment.

Section 1.

Neither slavery nor involuntary servitude, except as a punishment for crime whereof the party shall have been duly convicted, shall exist within the United States, or any place subject to their jurisdiction.

Section 2.

Congress shall have power to enforce this article by appropriate legislation.

AMENDMENT XIV

Passed by Congress June 13, 1866. Ratified July 9, 1868.

(**Note:** Article I, section 2, of the Constitution was modified by section 2 of the 14th amendment.)

Section 1.

All persons born or naturalized in the United States, and subject to the jurisdiction thereof, are citizens of the United States and of the State wherein they reside. No State shall make or enforce any law which shall abridge the privileges or immunities of citizens of the United States; nor shall any State deprive any person of life, liberty, or property, without due process of law; nor deny to any person within its jurisdiction the equal protection of the laws.

Section 2.

Representatives shall be apportioned among the several States according to their respective numbers, counting the whole number of persons in each State, excluding Indians not taxed. But when the right to vote at any election for the choice of electors for President and Vice-President of the

United States, Representatives in Congress, the Executive and Judicial officers of a State, or the members of the Legislature thereof, is denied to any of the male inhabitants of such State, being *twenty-one years of age*,[11] and citizens of the United States, or in any way abridged, except for participation in rebellion, or other crime, the basis of representation therein shall be reduced in the proportion which the number of such male citizens shall bear to the whole number of male citizens twenty-one years of age in such State.

Section 3.

No person shall be a Senator or Representative in Congress, or elector of President and Vice-President, or hold any office, civil or military, under the United States, or under any State, who, having previously taken an oath, as a member of Congress, or as an officer of the United States, or as a member of any State legislature, or as an executive or judicial officer of any State, to support the Constitution of the United States, shall have engaged in insurrection or rebellion against the same, or given aid or comfort to the enemies thereof. But Congress may by a vote of two-thirds of each House, remove such disability.

Section 4.

The validity of the public debt of the United States, authorized by law, including debts incurred for payment of pensions and bounties for services in suppressing insurrection or rebellion, shall not be questioned. But neither the United States nor any State shall assume or pay any debt or obligation incurred in aid of insurrection or rebellion against the United

---

[11] Changed by Section 1 of the 26th Amendment.

States, or any claim for the loss or emancipation of any slave; but all such debts, obligations and claims shall be held illegal and void.

Section 5.

The Congress shall have power to enforce, by appropriate legislation, the provisions of this article.

AMENDMENT XV

Passed by Congress February 26, 1869. Ratified February 3, 1870.

Section 1.

The right of citizens of the United States to vote shall not be denied or abridged by the United States or by any State on account of race, color, or previous condition of servitude--

Section 2.

The Congress shall have power to enforce this article by appropriate legislation.

AMENDMENT XVI

Passed by Congress July 2, 1909. Ratified February 3, 1913.

(**Note:** Article I, section 9, of the Constitution was modified by amendment 16.)

The Congress shall have power to lay and collect taxes on incomes, from whatever source derived, without apportionment among the several States, and without regard to any census or enumeration.

AMENDMENT XVII

Passed by Congress May 13, 1912. Ratified April 8, 1913.

(**Note:** Article I, section 3, of the Constitution was modified by the 17th amendment.)

The Senate of the United States shall be composed of two Senators from each State, elected by the people thereof, for six years; and each Senator shall have one vote. The electors in each State shall have the qualifications requisite for electors of the most numerous branch of the State legislatures.

When vacancies happen in the representation of any State in the Senate, the executive authority of such State shall issue writs of election to fill such vacancies: Provided, That the legislature of any State may empower the executive thereof to make temporary appointments until the people fill the vacancies by election as the legislature may direct.

This amendment shall not be so construed as to affect the election or term of any Senator chosen before it becomes valid as part of the Constitution.

AMENDMENT XVIII

Passed by Congress December 18, 1917. Ratified January 16, 1919. Repealed by amendment 21.

Section 1.

After one year from the ratification of this article the manufacture, sale, or transportation of intoxicating liquors within, the importation thereof into, or the exportation thereof from the United States and all territory subject to the jurisdiction thereof for beverage purposes is hereby prohibited.

Section 2.

The Congress and the several States shall have concurrent power to enforce this article by appropriate legislation.

Section 3.

This article shall be inoperative unless it shall have been ratified as an amendment to the Constitution by the legislatures of the several States, as provided in the Constitution, within seven years from the date of the submission hereof to the States by the Congress.

AMENDMENT XIX

Passed by Congress June 4, 1919. Ratified August 18, 1920.

The right of citizens of the United States to vote shall not be denied or abridged by the United States or by any State on account of sex.

Congress shall have power to enforce this article by appropriate legislation.

AMENDMENT XX

Passed by Congress March 2, 1932. Ratified January 23, 1933.

(**Note:** Article I, section 4, of the Constitution was modified by section 2 of this amendment. In addition, a portion of the 12th amendment was superseded by section 3.)

Section 1.

The terms of the President and the Vice President shall end at noon on the 20th day of January, and the terms of Senators and Representatives at noon on the 3d day of

January, of the years in which such terms would have ended if this article had not been ratified; and the terms of their successors shall then begin.

Section 2.

The Congress shall assemble at least once in every year, and such meeting shall begin at noon on the 3d day of January, unless they shall by law appoint a different day.

Section 3.

If, at the time fixed for the beginning of the term of the President, the President elect shall have died, the Vice President elect shall become President. If a President shall not have been chosen before the time fixed for the beginning of his term, or if the President elect shall have failed to qualify, then the Vice President elect shall act as President until a President shall have qualified; and the Congress may by law provide for the case wherein neither a President elect nor a Vice President elect shall have qualified, declaring who shall then act as President, or the manner in which one who is to act shall be selected, and such person shall act accordingly until a President or Vice President shall have qualified.

Section 4.

The Congress may by law provide for the case of the death of any of the persons from whom the House of Representatives may choose a President whenever the right of choice shall have devolved upon them, and for the case of the death of any of the persons from whom the Senate may choose a Vice President whenever the right of choice shall have devolved upon them.

Section 5.

Sections 1 and 2 shall take effect on the 15th day of October following the ratification of this article.

Section 6.

This article shall be inoperative unless it shall have been ratified as an amendment to the Constitution by the legislatures of three-fourths of the several States within seven years from the date of its submission.

AMENDMENT XXI

Passed by Congress February 20, 1933. Ratified December 5, 1933.

Section 1.

The eighteenth article of amendment to the Constitution of the United States is hereby repealed.

Section 2.

The transportation or importation into any State, Territory, or possession of the United States for delivery or use therein of intoxicating liquors, in violation of the laws thereof, is hereby prohibited.

Section 3.

This article shall be inoperative unless it shall have been ratified as an amendment to the Constitution by conventions in the several States, as provided in the Constitution, within seven years from the date of the submission hereof to the States by the Congress.

AMENDMENT XXII

Passed by Congress March 21, 1947. Ratified February 27, 1951.

Section 1.

No person shall be elected to the office of the President more than twice, and no person who has held the office of President, or acted as President, for more than two years of a term to which some other person was elected President shall be elected to the office of the President more than once. But this Article shall not apply to any person holding the office of President when this Article was proposed by the Congress, and shall not prevent any person who may be holding the office of President, or acting as President, during the term within which this Article becomes operative from holding the office of President or acting as President during the remainder of such term.

Section 2.

This article shall be inoperative unless it shall have been ratified as an amendment to the Constitution by the legislatures of three-fourths of the several States within seven years from the date of its submission to the States by the Congress.

AMENDMENT XXIII

Passed by Congress June 16, 1960. Ratified March 29, 1961.

Section 1.

The District constituting the seat of Government of the United States shall appoint in such manner as the Congress may direct:

A number of electors of President and Vice President equal to the whole number of Senators and Representatives in Congress to which the District would be entitled if it were a State, but in no event more than the least populous State; they shall be in addition to those appointed by the States, but they shall be considered, for the purposes of the election of President and Vice President, to be electors appointed by a State; and they shall meet in the District and perform such duties as provided by the twelfth article of amendment.

Section 2.

The Congress shall have power to enforce this article by appropriate legislation.

AMENDMENT XXIV

Passed by Congress August 27, 1962. Ratified January 23, 1964.

Section 1.

The right of citizens of the United States to vote in any primary or other election for President or Vice President, for electors for President or Vice President, or for Senator or Representative in Congress, shall not be denied or abridged by the United States or any State by reason of failure to pay any poll tax or other tax.

Section 2.

The Congress shall have power to enforce this article by appropriate legislation.

AMENDMENT XXV

Passed by Congress July 6, 1965. Ratified February 10, 1967.
(**Note:** Article II, section 1, of the Constitution was affected by the 25th amendment.)

Section 1.

In case of the removal of the President from office or of his death or resignation, the Vice President shall become President.

Section 2.

Whenever there is a vacancy in the office of the Vice President, the President shall nominate a Vice President who shall take office upon confirmation by a majority vote of both Houses of Congress.

Section 3.

Whenever the President transmits to the President pro tempore of the Senate and the Speaker of the House of Representatives his written declaration that he is unable to discharge the powers and duties of his office, and until he transmits to them a written declaration to the contrary, such powers and duties shall be discharged by the Vice President as Acting President.

Section 4.

Whenever the Vice President and a majority of either the principal officers of the executive departments or of such other body as Congress may by law provide, transmit to the President pro tempore of the Senate and the Speaker of the House of Representatives their written declaration that the President is unable to discharge the powers and duties of his office, the Vice President shall immediately assume the powers and duties of the office as Acting President.

Thereafter, when the President transmits to the President pro tempore of the Senate and the Speaker of the House of Representatives his written declaration that no inability exists, he shall resume the powers and duties of his office unless the Vice President and a majority of either the principal officers of the executive department or of such other body as Congress may by law provide, transmit within four days to the President pro tempore of the Senate and the Speaker of the House of Representatives their written declaration that the President is unable to discharge the powers and duties of his office. Thereupon Congress shall decide the issue, assembling within forty-eight hours for that purpose if not in session. If the Congress, within twenty-one days after receipt of the latter written declaration, or, if Congress is not in session, within twenty-one days after Congress is required to assemble, determines by two-thirds vote of both Houses that the President is unable to discharge the powers and duties of his office, the Vice President shall continue to discharge the same as Acting President; otherwise, the President shall resume the powers and duties of his office.

AMENDMENT XXVI

Passed by Congress March 23, 1971. Ratified July 1, 1971.
(**Note:** Amendment 14, section 2, of the Constitution was modified by section 1 of the 26th amendment.)

Section 1.

The right of citizens of the United States, who are eighteen years of age or older, to vote shall not be denied or abridged by the United States or by any State on account of age.

Section 2.

The Congress shall have power to enforce this article by appropriate legislation.

AMENDMENT XXVII

Originally proposed Sept. 25, 1789. Ratified May 7, 1992.
No law, varying the compensation for the services of the Senators and Representatives, shall take effect, until an election of Representatives shall have intervened.

APPENDIX B

RANGE OF DATES
FOR FIRST NATIONAL ELECTION[12]

Ratification	Eff. Date	Pres. Election	1st Nat. Election	Years After Ratification
11/10/25	11/10/27	11/11&12/28	11/9&10/30	5
11/13/25	11/13/27	11/11&12/28	11/9&10/30	5
11/10/26	**11/10/28**	**11/11&12/28**	**11/9&10/30**	**4**
11/11/26	**11/11/28**	**11/6&7/32**	**11/11&12/34**	**8**
11/13/26	**11/13/28**	**11/6&7/32**	**11/11&12/34**	**8**
11/5/27	11/5/29	11/6&7/32	11/11&12/34	7
11/8/27	11/8/29	11/6&7/32	11/11&12/34	7
11/5/28	11/5/30	11/6&7/32	11/11&12/34	6
11/8/28	11/8/30	11/6&7/32	11/11&12/34	6
11/5/29	11/5/31	11/6&7/32	11/11&12/34	5
11/8/29	11/8/31	11/6&7/32	11/11&12/34	5
11/5/30	**11/5/32**	**11/6&7/32**	**11/11&12/34**	**4**
11/6/30	**11/6/32**	**11/8&9/36**	**11/11&12/34**	**8**
11/8/30	**11/8/32**	**11/8&9/36**	**11/11&12/34**	**8**

---

[12] *See* page 142.

★ APPENDIX C

STATE DELEGATION VOTING POWER IN THE FIRST CONGRESS[13]

T he Percent column indicates the percentages (rounded) of the entire House represented by each State's delegation. The next column adds two Senate seats and compares any shift in total delegation power:

State	Reps.	Percent	+ Senate	Percent	% Change
Virginia	10	15.4%	12	13.2%	-2.2%
Massachusetts	8	12.3%	10	11.0%	-1.3%
Pennsylvania	8	12.3%	10	11.0%	-1.3%
New York	6	9.2%	8	8.8%	-0.4%
Maryland	6	9.2%	8	8.8%	-0.4%
Connecticut	5	7.7%	7	7.7%	---
North Carolina	5	7.7%	7	7.7%	---
South Carolina	5	7.7%	7	7.7%	---
New Jersey	4	6.2%	6	6.6%	0.4%
Georgia	3	4.6%	5	5.5%	0.9%
New Hampshire	3	4.6%	5	5.5%	0.9%

---

[13] *See* page 153.

Delaware	1	1.5%	3	3.3%	1.8%
Rhode Island	1	1.5%	3	3.3%	1.8%
TOTAL	65	100%	91	100%	---

⭐ APPENDIX D

STATE DELEGATION
VOTING POWER AFTER REAPPORTIONMENT
BASED ON THE 1790 CENSUS[14]

State	Reps.	Percent	% Change[15]	± Senate	Percent	% Change
Virginia	19	18.1%	2.7%	21	15.5%	-2.6%
Massachusetts	14	13.3%	1.0%	16	11.8%	-1.5%
Pennsylvania	13	12.4%	0.1%	15	11.1%	-1.3%
New York	10	9.5%	0.3%	12	8.9%	-0.6%
Maryland	8	7.6%	-1.6%	10	7.4%	-0.2%
Connecticut	7	6.7%	-1.0%	9	6.7%	---
North Carolina	10	9.5%	1.8%	12	8.9%	-0.6%
South Carolina	6	5.7%	-2.0%	8	5.9%	0.2%
New Jersey	5	4.8%	-1.4%	7	5.2%	0.4%
Georgia	2	1.9%	-2.7%	4	3.0%	1.1%
New Hampshire	4	3.8%	-0.8%	6	4.4%	0.6%

---

[14] *See* page 154.

[15] This column shows the percentage change from the original apportionment in the Constitution to the apportionment after the first census. The final column shows the percentage change for each State's delegation when its two Senators are added.

Delaware	1	0.9%	-0.6%	3	2.2%	1.3%
Rhode Island	2	1.9%	0.4%	4	3.0%	1.1%
Kentucky	2	1.9%	---	4	3.0%	1.1%
Vermont	2	1.9%	---	4	3.0%	1.1%
TOTAL	105	100%	---	135	100%	---

★ APPENDIX E

ELECTORAL COLLEGE
VOTING POWER OF THE TEN
LARGEST AND THE TEN SMALLEST
STATES BASED ON THE 2020 CENSUS[16]

LARGEST		SMALLEST	
State	Votes	State	Votes
1. California	54	41. New Hampshire	4
2. Texas	40	42. Maine	4
3. Florida	30	43. Montana	4
4. New York	28	44. Rhode Island	4
5. Pennsylvania	19	45. Delaware	3
6. Illinois	19	46. South Dakota	3
7. Ohio	17	47. North Dakota	3
8. Georgia	16	48. Alaska	3
9. North Carolina	16	49. Vermont	3
10. Michigan	15	50. Wyoming	3
TOTAL	254		34

---

[16] *See* page 180.

ACKNOWLEDGMENTS

A huge thank you to my law firm partner Peter G. Kelly, Sr., who took the time to read and go over the early draft with me page by page. Peter's wisdom from his many years in national politics and international democratic initiatives helped me hone the new systems I am proposing.

The historical background of grassroots movements that brought about the 18th, 19th, and 21st Amendments in Part Three was based on Chapters 3, 4, and 5 of Clement E. Vose's *Constitutional Change: Amendment Politics and Supreme Court Litigation Since 1900* (Lexington Books 1972). I first read this book in a course on the U.S. Constitution taught by Professor Vose in the Government Department at Wesleyan University.

Citations to and quotations from *The Federalist* are borrowed from Alexander Hamilton, John Jay & James Madison, *The Federalist* (George W. Carey and James McClellan eds., Liberty Fund 2001).

The text of the current U.S. Constitution and the Amendments in **Appendix A** is reprinted from the National Archives, www.archives.gov/founding-docs/constitution-transcript. The spelling and punctuation appear as in the original.

★ENDNOTES

---

[1] The standard convention in referring to particular amendments to the Constitution is to spell the number using letters, such as "Fourteenth Amendment," or to use Roman numerals, like "Amendment XIV." Both of these are cumbersome. It is easier to comprehend and visually recognize the number in ordinal numeric form, such as "14th Amendment." For the articles of the Constitution and the Restated Constitution, the convention of using Roman numerals is retained because they are fewer than ten in number and most people can recognize and understand Roman numerals I through X.

[2] Kristen Holmes, *Trump calls for the termination of the Constitution in Truth Social post,* CNN, https://www.cnn.com/2022/12/03/politics/trump-constitution-truth-social/index.htmlr.

[3] Elizabeth Rose, *Religious Freedom for Jews in Connecticut,* Teach It, https://teachitct.org/lessons/religious-freedom-for-jews-in-connecticut/.

[4] Center for Reproductive Rights, *State Constitutions and Abortion Rights, https://reproductiverights.org/state-constitutions-abortion-rights/.*

[5] *Know Nothing,* Wikipedia, https://en.wikipedia.org/wiki/Know_Nothing.

[6] *Secretary Mayorkas Announces New Immigration Enforcement Priorities,* Homeland Security (Sept. 30, 2021), https://www.dhs.gov/news/2021/09/30/secretary-mayorkas-announces-new-immigration-enforcement-priorities.

[7] N.Y. State Dept. of Motor Vehicles, *Learner permit written test and Driver's Manual in other languages,* https://dmv.ny.gov/driver-license/learner-permit-written-test-and-drivers-manual-different-languages.

[8] Ballotpedia, *Voting rights for people convicted of a felony,* https://ballotpedia.org/Voting_rights_for_people_convicted_of_a_felony.

[9] Meghan Keneally, *Skokie: The legacy of the would-be Nazi march in a town of Holocaust survivors,* ABC News (June 22, 2018),

https://abcnews.go.com/US/skokie-legacy-nazi-march-town-holocaust-survivors/story?id=56026742.

[10] Becky Little, *Why the Star-Spangled Banner is Played At Sporting Events*, History (Oct. 5, 2023), https://www.history.com/news/why-the-star-spangled-banner-is-played-at-sporting-events.

[11] Joseph L. Price, *History of the National Anthem*, Tampa Bay Rays, https://www.mlb.com/rays/history/national-anthem.

[12] *1968 Olympics Black Power Salute*, Wikipedia, https://en.wikipedia.org/wiki/1968_Olympics_Black_Power_salute.

[13] *Avery Brundage*, Wikipedia, https://en.wikipedia.org/wiki/Avery_Brundage.

[14] Mark Follman et al., *US Mass Shootings 1982-2024: Data from Mother Jones' Investigation*, Mother Jones (June 21, 2024), https://www.motherjones.com/politics/2012/12/mass-shootings-mother-jones-full-data/.

[15] Katherine Schaeffer, *Key facts about Americans and guns*, Pew Research Center (Sept. 13, 2022), https://www.pewresearch.org/short-reads/2023/09/13/key-facts-about-americans-and-guns/.

[16] *Second Amendment to the United States Constitution*, Wikipedia, https://en.wikipedia.org/wiki/Second_Amendment_to_the_United_States_Constitution.

[17] *States with or without the death penalty—2024*, Death Penalty Information Center, https://deathpenaltyinfo.org/states-landing.

[18] Alex Cohen and Wilfred U. Codrington III, *The Equal Rights Amendment Explained*, Brennan Center for Justice (Jan. 23, 2020), https://www.brennancenter.org/our-work/research-reports/equal-rights-amendment-explained.

[19] Tanya de Sousa et al., *The 2023 Annual Homelessness Assessment Report (AHAR) to Congress*, U.S. Dept. of Housing and Urban Development (Dec. 2023), https://www.huduser.gov/portal/sites/default/files/pdf/2023-AHAR-Part-1.pdf.

[20] As many foreigners wonder, why do we have a national government but 50 different sub-sovereignties with different laws, structures, and customs? We should rethink the utility of a dual system of government composed of a national government and 50 States with different laws and bureaucracies, but we should probably leave that issue to another day.

[21] *Office History*, Florida Dept. of State, https://dos.fl.gov/about-the-department/office-history/.

[22] George Washington, *Farewell Address (1796)*, National Constitution Center, https://constitutioncenter.org/the-constitution/historic-document-library/detail/george-washington-farewell-address-1796.

[23] Brian Bushard, *Voters Who Identify As Independents Skyrocket — As Democrats and Republicans Dwindle*, Forbes (Jan. 12, 2024), https://www.forbes.com/sites/brianbushard/2024/01/12/voters-who-identify-as-independents-skyrocket---as-democrats-and-republicans-dwindle/.

[24] *Elbridge Gerry*, Wikipedia, https://en.wikipedia.org/wiki/Elbridge_Gerry.

[25] While gerrymandering for State elections may violate sections of Article I of the Restated Constitution, such as Section 4 regarding voting and Section 13 regarding equal protection of the laws, it's up to Congress and the courts to address that problem.

[26] *Profiles*, United States Census Bureau, https://data.census.gov/profile?q=United%20States&g=010XX00US.

[27] Evan Andrews, *Why Is Election Day a Tuesday in November?*, History (July 10, 2024), https://www.history.com/news/why-is-election-day-a-tuesday-in-november.

[28] *Census Records*, National Archives, https://www.archives.gov/research/census.

[29] Troy E. Smith, *Connecticut Compromise*, Center for the Study of Federalism (2006), https://federalism.org/encyclopedia/no-topic/connecticut-compromise/.

[30] Kat Eschner, *The First US Census Only Asked Six Questions*, Smithsonian Magazine (Aug. 2, 2017), https://www.smithsonianmag.com/smart-news/first-us-census-only-asked-six-questions-180964234/.

[31] Jessie Krantz, *The 1790 Census and the First Veto*, National Archives (Apr. 4, 2022), https://prologue.blogs.archives.gov/2022/04/04/the-1790-census-and-the-first-veto/.

[32] *Unicameralism*, Wikipedia, https://en.wikipedia.org/wiki/Unicameralism.

[33] Noah M. Kazis, *American Unicameralism: The Structure of Local Legislatures*, 69 Hastings L.J. 1147, 1149 (2018).

[34] *States with a full-time legislature*, Ballotpedia, https://ballotpedia.org/States_with_a_full-time_legislature.

[35] Linton Weeks and Arnie Seipel, *Hey, Congress: Keep Your Day Jobs*, NPR (Dec. 12, 2010), https://www.npr.org/2010/12/28/132294306/hey-congress-dont-keep-your-day-jobs.

[36] Geoffrey Skelley, *How The House Got Stuck At 435 Seats*, FiveThirtyEight (Aug. 12, 2021), https://fivethirtyeight.com/features/how-the-house-got-stuck-at-435-seats/.

[37] Sean Ross, *How Congress Retirement Pay Compares to the Overall Average*, Investopedia (May 3, 2024), https://www.investopedia.com/articles/markets/080416/how-congress-retirement-pay-compares-overall-average.asp#:~:text=Since%202009%2C%20Congressional%20pay%20has%20been%20%24174%2C000%20per,minority%20leaders%20in%20the%20House%20and%20Senate%3A%20%24193%2C400.%29.

[38] Ballotpedia, *Filling vacancies in the U.S. Senate*, https://ballotpedia.org/Filling_vacancies_in_the_U.S._Senate.

[39] Ian Millhiser, *Is it constitutional to hold an impeachment trial for a former president?*, Vox (Feb. 8, 2021), https://www.vox.com/22242411/trump-impeachment-constitution-senate-trial-william-belknap.

[40] Ballotpedia, *Impeachment of federal judges*, https://ballotpedia.org/Impeachment_of_federal_judges.

[41] *2020 Census Apportionment Results*, United States Census Bureau (Apr. 26, 2021), https://www.census.gov/data/tables/2020/dec/2020-apportionment-data.html.

[42] *Presidential election results*, Politico (Nov. 8, 2022), https://www.politico.com/2020-election/results/president/.

[43] Tom Murse, *How Electoral Votes Are Awarded*, ThoughtCo. (Oct. 3, 2020), https://www.thoughtco.com/how-electoral-votes-are-distributed-3367484.

[44] Dave Roos, *5 Presidents Who Lost the Popular Vote But Won the Election*, History (updated July 12, 2024), https://www.history.com/news/presidents-electoral-college-popular-vote.

[45] Peter Carlson, *Although As Crooked As They Come, This Boston Politician Was Beloved*, HistoryNet (Aug. 29, 2023), https://www.historynet.com/michael-curley-politician/.

[46] Caitlin Yilek, *Trump White House failed to report 117 foreign gifts and some are missing, House Democrats say*, CBS News (Mar. 17, 2023), https://www.cbsnews.com/news/trump-foreign-gifts-missing-house-democrats-report/.

[47] David Roos, *Why Do 9 Justices Serve on the Supreme Court?*, History (updated Feb. 8, 2024), https://www.history.com/news/supreme-court-justices-number-constitution.

[48] John M. Yinger, *Origins and Interpretation of the Presidential Eligibility Clause in the U.S. Constitution*, Syracuse University (rev. Apr. 6, 2000), https://joyinger.expressions.syr.edu/citizenship/origins-and-interpretation-of-the-presidential-eligibility-clause-in-the-u-s-constitution/.

[49] Tom Murse, *Presidents Without College Degrees,* ThoughtCo. (updated Aug. 17, 2021), https://www.thoughtco.com/presidents-without-college-degrees-3368101.

[50] Robert S. Summers, *Presidents of the United States by Occupation,* POTUS, https://potus.com/presidential-facts/occupations/.

[51] *Reading Law*, Wikipedia, https://en.wikipedia.org/wiki/Reading_law.

[52] *Tapping Reeve House and Litchfield Law School*, Litchfield Historical Society, https://www.litchfieldhistoricalsociety.org/museums/tapping-reeve-house-and-law-school/.

[53] *1940 Statement of Principles on Academic Freedom and Tenure*, American Association of University Professors, https://www.aaup.org/report/1940-statement-principles-academic-freedom-and-tenure.

[54] *Mandatory retirement*, Ballotpedia, https://ballotpedia.org/Mandatory_retirement.

[55] *Impeachment of federal judges*, Ballotpedia, https://ballotpedia.org/Impeachment_of_federal_judges.

[56] *Impeachment Trial of Justice Samuel Chase, 1804-05,* United States Senate, https://www.senate.gov/about/powers-procedures/impeachment/impeachment-chase.htm.

[57] *On the Nomination PN422: Ruth Bader Ginsburg, of New York, to be an Associate Justice of the Supreme Court of the United States*, govtrack.us (Aug. 3, 1993), https://www.govtrack.us/congress/votes/103-1993/s232.

[58] JM Rieger and Madison Dong, *How senators voted on Ketanji Brown Jackson for the Supreme Court*, The Washington Post (updated Apr. 7, 2022), https://www.washingtonpost.com/politics/interactive/2022/ketanji-brown-jackson-confirmation-vote/.

[59] American Bar Association Standing Committee on the Federal Judiciary, *What It Is and How It Works* (2017), https://www.americanbar.org/content/dam/aba/administrative/govern ment_affairs_office/fjc-backgrounder.pdf.

[60] *Merrick Garland Supreme Court nomination*, Wikipedia, https://en.wikipedia.org/wiki/Merrick_Garland_Supreme_Court_nomi nation.

[61] Leigh Ann Caldwell, *Neil Gorsuch Confirmed to Supreme Court After Senate Uses 'Nuclear Option,'* NBC News (Apr. 7, 2017), https://www.nbcnews.com/politics/congress/neil-gorsuch-confirmed-supreme-court-after-senate-uses-nuclear-option-n743766.

[62] Carl Hulse, *How Mitch McConnell Delivered Justice Amy Coney Barrett's Rapid Confirmation*, The New York Times (updated Nov. 3, 2020), https://www.nytimes.com/2020/10/27/us/mcconnell-barrett-confirmation.html.

[63] *About the Judicial Conference*, United States Courts, https://www.uscourts.gov/about-federal-courts/governance-judicial-conference/about-judicial-conference.

[64] *Code of Conduct for United States Judges*, United States Courts, https://www.uscourts.gov/sites/default/files/code_of_conduct_for_unit ed_states_judges_effective_march_12_2019.pdf.

[65] Tom Kertscher, *What Ruth Bader Ginsburg said about Donald Trump*, PolitiFact (July13, 2016), https://www.politifact.com/article/2016/jul/13/what-ruth-bader-ginsburg-said-about-donald-trump/.

[66] Tierney Sneed, *What to know about the Justice Clarence Thomas recusal debate around his wife's texts*, CNN (updated Mar. 29, 2022), https://www.cnn.com/2022/03/29/politics/clarence-ginni-thomas-election-reversal-texts/index.html.

[67] Abbie VanSickle, *Clarence Thomas, in Financial Disclosure, Acknowledges 2019 Trips Paid by Harlan Crow*, The New York Times

(June 7, 2024), https://www.nytimes.com/2024/06/07/us/supreme-court-disclosures-gifts.html#:~:text=Justice%20Thomas%20did%20not%20report%20any%20gifts%20or,albums%20worth%20%242%2C000%20from%20Terrence%20and%20Barbara%20Giroux.

[68] Kelsey Reichmann, *Alito kicks up ethics questions with new undisclosed gifts from billionaire donors*, Courthouse News Service (June 21, 2023), https://www.courthousenews.com/alito-kicks-up-ethics-questions-with-new-undisclosed-gifts-from-billionaire-donors/.

[69] Zoe Richards, *Chief Justice Roberts declines to testify at Senate's Supreme Court ethics hearing*, NBC News (Apr. 25, 2023), https://www.nbcnews.com/politics/supreme-court/chief-justice-roberts-declines-testify-supreme-court-ethics-rcna81470.

[70] *Code of Conduct for Justices of the Supreme Court of the United States*, U.S. Supreme Court, https://www.supremecourt.gov/about/Code-of-Conduct-for-Justices_November_13_2023.pdf.

[71] Historical and Revision Notes, 28 United States Code § 1332, House of Representatives, https://uscode.house.gov/view.xhtml?req=granuleid:USC-2007-title28-section1332&num=0&edition=2007.

[72] Dave Roos, *How Do New States Become Part of the U.S.?*, How Stuff Works (updated Jan. 19, 2022), https://people.howstuffworks.com/new-state-in-us.htm#:~:text=Other%20states%20were%20carved%20out%20of%20existing%20states%3A,Atlas%20and%20West%20Virginia%20Archives%20and%20History%20%5D.

[73] Johnna Kaplan, *Northeast Ohio is Built Like New England Because It Used to Be Owned by Connecticut*, Atlas Obscura (Aug. 17, 2016), https://www.atlasobscura.com/articles/northeast-ohio-is-built-like-new-england-because-it-used-to-be-owned-by-connecticut.

[74] *Gettysburg Casualties: Total Dead and Wounded at the Battle of Gettysburg*, HistoryNet, https://www.historynet.com/gettysburg-casualties/#:~:text=George%20Gordon%20Meade%E2%80%99s%20Army%20of%20the%20Potomac%20lost,and%2010%2C790%20were%20missing%20%285%2C365%20Union%2C%205%2C425%20Confederate%29.

[75] Leo Shane III, *Pence — not Trump — asked Guard troops to help defend Capitol on Jan. 6, panel says*, Military Times (June 10, 2022), https://www.militarytimes.com/news/pentagon-congress/2022/06/10/pence-not-trump-asked-guard-troops-to-help-defend-capitol-on-jan-6-panel-says/.

[76] *The Federalist and the Republican Party*, PBS, https://www.pbs.org/wgbh/americanexperience/features/duel-federalist-and-republican-party/.

[77] Shannon Pettypiece, *Marjorie Taylor Greene calls for a 'national divorce' between liberal and conservative states*, NBC News (Feb. 20, 2023), https://www.nbcnews.com/politics/congress/marjorie-taylor-greene-calls-national-divorce-liberal-conservative-sta-rcna71464.

[78] *Originalism*, Wikipedia, https://en.wikipedia.org/wiki/Originalism.

[79] Doori Song, *Judicial Pragmatism: Strengths and Weaknesses in Common Law Adjudication, Legislative Interpretation, and Constitutional Interpretation*, 52 UIC J. Marshall L. Rev. 369 (2019).

[80] *Proposals to Amend the U.S. Constitution: Fact Sheet*, Congressional Research Service (Mar. 14, 2024), https://crsreports.congress.gov/product/pdf/R/R47959.

[81] Kinsey Crowley, *Two years ago, SCOTUS overturned the right to an abortion. Here is how each state changed*, USA Today (updated June 24, 2024), https://www.usatoday.com/story/news/politics/2024/06/23/state-by-state-abortion-laws-dobbs-anniversary/73769814007/.

[82] *Maine becomes second state to bar Trump from 2024 ballot*, WMTW, https://www.wmtw.com/article/trump-barred-maine-ballot/46246073.

[83] *The day the Constitution was ratified*, National Constitution Center (June 21, 2024), https://constitutioncenter.org/blog/the-day-the-constitution-was-ratified.

[84] Russ Feingold, *Warning: A "Convention of States" Is Practicing to Rewrite the Constitution*, The Nation, https://www.thenation.com/article/politics/convention-states-constitution/.

[85] Charlotte Greene, *Constitutional Topic: Ratification Conventions*, The U.S. Constitution Online (Apr. 23, 2024), https://www.usconstitution.net/consttop_acon-html/.

ABOUT THE AUTHOR

R ichard S. Order is a trial lawyer at Updike, Kelly & Spellacy, P.C. in Hartford, Connecticut and primarily handles business disputes in lawsuits, arbitrations, and mediations. He graduated from Wesleyan University with a major in Classics and attended the Intercollegiate Center for Classical Studies in Rome during a semester abroad. He graduated from Columbia University School of Law where he was the Managing Editor of the *Columbia Human Rights Law Review*. In 2021, he received the Connecticut Bar Association's Honorable Anthony V. DeMayo Pro Bono Award for his representation of dozens of survivors of domestic abuse seeking restraining orders.

www.ingramcontent.com/pod-product-compliance
Lightning Source LLC
Chambersburg PA
CBHW071137130626
46553CB00004B/1408